OTHERWORLDS

Otherworlds

*Fantasy and History
in Medieval Literature*

AISLING BYRNE

OXFORD
UNIVERSITY PRESS

OXFORD
UNIVERSITY PRESS

Great Clarendon Street, Oxford, OX2 6DP,
United Kingdom

Oxford University Press is a department of the University of Oxford.
It furthers the University's objective of excellence in research, scholarship,
and education by publishing worldwide. Oxford is a registered trade mark of
Oxford University Press in the UK and in certain other countries

First Edition published in 2016

Impression: 1

Published in the United States of America by Oxford University Press
198 Madison Avenue, New York, NY 10016, United States of America

British Library Cataloguing in Publication Data
Data available

Library of Congress Control Number: 2015939411

ISBN 978–0–19–874600–3

Printed in Great Britain by
Clays Ltd, St Ives plc

Acknowledgements

This book began as a doctoral project at St John's College, Cambridge and was completed during my time as Fitzjames Research Fellow in Old and Middle English at Merton College, Oxford. I am grateful to the Gates Cambridge Trust for funding my graduate work at Cambridge. I also benefited from the support of Cambridge University's Domestic Research Studentship scheme.

Joanna Bellis, Venetia Bridges, Paul Byrne, Elizabeth Dearnley, Victoria Flood, Joni Henry, Megan Leitch, and Emily Wingfield all generously read and commented on sections of this work. The work is considerably the richer for their keen eyes and their scholarship.

I am grateful to my teachers over the years. Brigitte Erwin nurtured my love of things literary and things medieval at an early point. At University College Dublin, Ron Callan and Alan Fletcher were generous with their guidance. To Neil Cartlidge I owe a particular debt, not only for first introducing me to the otherworld of *Sir Orfeo*, but also for the encouragement and guidance he gave me in pursuing medieval studies beyond my degree.

Thanks are also due to Jacqueline Tasioulas, and to my examiners Corinne Saunders and Christopher Page, who read and commented on this study. The suggestions of the two anonymous readers appointed by Oxford University Press were invaluable, as was the assistance of Rachel Platt. Numerous other people have contributed, chief among them are Elizabeth Archibald, Elizabeth Boyle, Chera Cole, Robert Easting, Emily Guerry, Hilary Larkin, Charles MacQuarrie, Máire Ní Mhaonaigh, Tom MacFaul, Richard McCabe, Simon Meecham-Jones, Sophie Page, Geraldine Parsons, Thomas Phillips, James Wade, Julia Walworth, Michael Whitworth, and Barry Windeatt. This book also owes a great deal to the insights of my students at Cambridge and at Merton. Patrick has helped greatly with both the large things and the small—his kindness and good cheer have made the final phase of this project the happiest of times.

Before I came to Cambridge, I was told that Helen Cooper was 'excellent in every way'. Her unfailing generosity and insight as a supervisor proved that there was no exaggeration in that description. I could not have asked for a better teacher.

My sisters, Caitríona and Maria, have entertained and sustained me with their boundless good humour. I owe most to my parents, Miriam and Paul, who imbued me with their love of learning, and who have given me so much throughout my life. *Buíochas ó chroí libh.*

Contents

List of Illustrations   ix
List of Abbreviations   xi

Introduction: Worlds within Worlds   1
Sources of Belief and the Celtic Connection   7
Real Otherworlds?   10
'He com into a fair cuntray': Words for Literary Worlds   12
Fiction into History   21

1. **Imagining Otherworlds**   25
   Pseudo-Mimesis   30
   Otherworld Excess and the Perils of Desire   43
   Mapping Gender   53
   Death and Deathlessness   58

2. **Otherworlds and the Afterlife**   68
   Owein in the Otherworld   74
   Biblical Sources and 'Celtic' Otherworlds   87
   Otherworlds in the Ocean: Scripture and Syncretism   97

3. **Supernatural Authorities**   107
   Kingship, Rulers, and Otherworld Realms   112
   Appropriating Avalon   119
   Alexander's Journey to the Earthly Paradise   129

4. **Archipelagic Otherworlds**   141
   The North Atlantic *Orbis Alter*   143
   These Other Edens   152
   Islands of Magic   159
   Monstrous Peripheries   167

Conclusion: Points of Departure   184

Bibliography   187
Index   207

List of Illustrations

3.1. The Luck of Edenhall   108

4.2. World Map from Oxford, St John's College MS 17, f. 6r.   144

List of Abbreviations

The following abbreviations are used throughout this book:

ANTS	Anglo-Norman Text Society
BL	British Library
cpt	chapter
CUL	Cambridge University Library
EETS	Early English Text Society
e.s.	Extra Series
ITS	Irish Texts Society
MED	*Middle English Dictionary*
n.s.	New Series
OED	*Oxford English Dictionary*
o.s.	Original Series
RS	Rolls Series
STS	Scottish Text Society

Introduction

Worlds within Worlds

When Sir Orfeo pursues the fairy hunt through the hollow hillside, he travels through darkness for a time before suddenly emerging into a bright and beautiful country. The anonymous poet writes:

> He com in-to a fair cuntray,
> As briȝt so sonne on somers day,   [as sun
> Smoþe & plain & al grene
> —Hille no dale nas þer non y-sene.[1]   [none to be seen

Nearby he sees a great castle that is 'clere and schine as cristal'.[2] Its buttresses are of red gold, its vaulting is adorned with enamel, and the dwellings within are of precious stones. The mounting sense that this realm might be a very different sort of place to the world Orfeo knows is quickly confirmed. We are told that the land never experiences darkness when night falls, because the precious stones shine as brightly as the sun at noon. Yet, for all its apparent strangeness, there is also a lot that is very familiar about *Sir Orfeo*'s 'fair cuntray'. The motifs the poet uses are typical of medieval accounts of what we usually term 'the otherworld'. The entry through the hillside, the land's beauty, copious quantities of precious stones, and rich materials, even the freedom from night-time darkness wrought by an unnatural light source, are all highly conventional motifs. In other narratives, otherworld spaces often feature beautiful gardens, fountains, fruitful trees, refined bird song, a beautiful palace, or a pavilion. A distortion of spatio-temporal rules is also frequent—the length of sojourns in the otherworld may be entirely at odds with the time that has passed in the actual world. The boundary between worlds may, as in *Sir Orfeo*, be a passage through a hollow hill, but it also frequently takes

---

[1] *Sir Orfeo*, edited by A. J. Bliss (Oxford: Oxford University Press, 1954), p. 31, ll. 351–4.
[2] *Sir Orfeo*, edited by Bliss, l. 358.

the form of a water barrier (whether the sea or a river) or it may be located at the bottom of a lake. This group of recurring motifs makes such realms so immediately recognizable that many of the problems inherent in conceptualizing 'otherworlds' in a medieval context can be, and have been, overlooked. This book is about these problems and the imaginative opportunities they create.

Numerous medieval texts feature unfamiliar realms that operate according to very different laws to those of the actual world. These places cannot be easily subsumed into the idea of the afterlife, Christian or otherwise. Realms of this sort survive in the earliest vernacular literatures of Ireland and Wales. In this respect, the literature of these regions seems more precocious than that of England. What survives of Old English writing or of the Latin texts of Anglo-Saxon England supplies little in the way of otherworld encounters.[3] The murky depths of Grendel's mere are perhaps the closest we get. It is only after the Norman invasion that otherworld accounts begin to proliferate and their emergence in the twelfth and thirteenth centuries goes hand in hand with a widespread fascination with the marvellous that characterized the courtly writing of that period.[4]

The classic work of modern scholarship on this topic is Howard Rollin Patch's 1950 study, *The Other World According to Descriptions in Medieval Literature*. Patch established beyond doubt the continuities between the motifs used in otherworld descriptions across a wide variety of places and periods.[5] The book is a valuable resource but, as several reviewers noted on

---

[3] The surviving corpus of Old English writing does not, of course, lack beings that might be considered 'otherworldly'; see, for instance, Alaric Hall, *Elves in Anglo-Saxon England: Matters of Belief, Health, Gender and Identity* (Woodbridge: Boydell, 2007). However, visits to or descriptions of the realms whence these beings come do not feature prominently.

[4] Increased interest in otherworld narratives may be yet another response to the set of interconnected social and cultural currents we usually associate with the twelfth century. Those that seem most immediately relevant are a widespread preoccupation with the limits of the natural and the supernatural among the learned elites, the rise of the knightly class and the growth of courtly literary culture that attended it, and a burgeoning appreciation for a mode of writing that might be more readily classified as 'fiction' than that which went before. Robert Bartlett outlines learned approaches to the supernatural in the same period in *The Natural and the Supernatural in the Middle Ages* (Cambridge: Cambridge University Press, 2008). For an exploration of why the rise of the knightly class might have fed an interest in marvels, see Jacques Le Goff, 'The Marvelous in the Medieval West', in *The Medieval Imagination* by Jacques Le Goff, translated by Arthur Goldhammer (Chicago: University of Chicago Press, 1988), 27–44. On the twelfth century as a key point of development for certain sort of vernacular fiction, see D. H. Green, *The Beginnings of Medieval Romance: Fact and Fiction, 1150–1220* (Cambridge: Cambridge University Press, 2002).

[5] Howard Rollin Patch, *The Other World According to Descriptions in Medieval Literature* (Cambridge, MA: Harvard University Press, 1950).

its publication, it is a largely taxonomic exercise.[6] This is unsurprising given the sheer number of texts covered and the fact that Patch's primary motivation in producing his study was to trace potential primitive sources for otherworld depictions.[7] Investigation into the literary properties of these places falls outside the scope of *The Other World*. Robert O. Payne summarized some of the outstanding issues in his 1951 review of the book: 'The question remains, however: What do they [otherworld themes and motifs] do to the surroundings into which they are brought? And, conversely, what has the artist in the particular case done with them? What effect does a particular treatment have upon the course of the tradition?'[8] Although it was not Patch's stated purpose, a great merit of *The Other World* from the perspective of literary studies is that it brought the wide range of otherworld material from a variety of places and periods together in a single work of reference, laying the (necessarily extensive) groundwork for further investigation of these realms. However, since 1950 there has been little attempt to address this body of material as a whole, and to build on Patch's initial efforts.

This is somewhat surprising; particularly, in light of the recent upsurge in interest in the role of the supernatural in medieval literature and in the genre with which such marvels and magic are most frequently associated, romance. Magic, marvels, and the supernatural have undergone something of a scholarly rehabilitation since the 1980s, in part, because of an increased interest in beings, communities, and concepts traditionally considered marginal. The trend finds its more obvious manifestation in the preoccupation of various strands of cultural studies with the idea of 'the Other'. Medievalists have found this a particularly fruitful area of exploration. After all, medieval culture had a pronounced appetite for monsters, giants, witches, werewolves, and other oddities. Scholarship focusing on medieval accounts of marginal or hybrid figures has flourished.[9] And, of course, this work on alterity has a natural affinity with influential theoretical discourses,

---

[6] See reviews by George Kane in *The Modern Language Review*, 46 (1951), 475–6; C. S. L.[ewis] in *Medium Aevum*, 20 (1951), 93–4; Robert O. Payne in *Comparative Literature*, 3 (1951), 366–8.

[7] Patch, *Other World*, pp. 1–5.

[8] Payne, 'Review of Patch, *Other World*', 367.

[9] See, for instance, Asa Simon Mittman, *Maps and Monsters in Medieval England* (London: Routledge, 2006); John Block Friedman, *The Monstrous Races in Medieval Art and Thought* (Cambridge, MA: Harvard University Press, 1981); David Williams, *Deformed Discourse: The Function of the Monster in Mediaeval Thought and Literature* (Montreal: McGill-Queen's University Press, 1996). On visual representations of monstrosity, see Friedman, *The Monstrous Races*, and Alixe Bovey, *Monsters and Grotesques in Medieval Manuscripts* (Toronto: University of Toronto Press, 2002). For a cultural-historical reading of this material, see Caroline Walker Bynum, *Metamorphosis and Identity* (New York: Zone Books, 2001).

like postcolonialism, where similar emphases are prevalent.[10] As Lorraine Daston and Katharine Park note:

> [W]ork on deviance and normalcy has contributed to the fascination with the extraordinary and the marginal... Wonder and wonders have risen to prominence on a wave of suspicion and self-doubt concerning the standards and sensibilities that had long excluded them (and much else) from respectable intellectual endeavours.[11]

These questioned 'standards and sensibilities' are as much aesthetic as they are social or political. The last few decades have also seen medieval literary studies engage more closely with modes of writing previously regarded less 'serious' and less 'literary'. Romance, particularly romance that responds to popular rather than to courtly tastes, has been the most notable beneficiary of this shift. Under the influence of new historicist thinking, chronicle writing, broadly conceived, has also been re-approached as a subject of literary study. Otherworld accounts are most frequently associated with these two (seemingly contrasting) modes of writing.

Although widespread interest in deviance and in the margins might seem to provide fertile ground for fresh engagement with medieval otherworlds, the last few decades have seen comparatively few attempts to address the topic directly. In Celtic studies, John Carey and Patrick Sims-Williams have produced a number of important papers on the depiction of the otherworld in Irish and, to a lesser degree, Welsh literature.[12] Most recently, Alfred Siewers has contributed a re-reading of Irish otherworlds in light of contemporary ecocritical theory.[13] In English studies, the most notable recent accounts are chapters on the topic produced by Jeff Rider

---

[10] Jeffrey Jerome Cohen has been a particularly vocal advocate for the connection between the medieval monstrous and the formation of political, particularly (proto)colonial, identities. See, for instance, his *Hybridity, Identity, and Monstrosity in Medieval Britain: On Difficult Middles* (New York: Palgrave Macmillan, 2006) and 'Hybrids, Monsters, Borderlands: The Bodies of Gerald of Wales', in *The Postcolonial Middle Ages*, edited by Jeffrey Jerome Cohen (New York: Palgrave Macmillan, 2001), pp. 85–104.

[11] Lorraine Daston and Katharine Park, *Wonders and the Order of Nature, 1150–1750* (New York: Zone Books, 1998), p. 10.

[12] John Carey, 'Time, Space, and the Otherworld', *Proceedings of the Harvard Celtic Colloquium*, 7 (1987), 1–27; Patrick Sims-Williams, 'Some Celtic Otherworld Terms', in *Celtic Language, Celtic Culture: A Festschrift for Eric P. Hamp*, edited by A. T. E. Matonis and D. F. Melia (Van Nuys, CA: Ford & Bailie, 1990), pp. 57–81; John Carey, 'The Irish Otherworld: Hiberno-Latin Perspectives', *Éigse*, 25 (1991), 154–9. For a broader perspective on the ways in which Christian learned elites engaged with otherworld accounts in Ireland, see John Carey, *A Single Ray of the Sun: Religious Speculation in Early Ireland* (Aberystwyth: Celtic Studies Publications, 1999), pp. 1–38.

[13] Alfred K. Siewers, *Strange Beauty: Ecocritical Approaches to Early Medieval Landscape* (New York: Palgrave Macmillan, 2009).

and Corinne Saunders.[14] Yet, it cannot be denied that this output does not amount to a particularly extensive body of scholarship, particularly when placed beside the numerous papers and volumes exploring other aspects of the medieval fantastical, like monsters, and of other marvellous spaces like Asia. The relative neglect may in part be due to the particular emphasis the discourse of 'the Other' places on reading texts in the light of specific political or religious ideologies. These are the sorts of day-to-day historical realities from which the otherworld appears (on the surface at least) to offer outright escape. Despite this problem, some scholars have tried to draw the otherworld into this discourse. Rider's deft definition of the otherworld in *The Cambridge Companion to Medieval Romance* suggests that it is any world other than that of the 'aristocratic society...at the center of the fictive worlds proposed by most medieval romances', a definition that encompasses any space inhabited by beings who might be considered, to a greater or lesser extent, 'other'.[15] However, in solving one problem, another is created: by allowing such a vast scope to the category of the otherworld, we risk stretching the semantic range of the term to the point where its utility is limited.

When medievalists use the term 'otherworld', it can mean any number of things, including the next world, the world of the fairies, an imaginary fantastical realm, or, less frequently, far-flung corners of the globe such as the wondrous East or the Antipodes. And, in a sense, the breadth of reference accorded to this one term is appropriate: what these realms have in common is the fact that what would be considered supernatural in the actual world is entirely natural in these locations. This is how Carey defines the term 'otherworld' in his analysis of Irish narratives. It is, he writes, 'a minimal designation for any place inhabited by supernatural beings and itself exhibiting supernatural characteristics'.[16] Thinking about otherworlds in this manner is certainly compelling and has particular utility in the context of Irish otherworld narratives; however, in the broader medieval context, it may again be too capacious a definition. Should, for instance, the past be thought of as an otherworld? After all, the observation that marvels and wonders were more common in previous times than the present is not unusual in medieval writing, famously

---

[14] Jeff Rider, 'The Other Worlds of Medieval Romance', in *The Cambridge Companion to Medieval Romance*, edited by Roberta L. Krueger (Cambridge: Cambridge University Press, 2000), pp. 115–31; Corinne Saunders, *Magic and the Supernatural in Medieval English Romance* (Cambridge: D. S. Brewer, 2010), see, in particular, Chapter 5: 'Otherworld Enchantments and Faery Realms', pp. 179–206.

[15] Rider, 'The Other Worlds of Medieval Romance', p. 115.

[16] John Carey, 'Time, Space and the Otherworld', *Proceedings of the Harvard Celtic Colloquium*, 7 (1987), 1–27 (p. 1).

providing the point of departure for Chaucer in *The Wife of Bath's Tale*.[17] Or can the outer reaches of the contemporary medieval world be thought of in this way, as the title of Mary B. Campbell's account of late medieval travel writing, *The Witness and the Other World*, implies?[18] Another approach might be to discuss these realms in terms of specifics rather than generalities, focusing on particular types of otherworlds, rather than on the otherworld as an overarching concept. Such an approach is relatively widespread in analysis of literatures in the Celtic languages, where the range of authentically medieval signifiers for otherworlds is considerably greater than that available to the scholar of medieval English literature. But these terms are obviously of limited utility when exploring very similar otherworld depictions from other cultural and linguistic traditions.

My main interest in this book is literature from England, whether in English, French, or Latin. However, I have chosen to frame this literature within the wider context of the insular world. In practice, this means engaging with the literature of the Celtic languages and with Latin writing from the other regions of Britain and Ireland. In the following, I take 'insular' to mean Britain, Ireland, and surrounding islands like the Isle of Man. The geographical limits of this study do not present themselves naturally. As Patch's work demonstrated, the pervasiveness and similarities of otherworld accounts makes zooming in on clearly demarcated geographical contexts challenging. What, if anything, is distinctive about otherworld accounts from England as opposed to, for instance, any region in Continental Europe? The continuities seem far more obvious than the differences. Accordingly, this book started out being about texts from medieval England, but rapidly spilled over beyond those boundaries. This was not just a function of the cross-cultural similarities of otherworld accounts in the Middle Ages. As we will see, otherworld depictions in the Celtic languages, and from Ireland in particular, have played an important role in scholarship on this topic in English studies. It seemed important to engage with this material as well and I have done so in two principal ways. Firstly, I have looked again at some of the claims that have been made for the influence of Celtic language material on English otherworld accounts. Secondly, the material from beyond England and English-speaking regions has a comparative value, a means of framing and illuminating, by comparison and contrast, the texts from England, even in instances where no line of clear influence is likely or possible. Such comparisons will

---

[17] Geoffrey Chaucer, 'The Wife of Bath's Tale', in *The Riverside Chaucer*, edited by Larry D. Benson, 3rd edn (Oxford: Oxford University Press, 1987), pp. 116–22, ll. 857–64.
[18] Mary B. Campbell, *The Witness and the Other World: Exotic European Travel Writing, 400–1600* (Ithaca, NY: Cornell University Press, 1991).

attempt to show that thematic similarities between otherworld narratives can often be accounted for by the fact that the otherworld lends itself to the treatment of certain themes, such as death, gender, authority, and territorial politics. This approach places the emphasis on the inherent characteristics of the otherworld motif, and on how these were recognized and exploited by a range of authors, rather than on extra-textual beliefs. Chapter 4 tries to bring these two approaches together, highlighting how similarities between English and Celtic otherworld accounts can be rooted in the distinctive archipelagic geography of the region, rather than attributed to clear textual lineages.

This is a literary study, rather than a cultural history, of otherworld depictions. I have structured chapters and sections on the basis of thematic relationships rather than by any sort of historical timeline. I have used 1500 as a rough end point for this study. For obvious reasons, a chronological starting point is not readily pinpointed. In theory, the literature of the early Middle Ages falls within the scope of this study. In practice, relevant material from England, in the vernacular or in Latin, is almost non-existent before the twelfth century. The earlier period is therefore represented by texts from other regions, especially Ireland. These potentially take us back as early as the eighth century, though the earliest manuscript survivals are from the central Middle Ages.

This study questions several (usually tacit) and interrelated assumptions that tend to dominate work on medieval otherworlds. The remainder of these introductory comments will explore three of the most influential of these assumptions, before finally moving towards a working definition of the otherworld. The first of these assumptions is the idea that when an otherworld is depicted in a text, it is a straightforward mimesis of a range of beliefs (usually assumed to be pagan beliefs, archaic or contemporary, coherent or garbled) prior and external to the text. The second assumption that I would like to probe is that it is possible to think of the 'otherworld' as a proper noun, a parallel reality distinguished from the actual world entirely in ontological terms. The third is that the modern term 'otherworld', with its wide range of meanings and connotations, is readily applicable to the medieval situation.

SOURCES OF BELIEF AND THE CELTIC CONNECTION

The first of these assumptions—that of the influence of prior, extra-textual belief systems—gestures towards the singularity of otherworld realms in the context of medieval accounts of marvels and the supernatural with which they are often grouped. Phenomena such as fairy visits are interruptions of the quotidian world that may *imply* another world that lies beyond our own but, because they take place in this world, they tend to register merely as aberrations in the ordinary course of nature. By contrast, visits to other-worlds represent a completely immersive experience of alterity; they are not merely aberrations in nature, but suggest the presence of another nature entirely. The assumption that such alternative realities point to alternative cosmologies, possibly derived from extra-textual beliefs, flows naturally from this immersive quality.

Much of the research on the otherworlds in Welsh and Irish literature continues to focus on how far literary representations may illuminate actual beliefs, past or present, and I think it is very difficult to look at the treatment of otherworlds in medieval English scholarship without acknowledging the role played by perceptions of the Celtic associations of these depictions. Indeed, such are the similarities between English and Celtic (usually Irish) depictions of the otherworld that it is hard to discuss the former without reference to the latter. Among scholars of English literature, there has been a tendency to assume that the English material is influenced by the—generally much earlier—Celtic material.[19] All too often, 'Celtic' tends to serve as a catch-all term for those things in medieval English texts that are supernatural and intractable, like otherworld spaces, and the depth of the disciplinary divide between Celtic studies and English studies tends to discourage many from probing any further. The persistent influence of this perception and the extent to which it is, in many ways, a dead end is summed up well in Saunders' recent account, where she notes 'Celtic tales of the supernatural seem to have been particularly formative [though] such influences are notoriously difficult to trace'.[20]

The persistence of such thinking is all the more remarkable because there is a strong case for arguing that Celtic language literatures do not display a significantly greater interest in otherworldly locations than English literature. Indeed, referring to 'Celtic' otherworld literature is somewhat misleading, since accounts of such realms are not a universal feature of narratives in those languages; they are, for instance, considerably rarer in the surviving corpus of Welsh texts than in their Irish

---

[19] Such assumptions are a rare instance of the continuing influence of the so-called 'anthropological approach' in medieval English studies. See further, C. S. Lewis, 'The Anthropological Approach', in *English and Medieval Studies Presented to J. R. R. Tolkien on the Occasion of his Seventieth Birthday*, edited by Norman Davis and C. L. Wrenn (London: Allen and Unwin, 1962), pp. 219–30.

[20] Saunders, *Magic and the Supernatural*, p. 180.

counterparts.[21] The perception of Celtic influence stems from a variety of sources. The most obvious is the modern tendency to associate the Celtic cultures themselves with that which is visionary, mystical, and other-worldly.[22] The particular fame (both medieval and modern) of three 'other-world' narratives that have connections with Ireland, the *Navigatio Sancti Brendani Abbatis* (The Voyage of Saint Brendan the Abbot), the *Visio Tnugdali* (The Vision of Tnugdal), and the *Tractatus de Purgatorio Sancti Patricii* (The Account of Saint Patrick's Purgatory), may also be a factor. However, these texts owe far more to Western European Christian culture than to any putative Celtic substratum.

In this respect, this book takes its cue from a growing body of work in Celtic studies that stresses the extent to which medieval Celtic, particularly medieval Irish, culture was part of the European mainstream. It also argues that the seeming Celticity of Middle English otherworld accounts can sometimes be overstated. A case in point is the *Orfeo* description above, which commentators and editors have routinely dubbed 'Celtic', but which does not draw on any source as heavily as the description of the New Jerusalem in the Johannine Apocalypse.[23]

Adducing Celtic sources would not be so problematic if it had not deferred engagement with some of the more intractable elements in medieval English literature. It is only a small step from ascribing a motif to a Celtic source to placing the exploration of that motif beyond the scope of the discipline of English studies. Whatever its merits as a piece of literary archaeology, assuming a 'Celtic' source for otherworld depictions still does not explain the continuing use and elaboration of the notion of the otherworld by authors throughout the Middle Ages.

Of course, downplaying the extent to which otherworlds embody coherent belief systems is not to imply that such systems were entirely absent in all such treatments. One of the most obvious challenges posed

---

[21] This point has been made recently by Barry J. Lewis, 'Celtic Ecocriticism', *Cambrian Medieval Celtic Studies*, 59 (2010), 71–81 (p. 72). The comparative rarity of otherworld accounts in Welsh might, in part, be explained by the relatively small size of the surviving Welsh corpus, or by local factors that contributed to the sorts of texts that survived, but it is a state of affairs which should provide a further caution against talking too sweepingly about 'Celtic' otherworld accounts.

[22] Patrick Sims-Williams, 'The Visionary Celt: The Construction of an Ethnic Preconception', *Cambridge Medieval Celtic Studies*, 11 (1986), 71–96. Sims-Williams cites a passage from Ernest Renan's influential *La Poésie des races celtiques* (1854), where entering the Celtic regions is compared to crossing into another world, and notes that '[t]he simile is seductive; if Celtia is such another world, would we not expect its natives to be attuned to the Otherworld?' (p. 82). Helen Fulton takes a similar tack in 'Magic and the Supernatural in Early Welsh Arthurian Narrative: *Culhwch ac Olwen* and *Breuddwyd Rhonabwy*', *Arthurian Literature*, 30 (2013), 1–26.

[23] Ad Putter, 'The Influence of Visions of the Otherworld on Some Medieval Romances', in *Envisaging Heaven in the Middle Ages* (London: Routledge, 2006), pp. 237–51. For further discussion, see the section entitled 'Biblical Sources and 'Celtic' Otherworlds' in Chapter 2.

by the all-encompassing term 'otherworld' is its frequent application to the
Christian afterlife in modern parlance. To take one prominent example of
this use among many, Robert Easting's 1997 bibliography of visions of
the afterlife was entitled *Visions of the Other World in Middle English*.[24]
Nonetheless, the distinction between secular and religious otherworlds is
not as absolute as it might at first appear. Descriptions of religious otherworlds frequently utilize imagery that echoes that of more secular realms.
This partly results from the fact that both are, to some extent, drawing on
the same pool of biblical and apocryphal imagery. However, the similarity
in the lexicon of images is particularly pronounced in texts where the entry
into the otherworld is physical rather than spiritual or psychological; in
other words, in accounts of otherworld journeys rather than of otherworld
visions or dreams. Depictions of the Earthly Paradise derived from biblical
accounts describe a bucolic idyll arrayed with precious metals and stones,
imagery which is pervasive throughout more secular otherworld descriptions. Furthermore, the boundaries that divide this world and the otherworld in medieval texts also appear in journeys to specifically religious
realms; for instance, in the *Tractatus de Purgatorio Sancti Patricii*, Sir
Owein travels to Purgatory by way of a cave-opening, and elsewhere Saint
Brendan voyages across the sea to attain the Earthly Paradise.

REAL OTHERWORLDS?

A second problem in employing the modern term 'otherworld' in critical
parlance arises, in many cases, from the underlying assumption that the
definition of the otherworld is predicated on the question of ontology: a
literary world is 'other' because it is 'unreal' or non-existent outside the
realm of the imagination. This is why scholars have readily dubbed such
sites as the islands encountered by Saint Brendan and the Earthly Paradise
as 'otherworlds' even though they were widely believed to lie within the
earth's geography in the Middle Ages and, indeed, appear on numerous
medieval maps. As it happens, a location identified as 'Brendan's Island'
appeared on maps as late as the eighteenth century, while the non-existent
Brazil Rock, a version of the legendary Hy Brasil, was not finally removed
from charts until 1865 (presumably based on logic that was the naval
equivalent of Pascal's wager).[25] Since many of these worlds incorporate

---

[24] Robert Easting, *Visions of the Other World in Middle English*, Annotated Bibliographies of Old and Middle English Literature, 3 (Cambridge: D. S. Brewer, 1997).
[25] See Barry Cunliffe, *Facing the Ocean: The Atlantic and its Peoples* (Oxford: Oxford
University Press, 2000), p. 14. Barbara Freitag gives an overview of the history of this

elements that might be described as fantastic, the lack of distinction is not surprising, but it is more than a little anachronistic to apply modern notions of what might or might not be 'real' to the products of medieval culture. The problem here is one that has bedevilled scholars attempting to deal with medieval ideas of the supernatural in general. Jacques Le Goff's observation on the subject is representative:

> [there was no] psychological, literary, or intellectual category that corresponds exactly to what, in French, we call *le merveilleux*, the marvellous. Where we see an intellectual construct or a literary genre, medieval clerics and their students saw a world of objects, a collection rather than a category.[26]

In one sense, this is unsurprising. The common denominator necessary for treating marvels as a homogenous category, a firm belief in the unreality of those marvels, did not exist in the Middle Ages. That the fantastical was coterminous with the fictional was by no means a given in the premodern, or more precisely, pre-Enlightenment, world.[27]

The natural inference to draw from medieval perceptions of the marvellous as 'a collection rather than a category' is the plurality of potential medieval attitudes to the supernatural and the fantastical. The notion of the otherworld is no different. We cannot assume that medieval writers and readers in all places and at all times believed absolutely in the reality of such places. For instance, the idea of an inhabited inaccessible Antipodean realm was a vexed question for much of the Middle Ages, and, despite the wide influence of the Brendan legend, not everyone believed that the saint had actually seen the various islands described in accounts of his voyage.[28] The existence of the Earthly Paradise was biblically sanctioned and

---

mythical location from the fourteenth century to the present day in *Hy Brasil: The Metamorphosis of an Island, from Cartographic Error to Celtic Elysium*, Textxet Studies in Comparative Literature 5.69 (Amsterdam and New York: Rodopi, 2013). For a treatment of medieval attempts to locate Eden on the map, see Alessandro Scafi, *Mapping Paradise: A History of Heaven on Earth* (London: British Library, 2006).

[26] Jacques Le Goff, *Medieval Imagination*, pp. 27–44.

[27] A point made by Daston and Park, *Wonders and the Order of Nature*, p. 15.

[28] On approaches to the issue of the Antipodes, see Alfred Hiatt, *Terra Incognita: Mapping the Antipodes Before 1600* (London: British Library, 2008), pp. 38–60. On the Brendan legend, see, for instance, the opinions of Vincent of Beauvais, Nicolaus de Bibera, and the author of a satire on the Brendan legend preserved in Oxford, Lincoln College MS 27: Vincent of Beauvais, *Bibliotheca Mundi seu Speculi Maioris: Speculum historiale* (Douai: Baltazar Belierus, 1624; repr. Graz: Akademische Druck- und Verlagsanstalt, 1965), p. 843; Nicolaus de Bibera, *Carmen Satiricum*, edited by Theobald Fischer, Geschichts-quellen der Provinz Sachsen, I: Erfurter Denkmäler (Halle: Buchhandlung des Waisen-hauses, 1870), ll. 1550–65; the Lincoln 27 poem is attributed to an author called 'David' and is edited and translated by David Howlett as: 'Hic poeta qui Brendani vitam vult describere', in *The English Origins of Old French Literature* (Dublin: Four Courts Press, 1996), pp. 112–15.

indisputable, but the hope that it might still exist within the temporal sphere faded as the history of exploration advanced. Conversely, Purgatory became more central to Christian belief as time went by, but the notion that it might be accessed at various geographic locations, most prominent among them Lough Derg in Ireland, was less widely accepted.[29] The challenge these locations present to the cultural historian is not so much that their existence was a matter of widespread belief or disbelief, but that they gave rise to widely varied degrees of belief and, in some instances, a certain agnosticism.[30]

The range of medieval attitudes to the existence of these realms suggests that one needs to tread carefully when considering the notion of other-worlds in medieval thought and culture. It also implies that the 'otherness' of these worlds is not as secure and absolute as that accorded to the otherworlds of, say, modern fantasy literature. They are 'other' only insofar as they are removed from the actual world the author inhabits and operate in ways that are unfamiliar to the text's readership; their reality or unreality may be a matter of interest, but it does not define them as otherworlds. This ontological uncertainty is, in some ways, an artistic strength, since it suggests that the distinction between 'this' worldly experience and the otherworldly is not as fixed and as clear as modern critical discourse might suggest.

'HE COM INTO A FAIR CUNTRAY': WORDS FOR LITERARY WORLDS

The final, and perhaps the most important, problem is the lexical one— how suited is the modern term 'otherworld' to the description of such realms in medieval writing? The *Oxford English Dictionary*'s entry for 'otherworld' reflects the broad scope and somewhat vague connotations of the modern term. It lists the term's application to the afterlife, which it then glosses more expansively as the 'realm of the supernatural', and then proceeds to note its application to strange and usually fantastical realms, allowing that these also may be said to constitute a 'supernatural realm'. Tellingly, the dictionary also elaborates this use of the term as 'imaginary worlds', suggesting that fantastical 'supernatural realms' might typically be

---

[29] The fullest treatment of these sceptical accounts is Robert Easting, 'Purgatory and the Earthly Paradise in the *Tractatus de Purgatorio Sancti Patricii*', *Cîteaux: Commentarii Cistercienses*, 37 (1986), 23–48.

[30] Robert Bartlett, *England under the Norman and Angevin Kings, 1075–1225* (Oxford: Clarendon Press, 2000), p. 690.

considered non-existent. Such definitional problems associated with the modern term 'otherworld' are compounded by a rarely recognized philological problem: no term of comparable semantic range appears to have existed in the Middle Ages. The situation is similar to that which obtains in the case of related modern terms and concepts, like 'marvels'. These are categories where the gulf between the modern and the medieval can be particularly deep and where terminology has so completely altered or shifted meaning that appropriate scholarly engagement can be particularly difficult. To be sure, the absence of a lexical marker for something does not necessarily imply the essential irrelevance of the entity to the culture in question, but it does at least caution us not to propose overly neat definitions of the object under discussion and encourages us to interrogate the precise understanding of the idea in the period. In other words, I am not arguing that the broad category intuited by modern scholarship does not exist, but it does not necessarily exist on the terms we often assume it does.

The relative lack of comment by scholars on this lexical lacuna results, in part, from it being all too rarely recognized. There are numerous authentically medieval words and phrases that lend themselves to the translation 'otherworld' but which, in reality, are by no means cognate with the modern term. A close examination of some of the most persistently used of these terms emphasizes the extent to which the modern use of 'otherworld' elides the complexity of the medieval situation. Unsurprisingly, the linking of an adjective meaning 'other' to a noun meaning 'world' does occur in Old and Middle English. However, in each case there is no sense that this combination is particularly privileged: in most instances the term designating 'other' could easily be replaced by 'next' with no loss to the meaning. The earliest instance of the collocation of 'other' and 'world' offered by the *OED* is from an Old English homily which speaks about how a man thought to be dead returned to life and recounted his vision 'on ðære oðre weorulde'.[31] This and later examples from the Middle Ages cannot reasonably be described as compound words, and the scope of the phrase is limited and highly specific; in most instances it designates the afterlife of Christian belief. Other such turns of phrase where reference to the afterlife seems not to be intended also fall short of the modern concept. The Middle English poem *The Wars of Alexander* suggests a female character was so beautiful that she seemed

---

[31] Wulfstan, *Wulfstan: Sammlung der ihm zugeschriebenen Homilien nebst Untersuchungen über ihre Echtheit*, edited by Arthur Sampson Napier, Sammlung englischer Denkmäler in kritischen Ausgaben, 4 (Berlin: Weidmannsche Buchhandlung, 1883), p. 205.

like 'An elfe out of anothire erde or ellis an aungell'.[32] We are not looking at a compound here either, and Middle English *erd* can mean another region or part of the world as readily as it may describe the earth as a whole. The use of the term 'otherworld' to denote a fantastic and imaginary realm is modern; the *OED*'s first citation for it is from 1804, entirely apt for the very post-Enlightenment emphasis on unreality that the definition implies.

The paradigmatic use of a phrase meaning 'other world' in Latin occurs in Book One of Lucan's *Pharsalia,* a first-century text that was particularly well known throughout medieval Europe.[33] *Orbis alius* is used to denote the destination of the spirits of the dead in Lucan's description of the teaching of Gaulish druids. Apart from the fact that the reference to an *orbis alius* is clearly a reference to an existence after death, the passage illuminates little about the location or properties of the realm under discussion. Indeed, as Salomon Reinach suggests, *orbis* could have a wider semantic range in classical Latin than merely 'globe', referring also, though less frequently, to other countries and regions of the world.[34] Therefore, it cannot be taken for granted that some celestial realm is under discussion here; indeed, in the Middle Ages, writers sometimes use similar terminology when referring to the Antipodes or to far-flung regions of the earth. In the eighth century, the cleric Virgil of Salzburg was criticized by Pope Zachary for apparently teaching that there was an inhabited *alius mundus* beneath the earth.[35] The ninth-century Irish geographer Dicuil describes how Ceylon was thought of as an *orbis alter* until Alexander's admiral reached it by boat.[36] In this light, it is not completely surprising that the Middle Irish version of the *Pharsalia, In Cath Catharda* (The Civil War), should interpret Lucan's description of an *orbis alius* as referring to the antipodes. *In Cath Catharda* recounts that the druids discovered through their magical arts that 'the souls

---

[32] *The Wars of Alexander*, edited by Hoyt N. Duggan and Thorlac Turville-Petre, EETS, s.s., 10 (Oxford: Oxford University Press, 1989), p. 167. This is an elaboration of the Latin source text where the comparison does not occur.

[33] 'They teach that the soul does not descend to the silent land of Erebis and the sunless realm of Dis below, but that the same breath still governs the limbs in a different scene [*orbis alius*]'. Lucan, *The Civil War, Books I–X*, edited and translated by J. D. Duff (London: William Heinemann, 1928), Book I, ll. 454–7.

[34] Salomon Reinach, 'Le mot *orbis* dans le latin de l'empire', *Revue Celtique*, 22 (1901), pp. 447–57.

[35] For a fuller discussion of Virgil's opinions, see John Carey, 'Ireland and the Antipodes: The Heterodoxy of Virgil of Salzburg', *Speculum*, 64 (1989), 1–10. Zachary's letter is edited in 'Die Briefe des Heiligen Bonifatius und Lullus', in *Monumenta Germaniae Historica, Epistolae Selectae*, 1, edited by Michael Tangl, 2nd edn (Berlin: Weidmann, 1955), pp. 178–9.

[36] Dicuil, *Liber de Mensura Orbis Terrae*, edited by J. J. Tierney (Dublin: Dublin Institute for Advanced Studies, 1967), pp. 80, 81.

of those that died in this [northern] temperate zone were taken southward through the torrid zone, and placed in other bodies in the southern temperate zone.'[37] The terms used here, *in mesraighthi deiscertaigh* (in the southern temperate zone) and *in mesraighthi tuaiscertaigh* (in the northern temperate zone), are also used in *In Cath Catharda*'s account of Alexander's exploits beyond the torrid zone.[38] It is possible that the Antipodean interpretation of Lucan's *alius orbis* may have been distinctively Irish, but it demonstrates that a phrase that we would readily translate as 'otherworld' did not automatically evoke a fantastical, non-existent, supernatural realm for premodern audiences.[39]

Although Latin variants on the term *orbis alius* were used in Ireland throughout the Middle Ages, there is no evidence to suggest that it might have any application to the fantastic regions that feature in the period's literature. Instead, Old and Middle Irish supply a rather wide range of terms for realms we might now gloss as otherworldly: *síd* (fairy mound), *Mag Mell* (Plain of Delights), *Tír Tairngire* (Land of Promise), *Tech Duinn* (House of Donn), and *Tír na mBeo* (Land of the Living), to name but a few.[40] Of all these terms, *síd* has been the subject of the most consistent analysis and the broadest applications.[41] However, in his discussion of otherworld terms in the Celtic languages, Patrick Sims-Williams argues convincingly that the scholarly tendency to speak of

[37] 'anmanna in lochta ba marbh isin mesraighthisea do / breith tresin tendtigi fodes & a tabairt i corpaibh ele isin / mesraighthi descertach.' *In Cath Catharda, The Civil War of the Romans: An Irish Version of Lucan's Pharsalia*, edited and translated by Whitley Stokes, in *Irische Texte mit Wörterbuch*, edited by Whitley Stokes and Ernst Windisch, 4 vols in 6 (Leipzig: S. Hirzel, 1880–1909), IV. 2 (1909), pp. 56–9, ll. 724–31. I have adapted Stokes' translation.

[38] *In Cath Catharda*, edited by Stokes, pp. 4–5.

[39] Although this distinction is important, it should also be borne in mind that the remote or unreachable regions of the world were generally thought to possess properties which, if not strictly supernatural, were certainly marvellous. Indeed, inaccessibility was no precondition for the fantastic, as Gerald of Wales had to go no further than Ireland to encounter a world he thought fantastical. His repeated references to Ireland as an *orbis alter* in the *Topographia Hibernica* are very firmly linked to the island's supposedly marvellous attributes (see further, Chapter 4 of this volume).

[40] This last term is generally restricted in application to the Christian Heaven in the medieval Irish tradition, but is used with reference to the fairy otherworld in *Echtrae Connlai*. See further, John Carey, 'The Rhetoric of *Echtrae Chonlai*', *Cambridge Medieval Celtic Studies*, 30 (1995), 41–65 (pp. 45–6). Carey suggests an origin for this Irish term in the Latin *terra uiuentium* as used in the Vulgate Bible. For an analysis that reads *Tír na mBeo* as a native Irish concept, see David Dumville, '*Echtrae* and *Immram*: Some Problems of Definition', *Ériu*, 27 (1976), 73–94 (p. 82).

[41] On the origins and connotations of the term, see Tomás Ó Cathasaigh, 'The Semantics of *síd*', *Éigse*, 17 (1978), 137–55, and Eric P. Hamp's note 'Varia X: Irish *síd* "tumulus" and Irish *síd* "peace"', *Études Celtique*, 19 (1982), 141–2.

'the otherworld' when discussing the *síde* is misleading.[42] The *síde* appear to have been conceived of as unlinked 'independent kingdoms', analogous, in Sims-Williams' terms, to the *túatha* of medieval Irish society rather than a single parallel world.[43] The afterlife had its own range of referents in Irish, including *alltar* (the world beyond) and *i-thall* (beyond). If the meanings of the constituent parts of a word are anything to go by, the Welsh term *annwfyn* appears to come closest to denoting a fantastical otherworld conceived of as a single location.[44] Its morphemes *an* and *dwyfn* appear to mean 'not world', or 'un-world' or, possibly, 'very deep'.[45] Unlike *síd*, the term appears to have denoted a single realm, but its use in Welsh literature is so rare that it is hard to come to any definite conclusions about its semantic range. The early Welsh poem *Preideu Annwfyn* suggests that *Annwfyn* is located across the sea and refers to it, or to places within it, as a 'mead feast fort' (*Gaer Vedwit*), a 'glass fort' (*Caer wydyr*), or, more enigmatically, a 'petrification fort' (*Gaer Rigor*), and a 'fort of impediment' (*Gaer Golud*).[46] *Preideu Annwfyn*'s description of Arthur and his men sailing to *Annwfyn* also sits a little oddly with the probable literal meaning of the term itself, which would appear to suggest an underworld rather than an island otherworld. Furthermore, its semantic components suggest that it cannot be considered an adequate term for the afterlife of Christian belief, except, perhaps, for the infernal regions.

This raises the question: what terms were employed when such realms were described by medieval writers? When considering this, it might be most useful to look at more self-consciously learned material. Latin writers, particularly chroniclers and authors of wonder collections, do not usually shy away from the ontological problems posed by encounters with the supernatural. After all, they offer numerous words to designate beings who did not fit into conventional categories of human or angelic.[47]

---

[42] Patrick Sims-Williams, 'Some Celtic Otherworld Terms', in *Celtic Language, Celtic Culture: A Festschrift for Eric P. Hamp*, edited by Ann T. E. Matonis and Daniel F. Melia (Van Nuys, CA: Ford and Bailie, 1990), pp. 57–81.

[43] Sims-Williams, 'Celtic Otherworld Terms', p. 63. For more on the *túatha*, see T. M. Charles-Edwards, *Early Christian Ireland* (Cambridge: Cambridge University Press, 2000), pp. 102–6. Modern scholars believe that there may have been in excess of one hundred such kingdoms in medieval Ireland.

[44] Sims-Williams, 'Celtic Otherworld Terms', p. 65.

[45] *Preideu Annwfyn*, in *Legendary Poems from the Book of Taliesin*, edited and translated by Marged Haycock (Aberystwyth: Cambrian Medieval Celtic Studies, 2007), pp. 433–51, ll. 22, 31, 28, 34.

[46] *Preideu Annwfyn*, edited by Haycock, pp. 433–51.

[47] On these creatures and terms for them, see C. S. Lewis, *The Discarded Image: An Introduction to Medieval and Renaissance Literature* (Cambridge: Canto, 1994) cpt 6; Bartlett, *England Under the Norman and Angevin Kings*, pp. 686–92; James Wade, *Fairies in Medieval Romance* (New York: Macmillan, 2011), pp. 4–5; C. S. Watkins, *History and*

Longaevi, lamias, and *incubi* are terms that could all now be translated as 'fairies', but beyond a tendency to group tales of such beings together in story collections, there is little evidence that an overarching medieval category for them existed. The variety of names proposed for these beings seems to reflect what Ronald Hutton describes as medieval writers' 'struggle' to create a single category for such phenomena from the existing terminology.[48] However, descriptions of encounters with marvellous realms offer no such variety of Latin terminology and there is little apparent effort to label or to categorize these places. This is despite the fact that Latin writers frequently relate otherworld encounters. The descriptions are particularly numerous in writings from the central Middle Ages when collections of *mirabilia* attained something approaching a generic status.[49] Some of these accounts are well known: the green children of Woolpit, the flying ship manned by sailors who cannot breathe earthly air, Elidyr and the fairy kingdom. As we will see, the motifs and themes that feature in these apparently historical accounts are cognate with those of more 'literary' sources like romances. The extent to which historical and literary accounts of otherworld encounters drew on the same motifs is striking and, indeed, the narrative structure of chronicled visits to fairy otherworlds often parallels that of romance.

Gervase of Tilbury's *Otia Imperialia* includes several tales which conform to the pattern typical of otherworld visitations: an account of a woman carried to the bottom of a lake to serve as a nurse for a 'drac' for seven years,[50] an account of a swineherd who visited a strange land by entering a cave in Derbyshire,[51] the story of a girl who was abducted to a palace of demons beneath a lake in Catalonia,[52] and that of a sailor who was taken on horseback to a distant land across the sea.[53] He also gives an account of a ship that was spotted sailing in the clouds, citing it as evidence for a realm of water above the earth.[54] Motifs familiar from the

---

the *Supernatural in Medieval England* (Cambridge: Cambridge University Press, 2007), pp. 19–20.

[48] Ronald Hutton, 'The Making of the Early Modern British Fairy Tradition', *The Historical Journal*, 57 (2014), 1135–56 (p. 1140).

[49] See further, Watkins, *History and the Supernatural.*

[50] Gervase of Tilbury, *Otia Imperialia: Recreation for an Emperor*, edited and translated by S. E. Banks and J. W. Binns (Oxford: Oxford University Press, 2002), III: 85, pp. 718–20.

[51] Gervase, *Otia Imperialia*, III: 45, pp. 642–5.

[52] Gervase, *Otia Imperialia*, III: 66, pp. 684–93.

[53] Gervase, *Otia Imperialia*, III: 63, pp. 678–83.

[54] Gervase, *Otia Imperialia*, I: 13, pp. 80–1. Similar stories appear in an Irish context in several sources; see further, Miceal Ross, 'Anchors in a Three-decker World', *Folklore*, 109 (1998), 63–75, and John Carey, 'Aerial Ships and Underwater Monasteries: The Evolution of a Monastic Marvel', *Proceedings of the Harvard Celtic Colloquium*, 12 (1992), 16–28.

wider body of otherworld narratives feature in all these accounts. The lake bottom dwelling of supernatural creatures is an entirely conventional motif. In the account of the sailor, we hear how a storm arose when a dolphin was struck by a spear thrown from a Mediterranean vessel. As the men aboard the ship were beginning to lose hope, a knight-like figure appeared, riding over the sea on horseback. The knight took the sailor who had struck the dolphin in exchange for calming the storm and rode off with him across the sea to a distant land. There the sailor found that the dolphin he had wounded was in fact a knight who had been enchanted. The sailor removed the spear and healed the wound himself, before being conveyed back to the ship.[55] The disjunction between the length of the journey and the time it took to make it is entirely typical of these accounts where the normal operations of time and space are frequently distorted. That the sea can appear solid to a supernatural being is not without precedent either; the author of the early Irish voyage tale *Immram Brain* (The Voyage of Bran), for instance, recounts a similar phenomenon.[56]

Perhaps the most archetypal of Gervase's accounts is the journey of a Derbyshire swineherd who enters a hillside cave while searching for a missing sow one winter day. The man wanders in darkness for a long time, before emerging into a bright and fertile country where it is clearly summer, not winter. A hollow hill is a conventional point of entry to the otherworld, and the swineherd's prolonged journey through the darkness and the disjunction between the seasonal cycle in the two worlds are both elements which conform to the traditional pattern of the otherworld journey, even though this otherworld contains no further fantastical elements. Gervase suggests that the disjunction in the seasonal cycle is evidence for the swineherd having happened upon an entrance to the Antipodes. The term used for the country the swineherd visits is *terra*, and the ontological continuity between it and the upper world is driven home by Gervase's overarching Antipodean interpretation. Similarly, Gervase contrasts the sea that he postulates as being above the earth in his account of the aerial ship with *nostra habitatio*, a phrase with far less totalizing implications than the translation 'the world we live in' offered by S. E. Banks and J. W. Binns.[57] These phrases, scattered though they are, develop a sense of continuity between the actual world and the otherworld, and emphasize how far any perception of strangeness and

[55] Gervase, *Otia Imperialia*, III: 63, pp. 678–83.
[56] *The Voyage of Bran Son of Febal to the Land of the Living: An Old Irish Saga*, edited and translated by Kuno Meyer and Alfred Nutt, 2 vols (London: David Nutt, 1895–1897), I (1895), p. 17.
[57] Gervase, *Otia Imperialia*, I: 13, p. 83.

alterity is contingent on perspective and might be relative rather than absolute. These lexical choices are potentially very important for our understanding of medieval otherworld descriptions. Describing a location as 'another country' has rather different implications from describing it as 'another world'. It suggests a degree of continuity between the actual world and the world being described, analogous to that between countries rather than between parallel realities.

On a lexical level, William of Newburgh's late twelfth-century account of two green-skinned children who emerged from a trench in the earth at Woolpit in Suffolk strikes a similar note to Gervase's accounts of otherworldly realms. The children spoke a strange language, could not eat most foodstuffs, and claimed they came from a place called St Martin's Land. They described St Martin's Land as being all green and existing in a permanent twilight. William too uses the word *terra* to refer to St Martin's Land throughout.[58] This sense of continuity between Woolpit and St Martin's Land is borne out in the insistence of the children that theirs is a Christian land.[59] The conventional markers of the otherworld, as related in literary texts, are readily observable: the land is reached through an opening in the earth, the children's movement between worlds is largely involuntary, and St Martin's Land exists in a perpetual twilight.[60]

A similar account is found in Gerald of Wales' near-contemporary *Itinerarium Kambriae*. He describes how the priest Elidyr ran away from home when he was a child and hid for two days under the bank of a river.[61] There, he was visited by two tiny men and was invited to follow them to their delightful country under the earth. Once there, the child was presented to the country's king and became a companion for the king's

---

[58] William of Newburgh, *The History of English Affairs, Book I*, edited and translated by P. G. Walsh and M. J. Kennedy, (Warminster: Aris and Phillips, 1988), pp. 114–17. The same events are also recorded by Ralph of Coggeshall a few years later; see *Radulphi de Coggeshall Chronicon Anglicanum*, edited by Joseph Stevenson, RS, 66 (London: Longmans, 1875), pp. 118–20.

[59] William, *History of English Affairs*, p. 116.

[60] The green children have received a good deal of scholarly attention in both historical and literary studies in recent years. John Clark provides an overview of the background to this episode and an exploration of the possible significance of 'St Martin's Land' in 'Martin and the Green Children', *Folklore*, 117 (2006), 207–14. Jeffrey Jerome Cohen offers a more literary approach, reading the story as a metaphor for alternative histories of England forced 'underground' by the Norman invasion in 'Green Children from Another World, or the Archipelago in England', in *Cultural Diversity in the British Middle Ages: Archipelago, Island, England*, edited by Jeffrey Jerome Cohen, The New Middle Ages (New York: Palgrave MacMillan 2008), pp. 75–94.

[61] Gerald of Wales, *Itinerarium Kambriae*, in *Giraldi Cambrensis Opera*, edited by J. S. Brewer and others, 8 vols, RS, 21 (London: Longman, 1861–1891), VI (1868), I: 8, p. 78.

son. The land was very beautiful, abounding in gold and, like St Martin's Land, perpetually in twilight. Elidyr returned periodically to the upper world, at first accompanied but later on his own, to visit his mother. She asked him to bring back one of the golden items that abounded in that land, so he stole a small golden ball. He was pursued from the country by two of the little men who eventually caught up with him on the threshold of his parents' house and retrieved the stolen object. The story concludes by relating how Elidyr attempted to enter the subterranean world again, without success. The account is a veritable checklist of motifs conventional to accounts of the otherworld. The entry point to the country, under the hollow bank of a river, is paralleled in numerous accounts of cliff openings and caves, as is the journey through darkness preceding an emergence into a beautiful countryside. The strange half-light is also a feature of the underground realm described in the *Tractatus de Purgatorio Sancti Patricii.* The diminutive size of its denizens recalls stories such as Walter Map's *De Herla Rege* (Of King Herla),[62] while their insistence on truth and lack of vice has something of the prelapsarian about it. Furthermore, the incident with the golden ball fits neatly into the tradition of precious objects being brought back from the otherworld. The language used by Gerald to describe this underground realm is similar to that used by both Gervase and William. The Latin term most frequently used to denote the beautiful country beneath the earth is *terra.* Writers working in a more 'fictional' mode make similar lexical choices. Although the anonymous poet of *Sir Orfeo* states that the fairy king's captives were 'in this warld y-nome', he describes the fairy kingdom into which his protagonist ventures as a 'fair cuntray', and refers to it thereafter as that 'lond'.[63] Similarly, the fairy mistress of Thomas of Erceldoune claims to come from 'ane oþer countree'.[64]

Just as modern attempts to interpret literary otherworlds as mere relics of past beliefs, or as non-existent locations, prove problematic and misleading in a medieval context, the modern term 'otherworld' itself falls short of adequately describing the medieval situation. The lexical markers that are used to refer to the realms which we tend to categorize as 'otherworlds' appear to have been both highly varied and relatively specific. No term emerges that encompasses all these realms at once.

---

[62] Walter Map, *De Nugis Curialium: Courtier's Trifles,* edited and translated by M. R. James, revised by C. N. L. Brooke and R. A. B. Mynors (Oxford: Oxford University Press, 1983), I: 11, pp. 26–31.

[63] *Sir Orfeo*, edited by Bliss, ll. 403, 327, 345, 450.

[64] *The Romance and Prophecies of Thomas of Erceldoune*, edited by James Murray, EETS, o.s., 61 (London: N. Trübner, 1875), p. 6, l. 93.

FICTION INTO HISTORY

So where does this leave us as far as the medieval 'otherworld' accounts are concerned? The term is certainly a convenient one, and it would be both futile and overzealous to suggest purging it from the scholarly lexicon. However, the terms on which medieval 'otherworlds' are understood need some examination and, perhaps, some adjustment. The fact that the terminology medieval writers appear to have used in speaking of these realms often highlights the relative rather than the absolute, and speaks of multiplicity rather than of a clear binary, suggests that the term 'otherworld' could profitably be drained of its absolutizing and dichotomizing associations in general scholarly use. Such a reappraisal of the term would allow for a more fruitful approach to these worlds. For instance, their immediate and ambiguous relation to the real world, which undoubtedly contributed to their imaginative force, would move into focus.

Let us return once more to the point where this discussion began, the fairy country described at length in *Sir Orfeo*. The fact that we immediately recognize that realm as a very particular kind of geographical space is not entirely a function of our own modern assumptions about fantastical otherworlds—the realm's resemblance to a very distinctive set of lands described in a whole range of texts is pronounced, and would have been more than evident to any medieval audience member who had heard a tale or two. In the absence of a clearly conceptualized category of the 'otherworld', it seems that the shared lexicon of motifs collected by Patch may not only point (as he argues) to shared and ancient sources for these depictions, but might be the primary and largely definitive signifier of the presence of a realm we like to call the 'otherworld' in literary texts. The markers of the otherworld come in the form of recurring images and themes. As such, it might be most helpful for scholars of medieval literature to think of the otherworld of medieval culture as primarily an *imaginative* (as opposed to an 'imaginary') field, rather than an ontological or ideological one. This has important implications for how otherworlds are treated in medieval scholarship. In particular, it suggests that, in negotiating the complex relationship between fiction and history, fiction might be a better starting point than has been previously thought.

From a narratological perspective, it might be more productive to avoid defining the otherworld as the place where the real and the natural gives way to the unreal and the supernatural, but instead to think of it as a wholly new horizon of expectations *within* the text. Beyond this horizon, the rules of engagement that have held true up to that point (and which are not necessarily those of the actual world) can no longer be taken for granted. Hans Jauss's notion is, of course, a tool developed for analysing and defining generic boundaries, rather than topographical or spatial boundaries within a narrative. However, the immersive nature of the otherworld encounter and the pronounced similarities between these spaces suggest that analytical models developed for dealing with genre might be readily applicable to these realms. Certain recent trends in the scholarship on medieval generic divisions dovetail with such an approach. In treating romance narratives, Helen Cooper has argued that medieval enthusiasm for re-using very conventional motifs in literary works should not be thought of as mindlessly repetitive but as creative variations on a theme.[65] Authorial originality lies not in the rejection of tradition, but in enlisting the semantic accretions which successive generations of authors have built up around a particular motif—what Cooper terms a 'meme'— to their own ends. In this respect, Cooper's argument provides a fresh approach to the defining of the notoriously polysemous genre of romance: motifs may serve as generic markers which enable audiences to recognize the relationships between individual texts and to place each text they encounter within a broader landscape of related narratives. The replication and recombination of these motifs is what draws these textual accounts together into a single family grouping. Similarly, it may be possible to think of the motifs of otherworld descriptions as signposts to the text's audience. Most fundamental among these markers, in that it is usually the first marker encountered in the text, is the otherworld boundary or entry point. Of all the subgroups of motifs associated with the otherworld (night-time light, jewelled landscapes, etc.), this is perhaps the smallest and most tightly knit group. The audience's expectations of the rules by which the narrative should operate are fundamentally altered through the cue given by the boundary between realms. If the encounter with the otherworld produces a shift in the horizon of expectations that the reader and the protagonist bring to bear on the action of the text, it may be thought of as analogous to the shift in cognitive expectation that takes place when encountering the fictional text itself. This means that in many narratives, the otherworld can be thought of as a fiction within a fiction.[66]

To think of otherworlds as primarily an imaginative field, rather than as a category defined by historical beliefs, encourages us to refigure the relationships we traditionally imagine between these realms and historical reality. It allows us to acknowledge the autonomy of medieval authors and places artistic creativity—so frequently sidelined in medieval literary

---

[65] Helen Cooper, *The English Romance in Time: Transforming Motifs from Geoffrey of Monmouth to the Death of Shakespeare* (Oxford: Oxford University Press, 2004), pp. 3–21.

[66] See further, Chapter 1.

studies—at the root of these descriptions.[67] In providing an experience analogous to fiction itself, the otherworld account holds up a mirror to the other realms depicted in the texts in which it features and introduces an extra perspective from which to view reality itself. What follows, therefore, takes the imaginative text as its starting point and proceeds from there to an appraisal of how the historical could be reshaped and influenced in the light of the imaginative. It is necessary to engage with history when considering the role of the otherworld in medieval writing, but desirable to do so on somewhat different terms than has traditionally been the case. Rather than focusing on how literary depictions of otherworlds draw upon established historical beliefs, this book suggests that it might be more fruitful to consider how the rhetoric of literary otherworlds is employed in an historical context. Taking this approach illustrates the imaginative impact of depictions of such realms and stresses the degree to which their depiction could impact on the actual world rather than constitute an escape from it.

The first chapter of this study, 'Imagining Otherworlds', develops an initial reading of otherworld encounters that highlights their role within the texts in which they are embedded, rather than their relationship to the historical context in which they are imagined; in Payne's terms, what otherworlds 'do to the surroundings into which they are brought'.[68] This chapter explores the ways in which authors build internally consistent fantastic realms that provide an incentive for the audience to 'make-believe'. It suggests that literary otherworlds, by their very nature, are well suited to the exploration of absolutes and profound difference, and that this quality is reflected in the themes most frequently associated with these realms in fiction: gender, desire, and death. The second chapter, 'Otherworlds and the Afterlife', presents the first of three 'historical' perspectives with which these fictional otherworlds interact. It addresses the relationship between the otherworld of Christian belief and depictions of more 'secular' otherworlds. While religious depictions of the afterlife constitute a 'special case' in having a clearly defined meaning derived from an ideology external to the text, they also share a lot of imaginative and thematic material with more secular otherworld descriptions. This chapter focuses on two of the most widely disseminated otherworld depictions: the *Tractatus de Purgatorio Sancti Patricii* and the *Navigatio Sancti Brendani Abbatis*. It considers the ways in which these texts are adapted throughout

---

[67] James Wade's recent book made fruitful use of such an approach in its treatment of the role of fairies in medieval writing. He makes the case for a 'new intentionality' that recognizes the 'world constructing powers of the author'. Wade, *Fairies*, p. 7.

[68] Payne, 'Review of Patch, *Other World*', 367.

the Middle Ages. In particular, it explores how these various adaptations blur the distinctions between the secular and the religious, the real and the imagined.

The third chapter of this study, 'Supernatural Authorities', expands this discussion into the sphere of worldly power, exploring the validating impact of the supernatural within and outside of literary narratives. The chapter starts by looking at a group of related Irish narratives where otherworld journeys play into ideas of kingship and succession. It proceeds to an analysis of the role of Avalon within the Arthurian tradition before exploring how Alexander's journey to the Earthly Paradise represents both the summit and the limit to the achievements of the 'greatest' human conqueror. Such political uses of otherworld imagery are most clearly visible from the third historical perspective that this book adopts: when texts rewrite actual world locations as otherworlds. The final chapter of this study, 'Archipelagic Otherworlds', attempts to refigure the relationship scholars have traditionally ascribed to the historical world and the fictive otherworld. Rather than seeing the narrative otherworld as merely a reflection of known or postulated historical beliefs, this chapter suggests that we can see the impact of literary otherworld accounts in how frequently and effectively imagery associated with them is applied in treatments of the history and geography of actual locations in the insular world.

1

Imagining Otherworlds

A significant number of medieval works—particularly romance texts—seek to negotiate such boundaries as the court and the wild, and the familiar and the 'other', but the depth of otherworldly difference makes it possible to distinguish these realms from other 'alien' spaces. No matter how exotic the territory encountered by the traveller in the actual world, be it the wilderness, the forest, or the marvellous East, the laws of nature do not usually shift and, when such realms prove themselves more apt to produce marvels than familiar locations, it is still understood that such phenomena are exceptions to the rule, not manifestations of an alternative set of rules. By contrast, otherworlds do not merely differ in man-made, mutable things like societal structures, or customs, or even in exotic flora and fauna, they are of another nature entirely: night may never occur there, seasonal differences may be elided, time may pass at a different rate, and space may have an entirely different value. The otherworld also stands out from many such realms in being thoroughly inassimilable. Although the physical boundaries between the worlds may be crossed—most frequently in romantic attachments that can form between otherworld beings and humans—there is never any real prospect of a thoroughgoing reconciliation between the two spheres. Their fundamental separateness from the actual world is stressed by the emphasis given to the boundaries between the real and the other in these accounts. On the brink of entry into the otherworld, at a hillside cave, or on a river bank, the audience's horizon of expectations shifts for a second time, and that of the narrative's human protagonist for the first time, enabling these discrete spaces within narrative texts to mimic the processes of fiction itself.

This is why, as I have outlined, the otherworld might be described as a fiction within a fiction. If the encounter with the otherworld produces a shift in the horizon of expectations the reader and the protagonist bring to bear on the action of the text, it may be thought of as analogous to the shift in cognitive expectation that takes place when encountering the narrative text itself. This is something John Carey has observed with reference to medieval Irish texts. He notes that there is often a 'parallelism between Otherworld and narrative world' and that certain characteristics

of the otherworld mimic those 'of the imagination itself—more specifically, of the imagination as expressed in narrative'.[1] The treatment of time
in otherworld accounts is a case in point: in these places 'time and space
can be telescoped at will', in the same way temporalities can be manipu-
lated in narrative.[2] Carey makes a connection between this quality of the
otherworld and the association of supernatural beings with artifice in Irish
mythology. They are often depicted as the first practitioners of various
arts, including poetry. Such an explicit and consistent association of
otherworld inhabitants with artifice is not present in other mythological
and literary traditions; however, the connection Carey makes between
the otherworld and products of the imagination can be discerned beyond
Ireland. Connecting the magical arts, with their world-constructing
powers, with art itself is a very natural thing to do. In most descriptions,
the otherworld is marked by a rather inorganic quality.[3] There is often a
stress on the spectacular, delicately crafted nature of palaces and other
dwellings. Objects are of the very finest quality and sumptuously decorated, while landscapes are adorned with gems and precious metals. The
Middle English *Sir Orfeo* seems to hint at a connection between a product
of creative art and the experience of the otherworld. Only two things are
compared to 'paradis' in the poem: Orfeo's musical performance and the
otherworld he encounters. In the early lines of the poem his music is
described in glowing terms:

> In al the warld was no man bore   [born
> That ones Orfeo sat bifore—
> And he might of his harping here—
> Bot he schuld thenche that he were   [think
> In on of the joies of Paradis,
> Swiche melody in his harping is.[4]

Several hundred lines later, as Orfeo first sees the fairy kingdom, precisely
the same comparison is made, and expressed in a very similar manner:

> No man may telle, no thenche in thought,   [nor think
> The riche werk that ther was wrought.
> Bi al thing him think that it is
> The proude court of Paradis.[5]

---

[1] John Carey, 'Otherworlds and Verbal Worlds in Middle Irish Narrative', *Proceedings of the Harvard Celtic Colloquium*, 9 (1990), 32–42 (pp. 31–2).
[2] Carey, 'Otherworlds and Verbal Worlds', p. 32.
[3] Carey, 'Otherworlds and Verbal Worlds', p. 32.
[4] *Sir Orfeo*, edited by Bliss, ll. 33–8.
[5] *Sir Orfeo*, edited by Bliss, ll. 372–5.

The initial vision of the landscape of fairyland seems to ravish Orfeo's senses in a fashion that parallels the effect his music has on others, the physical transportation from one world to another echoing the experience of sensory transport that the king's harping produces. The verbal linking of these overwhelming sensory experiences—one visual and one aural—stresses their status as the twin sources of power within the poem. Orfeo's harping takes on the quality of an enchantment; however, in stark contrast to otherworld magic, his spell binds by seduction rather than coercion.

In providing an experience analogous to fiction itself, the otherworld account holds up a mirror to the narrative world and introduces an extra perspective from which to view reality. This relationship might be expressed by borrowing and extending J. R. R. Tolkien's formulation where the reader's own world and the world of the fictional text are envisioned as 'primary' and 'secondary' worlds respectively.[6] In this perspective, otherworld realms in narratives may be considered 'tertiary' worlds. When contrasting worlds are brought together they inevitably prompt comparisons between them. The introduction of this third term of comparison—the tertiary world—into a narrative allows for a considerably broader range of interpretative permutations than the actual-fictional binary ordinarily permits. Tertiary worlds may also function as a means of enhancing the applicability of the text, pushing the secondary world closer to that of the reader by contrasting it with the overwhelming strangeness of the otherworld realm—the fantastical working to define the verisimilar.[7] Such counterpoint may invite empathy. For instance, Orfeo's encounter with the strange and sinister fairy realm renders the seemingly far-off world of ancient Thrace/Winchester more immediate and the emotional ties that lie at the heart of the romance more real to the text's audience. In this sense, otherworlds enhance the recognizability and further the 'realism' of the secondary world.

The flexibility of this tripartite arrangement is evident in the story of King Herla in Walter Map's *De nugis curialium* (Courtiers' Trifles).[8] Herla, a king of the ancient Britons, is visited by a man of tiny stature who rides a goat. This man claims he is also a king and makes an agreement with Herla that each will attend the other's wedding feast. The tiny king and his men provide Herla's feast with abundant food and

[6] J. R. R. Tolkien, 'On Fairy Stories', in *The Monsters and the Critics and other Essays* (London: Allen and Unwin, 1983), pp. 109–61.

[7] D. H. Green defines the three types of medieval narrative as the *historia*, the *argumentum*, and the *fabula*, terms which express a sliding scale that moves progressively away from reality and which seem to me to approximate rather closely to the difference between primary, secondary, and tertiary worlds (Green, *Beginnings of Medieval Romance*, pp. 6–9).

[8] Map, *De Nugis Curialium*, I: 11, pp. 26–31.

with vessels made from gold and precious stones, before departing for their own country. A year later, Herla is summoned to fulfil his side of the pact. He and his retinue ride through a cave in the side of a hill and find a beautiful land lit by lamps, rather than by the sun and moon, and enter a mansion, which Map likens to the palace of the sun described briefly in Ovid's *Metamorphoses*. After attending the wedding, Herla and his men are given gifts and a bloodhound by the king of the other country. They are warned against dismounting in their own land until the dog has leapt forwards. On re-emerging into daylight, they discover that, although it seemed that they had only spent three days away, centuries have passed in their own world, the rule of the Britons has been succeeded by that of the Anglo-Saxons, and Herla's own name has dwindled into legend. Some of his troops try to dismount, but turn to dust. Herla warns the remaining men to remain on their horses until the bloodhound leaps forward, but he never does so and the Britons are condemned to a perpetual wandering.

The story forms part of Map's satirical depiction of the court of Henry II, in his view a hell-like and restless place.[9] The account of King Herla's otherworld journey begins by stressing the applicability of the narrative to the audience's primary world ('One court and one only do stories tell of that is like our own'),[10] but it is not clear to which of the courts depicted in the text Map is referring until the close of the tale. The secondary world of the human court seems the most immediately recognizable narrative space. This realm engages the sympathies of the audience by stressing the very human awe and confusion of its inhabitants when they are confronted with the outlandish company and abundant wealth of the pygmy king. His tertiary world, accessed through a hillside and lit by many lamps, has sufficient richness, opulence, and (ostensible) courtesy to make it seem like an object of aspiration. Yet, by the end of the story, it becomes clear that the court which 'is like our own', or like Henry's, is that of the wandering Herla, who finds himself caught between two worlds, neither actual nor otherworldly, but in a sort of non-space, condemned to permanent restlessness.[11] We never hear enough about Herla's own court to ascertain whether his fate was deserved or not, and the precise position the realm of the pygmy king occupies on the spectrum of good and evil is never clarified. There is certainly something diabolical in the otherworld king's 'fiery' visage, red beard, and goat's hooves, but the explicit comparison Map makes is with Pan, rather than with the devil, though, of

[9] Map, *De Nugis Curialium*, I:10, pp. 14–17.

[10] 'Vnam tamen et solam huic nostre curie similem fuisse fabule dederunt'. Map, *De Nugis Curialium*, I: 11, p. 26.

[11] Map, *De Nugis Curialium*, I: 11, p. 31.

course, the iconography of these two figures regularly coalesces in this period.[12] The generosity, civility, and friendliness of these otherworld beings are stressed throughout the text. No hint of any malice is evident until Herla's men attempt to alight on their return to their world. Map's treatment of the otherworld multiplies the interpretative possibilities. The narrative's three distinct spaces—Henry's court, Herla's court, and the world of the pygmy king—never overlap or intersect and, as such, the relationship between them cannot be firmly established. The image in which the secondary and tertiary worlds might appear to combine, Herla's wandering court, is defined by its inability to inhabit a single fixed space.

Seeing the role of the otherworld within a narrative as an analogy for the operations of fiction itself is important for understanding the popularity of the otherworld as a narrative motif in medieval literature and the range of concerns that are often articulated through it. This interest in the inter-actions of widely different realms of experience may be one of the reasons why the otherworld comes into its own in romance (though the potential for immersive exploration of the magical and the supernatural must also be a contributory factor). Romance is characterized by its tendency to set up and then mediate oppositions. The intractable otherworld poses the most absolute opposition to the secondary world and stresses that the process of mediation is never easy and that the happily-ever-after reconciliations of romance are not foregone conclusions. By adding a third term of com-parison to the standard encounter between the actual and the fictional, the otherworld also multiplies the interpretative possibilities and, hence, the range of applications that the narrative may have to the reader's own world. It is this flexibility, borne of deeply entrenched difference, which allows the otherworld to perform so many roles within the plot and to bring together such a diverse range of themes in and across the texts in which it appears.

Medieval writers put the range of motifs and themes associated with the otherworld to a wide range of uses. On the broadest level, otherworld motifs can be divided into two categories: those that are central to the action of the plot and those that might seem more incidental. Motifs in this latter category are, nonetheless, crucial to otherworld accounts, because they are used to build highly detailed descriptions of these realms which give a degree of concreteness and, hence, believability to spaces that might otherwise be dismissed as merely fanciful. There are also a range of themes that are particularly characteristic of otherworld narratives; among

---

[12] Map, *De Nugis Curialium*, I: 11, p. 26. On the link between Pan and the devil, see Jeffrey Burton Russell, *Lucifer: The Devil in the Middle Ages* (Ithaca, NY and London: Cornell University Press, 1984), p. 68.

the most frequently explored are desire, gender, and death. The prevalence
of such themes is one of the paradoxes of otherworld narratives. The
degree of perspective offered by a tertiary world allows authors to use this
most fantastical of literary motifs to explore the weightiest of themes.
Although scholars have noted such themes in otherworld accounts before,
they have often linked their persistence to the influence of earlier texts or
of belief systems external to the texts themselves. The preoccupation with
death, for instance, reflects the sometimes porous boundary between
depictions of otherworlds and of afterlife realms.[13] However, an alternative interpretation is possible. It may be that the inherent qualities of
literary otherworlds, such as descriptive hyperbole, wish-fulfilment, excess,
and alterity, make such realms a particularly flexible tool for the exploration of that which is absolute, intractable, and deeply different.

What follows in this chapter asks why medieval authors, particularly
authors of romance, return so often to otherworlds: what made them such
a popular narrative vehicle? What were the imaginative challenges, opportunities, and significations of literary otherworlds? The way in which
otherworlds constitute a tertiary world is central to their interpretive
possibilities and implications. As a third term, otherworlds allow a more
multidirectional interpretative experience than that which is typically
allowed by the binary of the actual and fictional. We shall look first at
some recurring motifs, particularly those that seem, at first glance, to lack
deep narrative significance. Then I will take up some of the larger themes
that often feature in otherworld narratives.

PSEUDO-MIMESIS

A surprising number of motifs associated with the otherworld fail to
perform a clear narrative function. Their value seems to be almost entirely
ornamental, constituting what Roland Barthes termed 'insignificant notation'.[14] Features like gold and gemstones, beautiful music, year-round
summer, flowering plains, and night-time brightness rarely perform any
role in the story itself. Yet, otherworld settings seem to be an exception to
medieval authors' general (though by no means universal) lack of interest
in elaborately described landscapes. The realms of dream poetry are one of

---

[13] The relationship of otherworld narratives and afterlife accounts is discussed in
Chapter 2.
[14] Roland Barthes, 'The Reality Effect', in *The Novel: An Anthology of Criticism and
Theory, 1900–2000*, edited by Dorothy J. Hale (Oxford: Blackwell, 2006), pp. 229–34
(p. 231).

the most obvious exceptions to the sparing use of the *descriptio loci* in medieval narratives, but since dream landscapes are usually charged with allegorical meaning, the *descriptio* is central to the reading experience. By contrast, otherworld descriptions are, with very rare exceptions, completely unresponsive to allegorical modes of interpretation. Why, then, are extensive descriptions of otherworld spaces so numerous? The most obvious answer is that the descriptions proceed naturally from the author's desire to divert his audience with accounts of marvels and superlative beauty. However, there may be another motivation: this density of description induces the audience's willingness to make-believe. The shift from a relatively recognizable text world to one that is utterly fantastical may be more smoothly negotiated through a highly detailed, internally consistent account of the tertiary world.

There are various ways we might conceptualize this process. It is what Tolkien described as giving a realm 'the inner consistency of reality'[15] and it has some points of overlap with what Roland Barthes termed the 'reality effect'. Barthes' formulation, though neat, is somewhat problematic, since in medieval otherworld accounts the 'reality effect' is being produced in a situation that is completely without realism. Barthes does treat the medieval context, albeit briefly, in his essay. He characterizes medieval description as being 'constrained by no realism; its truth is unimportant' and he suggests that medieval literary descriptions have a primarily aesthetic function.[16] Be that as it may, insignificant notation in a medieval text can also serve purposes more akin to those Barthes ascribes to description in the modern novel. Although otherworld descriptions are by no means 'realistic', their level of detail creates the illusion that what they are describing might actually exist. This use of 'insignificant notation' in otherworld accounts might be termed *pseudo-mimesis*. These accounts have a level of detail that we would associate with a mimesis of reality, but what they are ultimately conveying is a fantasy.

In otherworld accounts, elaborate pseudo-mimetic descriptions can be a prerequisite for narrative action, at least for the sorts of alternative narrative actions fantastical locations allow. For instance, it is, in part, its noticeable lack of descriptive detail that renders the fairyland of *Sir Thopas* comically underwhelming. There appears to be no clear boundary between this particular otherworld and the actual world (it is merely in a secluded location) and Chaucer offers no description of it other than the vague comment that it is 'so wilde'.[17] The otherworld evoked by Chaucer

---

[15] Tolkien, 'On Fairy Stories', p. 139.   [16] Barthes, 'Reality Effect', p. 231.
[17] Geoffrey Chaucer, 'Sir Thopas', in *The Riverside Chaucer*, edited by Larry D. Benson, 3rd edn (Oxford: Oxford University Press, 1987), pp. 212–16, l. 803.

the Pilgrim fails to rehearse any of the conventions of the otherworld description and, as such, lacks any capacity to awe or to enchant and provides no incentive to make-believe. The necessity of extensive description to the narrative is perhaps best exemplified by the various medieval versions of *Lanval,* from Marie de France to the account by Thomas Chestre. Because the encounter with the fairy injects a whole set of new expectations into the plot, the audience's belief in the text's supernatural framework is crucial. *Lanval* does not explicitly remove its hero to his fairy mistress's otherworld realm until the very last lines of the poem. Deferral of the otherworld visit to the end of the text has the advantage of making that journey more climactic, but its postponement makes belief in the otherworld rules introduced early in the narrative more challenging. Description plays a large part in surmounting this obstacle. This narrative devotes considerable attention to describing the pavilion in which the fairy initially meets the knight. We have already had some hint that the knight may be close to the border of the otherworld. Marie describes how Lanval's horse starts to tremble and become agitated when the knight arrives at a river. He first sees the ladies who take him to the fairy's pavilion when he dismounts there.[18] Although Lanval never seems to cross the river, the hint that it might be an otherworld boundary paves the way for the marvels that follow.[19] Regardless of its precise position relative to the otherworld, this pavilion appears to be a space where the rules of the otherworld might be expected to operate. The suggestion is reinforced by the profusion of visual detail that echoes the conventional material of otherworld accounts. The depth of description is particularly marked in the Middle English versions. The author of *Sir Landevale* notes that the pavilion was 'With treysour i-wrought on euery syde' and that each pommel was worth the price of a city.[20] The pavilion is topped with the figure of a heron that holds a light-emitting carbuncle in his mouth. Thomas Chestre's version, *Sir Launfal,* describes the pavilion as the 'werk of Sarsynys', that has 'pomelles of crystal' and is surmounted by an eagle of burnished gold and enamel who has eyes of carbuncle: 'As the mone they schon anyght, / That spreteth [spreads] out ovyr all'.[21] The

[18] Marie de France, *Lanval*, in *Lais*, edited by A. Ewert (Oxford: Blackwell, 1978), pp. 58–74, ll. 45–56.

[19] A. C. Spearing, *The Medieval Poet as Voyeur: Looking and Listening in Medieval Love-Narratives* (Cambridge: Cambridge University Press, 1993), pp. 98–9.

[20] *Sir Landevale*, in *The Middle English Breton Lays*, edited by Anne Laskaya and Eve Salisbury (Kalamazoo, MI: Medieval Institute Publications, 1995), pp. 423–37, ll. 79–82.

[21] Thomas Chestre, *Sir Launfal*, edited by Laskaya and Salisbury, pp. 201–62, ll. 266, 272–3. A. C. Spearing explores how the various versions of this very visual description

crystal decoration is characteristically otherworldly and the role of the carbuncle in providing twenty-four hour illumination to a dwelling place is also a conventional otherworld motif. Both Marie de France and her Middle English adaptors stress the exceptional nature of the setting by noting that no earthly ruler could afford such luxury; Marie says that the riches of Semiramis and Octavian were inferior to these, while the Middle English versions make comparison with Arthur and Alexander.

Arthur and Alexander are interesting choices in this context since both made celebrated otherworld journeys that parallel certain elements in Lanval's own encounter; the former travelled to the realm of a well-disposed fairy and the latter in certain versions of his legend sought out the riches and beauty of the Earthly Paradise.[22] This apparent allusion to other encounters with the supernatural is very much in the spirit of the otherworld description. Willingness to make-believe is facilitated by the conspicuous intertextuality of otherworld accounts, where the same group of images is employed in multiple texts. Drawing attention to the resemblances between these realms is a strategy that elsewhere helps underscore the authenticity of religious visions of the afterlife, where descriptions usually have what R. Howard Bloch has called a 'collated quality'.[23] Since all afterlife visions purport to depict the same set of spaces, resemblance to previous accepted reports is an important element in authenticating individual experiences. This interest in authentication is obviously linked to the non-fictional nature of these texts, yet this 'collated quality' is also in evidence in otherworld accounts that are less invested in their own factuality. Such intertextual similarities in fictional material are all too frequently interpreted as a reflection of the pagan beliefs of an earlier age or of folkloric influences, but there is also the possibility that they might be partially or wholly a conscious strategy deployed by medieval authors. The 'collated' quality of otherworld narratives can provide a further aid to the process of 'make-believe' in implying that all these texts report experiences of the same set of realms.

Several elements in *Immram Brain*'s treatment of the otherworld suggest that it might be pseudo-mimetic. This Irish voyage narrative may date from as early as *c.*900, but it was read and copied as late as the fifteenth century and describes otherworld geography at considerable

---

relate to the poems' wider emphasis on the act of gazing in *Medieval Poet as Voyeur*, pp. 97–119.

[22] Both of these legends are discussed at further length in Chapter 3.

[23] R. Howard Bloch, *The Anonymous Marie De France* (Chicago: University of Chicago Press, 2003), p. 263.

length.[24] It tells of the wonders Bran the son of Febal and his men encounter on a voyage across the ocean to the Land of Women. Like King Herla and his men, they return after a year in the otherworld to discover that far more time has elapsed in their own world. When one of Bran's men touches the earth, he turns to dust. The text is a relatively short one, and the most sustained otherworld account comes in the song of a mysterious woman who appears in Bran's hall at the start of the narrative and convinces him to undertake the voyage. Although the text promises fifty quatrains (the number is specified twice in the opening lines of the text), no surviving manuscript delivers more than twenty-eight, yet, of these, twenty-two are given over to an often highly enigmatic description of an island paradise. Since it appears at an early stage of the narrative, this extensive and immersive description helps create an otherworldly horizon of expectations. The ratio of description to narrative in *Immram Brain* as a whole is strikingly high. Of the sixty-six sections observed by the text's modern editors, thirty-seven are given over to description of otherworld locations. Indeed, the linguistic evidence suggests that, in the case of this particular text, description may have given rise to narrative rather than the reverse. The text's most recent editor, Séamus Mac Mathúna, has suggested that quatrains 3–25 of the twenty-eight spoken by the otherworld woman at Bran's palace 'form the nucleus around which the remainder of the tale is built'.[25] These quatrains are, for the most part, a detailed account of the topography of the woman's island paradise. If Mac Mathúna's theory is correct, then the narrative is extrapolated from the otherworld description in a manner that echoes the strategy of creating whole narratives to explain toponyms in the Irish *dinnshenchas* (place-name lore) tradition.

The number of toponyms in these verses, most of them unattested in any other text, is striking. In all, there are twelve points where place names occur: *Eamhain* (mentioned three times; in paragraphs 3, 10, and 19), *Mag Findargat* ('White-silver Plain'; 5), *Mag Argatnél* ('Silver cloud Plain'; 8), *Aircthech* ('Bountiful Land'; 12), *Cíuin* ('Gentle Land'; 13), *Imchíuin* ('Very Gentle Land'; 21), *Mag Réin* ('Plain of the Sea'; 14), *Mag Mon* ('Plain of Sports', mentioned twice; 14, 23), and *Ildathach* ('Many-coloured Land'; 24). Of these names, only *Eamhain* is well attested elsewhere, though its range of reference is quite wide and its precise meaning can be rather ambiguous.[26] The seeming obscurity of most of these toponyms may be due, in part, to the relatively early date of the text and it is not impossible that they had a

---

[24] *Immram Brain: Bran's Journey to the Land of Women*, edited by Séamus Mac Mathúna (Tübingen: Niemeyer, 1985).

[25] *Immram Brain*, edited by Mac Mathúna, p. 295.

[26] For one interpretation of its resonances in this context, see *Immram Brain*, edited by Mac Mathúna, pp. 129, 295–6.

clear frame of reference at the time of the poem's composition. On the other hand, their absence from other similarly early texts—particularly other *immrama* and *echtrae*, all of which might be expected to deploy a comparable range of vocabulary—complicates such an assumption. At the very least, it seems clear that the later audiences of the text did not recognize the names. In the manuscript tradition of *Immram Brain*, the place names given above are glossed with phrases like *i.e. regio*, or *i.e. nomen regionis*. For instance, *Mag Argatnél* is glossed '.i. nomen regionis' in six manuscripts, *Ildathach* is glossed '.i. regio' in three manuscripts, and '.i. nomen regionis' in two, while *Cíuin* is glossed as an island ('insola') in four manuscripts, and 'nomen regionis' in another.[27]

The antiquity of this glossatorial tradition is difficult to determine. All but one of the manuscript witnesses to this text date from the fourteenth century or later; the earlier manuscript, *Lebor na hUidre* (Book of the Dun Cow), dates from *c.*1100, but preserves only the final few lines of *Immram Brain*,[28] and lacks the portions of the narrative that are glossed in later copies. Linguistic evidence is more instructive, but it must be derived from other recurring glosses to this text in which Irish is used rather than Latin. These Irish annotations appear to date from the Middle Irish period[29] (roughly from the tenth to the twelfth century), suggesting that, if the *Immram Brain* glosses originate as a group, the Latin toponym glosses quoted above are no later than the twelfth century. Such glosses suggest that the precise identity of these places might have been largely opaque to the text's medieval audiences from an early stage or, indeed, from the beginning. It is possible that the profusion of place names is a rhetorical strategy designed to enhance the tangibility of the land described through the inclusion of a large number of pseudo-factual details. There can be little doubt that these terms inject a degree of concreteness into the fantastical account, giving the woman's song the texture of an extensive verse topography, rather than a flight of fancy. A similar aid to the audience's make-believe is provided in the quatrain:

> There are thrice fifty distant isles
> In the ocean to the west of us;
> Larger than Erin twice
> Is each of them, or thrice.[30]

---

[27] See notes to the relevant lines in Mac Mathúna's edition, where the manuscript glosses are given.

[28] Royal Irish Academy MS 23 E 25, p. 121. *Lebor na hUidre: Book of the Dun Cow*, edited by R. I. Best and Osborn Bergin (Dublin: Royal Irish Academy, 1929), p. 306.

[29] *Immram Brain*, edited by Mac Mathúna, p. 25.

[30] 'Fil trí coícta inse cían / isind oceon frinn aníar; / is mó Érinn co fa dí / cach aí díïb nó fa thrí'. *Immram*, edited by Mac Mathúna, p. 37.

Populating the unmapped spaces of the Atlantic with islands of such number and size goes some way towards demystifying the ocean by the addition of concrete points of reference.

A similar pseudo-mimetic process may underlie enigmatic references in the Middle English versions of the *Lanval* story. Both *Sir Landevale* and Thomas Chestre's later *Sir Launfal* significantly expand the account given in Marie's poem where the fairy's origins, and indeed her status as a fairy, go unmentioned until she takes Lanval away with her to Avalon in the final lines. In *Sir Landavale*, by contrast she is identified as a fairy, she is:

> The kynges daughter of Amylione,—
> That ys an ile of the fayre
> In occian fulle faire to see.[31]   [the west

Thomas Chestre's text is even more detailed:

> The kinges doughter of Olyroun,
> Dame Triamour that highte;   [named
> Her fader was King of Fairie,
> Of Occient, fer and nighe,
> A man of mochell mighte.[32]   [great

Such locational specificity is notable in these poems, which otherwise display a certain vagueness about locations in general. The references to 'occian' and 'Occient' suggests the usual association of the Western ocean with supernatural utopias. The place names 'Amylione' and 'Olyroun' are less easily accounted for. The former has been interpreted by G. L. Kittredge as a corruption of Marie's 'Avalon'.[33] Minim confusion seems the likeliest culprit here, given the wide variety of attested Middle English spellings of Avalon.[34] A detail from the final lines of *Sir Landevale* also reinforces the idea that 'Amylione' is a misreading of an exemplar's rendering of Avalon: here Lanval's final destination is described as a location known to every Briton ('. . . a joly yle / That is clepyd [called] Amylyon / That knowith every Brytan.').[35] 'Amylione', a location attested nowhere else in the surviving corpus, seems a poor candidate for such a description, whereas Avalon is a perfect fit. *Sir Launfal*'s 'Olyroun' is a more interesting case and has the hallmarks of a conscious adaptation of

---

[31] *Sir Landevale*, edited by Laskaya and Salisbury, ll. 90–2.

[32] Thomas Chestre, *Sir Launfal*, ll. 278–81.

[33] For a discussion, see G. L. Kittredge, 'Launfal', *The American Journal of Philology*, 10 (1889), 1–33, (pp. 13–14).

[34] Robert W. Ackerman, *An Index of the Arthurian Names in Middle English* (Stanford, CA: Stanford University Press, 1952), p. 21. The distance of 'Amylione' from attested spellings like 'Auelione' and 'Auailun' is not all that great.

[35] *Sir Landevale*, edited by Laskaya and Salisbury, ll. 532–4.

Marie's Avalon. Kittredge suggests that a reference may be intended to the island of Oléron off the coast of Brittany, but, although this seems plausible, this identification clarifies little, since no other text associates that island with a fairy kingdom. Matters are further complicated by the fact that the word is also reminiscent of the 'Île de Ore' where the supernatural lady dwells in *Le Bel Inconnu* and its English adaptation *Lybeaus Desconus*.[36] The textual evidence is insufficient to allow for a clear identification of this place, and perhaps searching for such identification is beside the point; after all, real-world referents are rarely sought for in the invented names of more modern fiction. Its cultural and intertextual resonances mean that 'Olyroun' is a thoroughly believable name for a supernatural island. Like the place names in *Immram Brain*, 'Olyroun' is concrete enough to command belief while also retaining enough non-specificity to maintain a sense of mystique.

Extensive pseudo-mimetic descriptions that encourage the audience to make-believe are particularly important in stories where supernatural encounters produce situations that contravene moral laws observed in the actual world. The potentially problematic sexual behaviour related in *Lanval* may contribute to the intense focus on otherworldly description in the various versions of the story. On the face of it, the extramarital liaison between the fairy and the knight can only be divested of its seeming immorality if the alterity of the fairy, unfettered by the ethics of the actual world, is firmly established. The descriptive richness that, on one level, renders the unfamiliar otherworld landscape more tangible could also be directed at establishing a very clear defamiliarization of the narrative's context. *Imramm Brain* may be read as exhibiting a similar impulse. In the course of his voyage, Bran encounters the sea deity Manannán mac Lir, who informs him that the inhabitants of the otherworld operate according to a different moral law:

> A beautiful game, most delightful,
> They play sitting at the luxurious wine,
> Men and gentle women under a bush,
> Without sin, without crime.[37]

Such 'play' seems to be encouraged by the living arrangements during the time Bran's company spend in the Land of Women: the account notes that 'they went into a large house, in which was a bed for every

---

[36] *Lybeaus Desconus*, in *Codex Ashmole 61: A Compilation of Popular Middle English Verse*, edited by George Shuffleton (Kalamazoo, MI: Medieval Institute Publications, 2008), pp. 111–64, l. 1317.

[37] 'Clu(i)che n-aímin n-inmeldag / aigdit fri find-imborbag, / fir is mná míne fo doss / cen peccad cen immarboss.' *Immram Brain*, edited by Mac Mathúna, p. 40.

couple, even thrice nine beds',[38] and leaves the audience to draw their own conclusions. Throughout the text, the descriptive depth with which the otherworld is constructed reinforces the impression that the laws of the actual world do not apply here. The point is driven home by another assertion of Manannán's—he claims that otherworld beings are immortal because 'the sin has not come to us'.[39] Because of, rather than despite, the fact it is described in very concrete terms, the otherworld remains necessarily 'other', and so allows for a wide range of behaviours that sit uneasily in the actual world.

The sort of rich description used in otherworld accounts can also lend itself to evoking the ambiguous and the intractable. Describing the supernatural presents a very particular set of problems and opportunities, of which the long account of the Green Knight when he enters Arthur's court is one of the best-known examples. The *Gawain*-poet's description is not short on information, but the profusion of detail tends to deepen the ambiguity of the figure rather than clarify it; the Green Knight manages to be courteous and wild, jolly and threatening, his size is never clearly established and his status as fairy or demon is not at all obvious.[40] Such detailed yet conflicting description of the supernatural has a destabilizing effect in a text like *Sir Orfeo*, whose otherworld realm is never fully explicable by the interpretative strategies that the poem's rich description nonetheless appears to prompt.[41] Abundant detail serves to deepen the mystery of a supernatural encounter in a particularly memorable fashion in the twelfth-century Anglo-Norman romance *Amadas et Ydoine*. One night while grieving over the tomb of his lover Ydoine, Amadas suddenly sees more than a thousand people in fine clothing approaching him in two companies.[42] A group of clerks bears a bier with a body covered in a golden cloth; they stop outside the walls of the graveyard and place the bier on the ground. On the other side of the cemetery, another host dismounts and Amadas's eyes fix on one particularly richly equipped,

---

[38] 'lotar íarom i tegd(a)is máir. Ar-ránic imdai cecha lámamn(a)e and .i. trí noí n-imdæ', *Immram*, edited by Mac Mathúna, p. 44.

[39] 'nín-táraill int immarbuss', *Immram*, edited by Mac Mathúna, p. 40.

[40] See further, Helen Cooper, 'The Supernatural', in *A Companion to the Gawain-Poet*, edited by Derek Brewer and Jonathan Gibson (Woodbridge: D. S. Brewer, 1997), pp. 277–91 (p. 287).

[41] For discussion of how the poem's otherworld seems to be a symbol of the unknowable and the chaotic, see Derek Pearsall, 'Madness in *Sir Orfeo* ', in *Romance Reading on the Book: Essays on Medieval Narrative Presented to Maldwyn Mills*, edited by Jennifer Fellows and others (Cardiff: University of Wales Press, 1996), pp. 51–63, and Neil Cartlidge, 'Sir Orfeo in the Otherworld: Courting Chaos?', *Studies in the Age of Chaucer*, 26 (2004), 195–226.

[42] *Amadas et Ydoine*, edited by John R. Reinhard (Paris: Honoré Champion, 1926), ll. 5611–20. There is an English translation: *Amadas and Ydoine*, translated by Ross G. Arthur (New York: Garland, 1993).

riderless white horse which is arrayed in cloth, gold, and gems; the bells on the harness play a strange and beautiful melody, but everything else is silent.[43] The effect is decidedly eerie, but the uncanny nature of the scene only becomes fully evident as the narrative progresses. A beautiful knight in rich golden armour rides up to Amadas and challenges him. He tests Amadas's loyalty to Ydoine by claiming to have been the lady's lover, and a bitter duel ensues. The confrontation occupies nearly seven hundred lines of the narrative, but at no point does the remainder of the vast and mysterious host play any role.

In a romance that is by no means economical with words, the significance of the great host is never revealed, and details like the beautiful white horse and the body on the bier are left unexplained. The entire tableau seems surplus to the requirements of the plot. The scene might be read as a means of establishing the immense power of the forces confronting Amadas, but even from that perspective it seems to labour the point. The fraught and lengthy encounter with the supernatural knight, where Amadas is almost killed on more than one occasion, makes his peril clear enough. Indeed, everything about the scene itself seems excessive: the vast number of people, the richness of their attire, and their superlative beauty all add up to an experience of descriptive overload. Not only does the description establish an otherworldly context for the action of the plot, but it goes some way towards conveying a realm of experience that neither Amadas nor the audience can adequately comprehend. The effect is highly ambiguous, but it is an ambiguity borne of too much detail rather than too little. Otherworld descriptions require a high level of detail, since—as *Sir Thopas* amply demonstrates—the otherworld that is too vaguely sketched tends to lack any real threat or allure, yet some authors seem to have exploited this requirement by pushing the extent and depth of their descriptions beyond the point where they merely facilitate make-believe, to produce effects that are memorably bizarre and haunting.

The uses and meanings of this sort of excess are explored in Neil Cartlidge's important article on the otherworld account in *Sir Orfeo*.[44] His analysis of the precursors of *Orfeo*'s uncanny otherworld description (including *Amadas et Ydoine*) concludes that these sort of descriptions of the otherworld are carefully crafted in order to allow authors to 'court chaos as a mood, as an idea'.[45] He highlights a particularly illustrative instance of how otherworld excess operates in *The Peterborough*

---

[43] *Amadas*, edited by Reinhard, ll. 5635–46.
[44] Cartlidge, 'Sir Orfeo in the Otherworld'.
[45] Cartlidge, 'Sir Orfeo in the Otherworld', 203.

Chronicle.[46] In the entry for the year 1127, the *Chronicle* describes how a Wild Hunt featuring huge black riders mounted on goats was seen in and around Peterborough. In contrast to *Amadas* and many other texts, we are guided in our interpretation of the meaning of this otherworld incursion. *The Peterborough Chronicle* connects this alarming event in the locality to the arrival of the corrupt abbot Henry of Poitou.[47] Yet, this is not as easy an interpretative refuge as it first appears. The sign and the signified are dramatically out of proportion to each other, making the connection seem 'magnificently overdetermined'.[48] This mismatch may not necessarily be a literary misstep, since, as Cartlidge notes, 'The strain of attempting to confine the tumultuously unconfinable significance of the Otherworld only serves to suggest something of the author's own sense of stress in the face of what he regards as an act of profound wickedness'.[49] We can extend this interpretation to other texts. For instance, the disturbing excess of the otherworldly host of *Amadas* evokes the awfulness of Ydoine's loss to an extent that would not be possible with a more readily analysable signifier.

The fact that effective otherworld descriptions are inherently excessive also makes them very susceptible to parody. There is a fine line between the uncanny effect of the great host in *Amadas* and descriptions that are merely ridiculous. Elaborate set-piece depictions that itemize the make-up of their subject tend to be most frequently associated with comedy in medieval vernacular literatures.[50] The fourteenth-century Hiberno-English *Land of Cokaygne* exhibits the same tendency towards descriptive superfluity as *Amadas*, but its effects are more comedic and pleasurable than haunting and disturbing.[51] Its author knows the conventions of otherworld accounts all too well and rehearses them to the point of descriptive redundancy. The work begins by claiming that '[t]hogh Paradis be miri and bright, / Cockaygn is of fairer sight'.[52] Paradise, so often the standard against which earthly beauty and comfort is measured, is

[46] *The Peterborough Chronicle, 1070–1174*, edited by Cecily Clark, 2nd edn (Oxford: Clarendon Press, 1970), p. 50.

[47] *Peterborough Chronicle*, edited by Clark, pp. 48–9.

[48] Cartlidge, 'Sir Orfeo in the Otherworld', 202–3.

[49] Cartlidge, 'Sir Orfeo in the Otherworld', 203.

[50] Cooper, *English Romance*, pp. 16–17. Indeed, as early as the second century, Lucian's *True History* had demonstrated the comic potential of fantastical journeys (Lucian, *The True History*, in *The Works of Lucian of Samosata*, translated by H. W. Fowler and F. G. Fowler, 4 vols (Oxford: Clarendon Press, 1905) II, 136–72).

[51] *Land of Cockaygne*, in *Anglo-Irish Poems of the Middle Ages*, edited by Angela Lucas (Dublin: Columba Press, 1995), pp. 46–72. On the Land of Cockaygne in medieval literary tradition, see Herman Pleij, *Dreaming of Cockaigne: Medieval Fantasies of the Perfect Life*, translated by Diane Webb (New York: Columbia University Press, 2001).

[52] *Land of Cockaygne*, edited by Lucas, ll. 5–6.

comically divested of its desirable qualities: accounts of the abundance of fruit in Eden are interpreted as meaning a corresponding lack of meat, the poet laments that Paradise has no drinking halls, only 'grasse and flure and grene ris', and notes that, since only Enoch and Elijah dwell there, it must be a lonely place.[53] He then goes on to enumerate the wonders of Cokaygne. At an early stage in the description, the poem moves into rhetoric typical of descriptions of paradise-like locations:

> Ther is mani swete sighte,
> Al is dai, nis ther no nighte.
> Ther nis baret nother strif,   [conflict
> Nis ther no deth ac euer lif.   [but
> Ther nis lac of met no cloth,
> Ther nis man no womman wroth.
> Ther nis serpent, wolf no fox...[54]

However, at this point, the description begins to press the rhetorical flourish towards the point of absurdity, eliminating features of the actual world that are by no means inimical to happy living:

> Hors no capil, kowe no ox,   [gelding
> Ther nis schepe, no swine, no gote
> Ne non horwgh, la, God it wote.[55]   [dung

The implication is that the daily grind of agricultural work is unnecessary in this fruitful island, but the lines carry the description so far from its original emphasis on the absence of life-threatening creatures that it appears absurd. The *Land of Cokaygne* deploys a wide range of motifs associated with Paradise in its description of its Atlantic island. Like Paradise, Cokaygne has four rivers, of oil, milk, honey, and wine;[56] no one dies there and there is twenty-four-hour daylight. Like the New Jerusalem, the monastic cloister on the island has pillars of crystal, there are many birds who sing all day and night, and, in an apparent reference to the Tree of Life in Eden, there is a beautiful tree which is described at length, but whose significance, in the end, appears to be merely aesthetic, rather than symbolic.[57] Gold and gems abound on the ground and in streams, and the poet, in a move that parallels numerous otherworld

---

[53] *Land of Cockaygne*, edited by Lucas, ll. 7–16.

[54] *Land of Cockaygne*, edited by Lucas, ll. 25–31.

[55] *Land of Cockaygne*, edited by Lucas, ll. 32–4.

[56] *Land of Cockaygne*, edited by Lucas, ll. 45–6. The four rivers of Paradise: Tigris, Euphrates, Geon, and Phison are associated with these substances in the popular *Apocalypse of St Paul: The Apocryphal New Testament*, translated by M. R. James (Oxford: Clarendon Press, 1924), p. 538.

[57] *Land of Cockaygne*, edited by Lucas, ll. 67–8, 95–100.

accounts, gives a catalogue of the specific jewels to be found there.[58] The comedy of *The Land of Cokaygne* is heavily dependent on its intertextuality and it is best read against the backdrop of medieval otherworld narratives. Most other writers treat such motifs with seriousness, particularly in accounts of Eden, and that seriousness serves to counterpoint the comical aspects of *Cokaygne*. These associations give the poem its distinctive comic texture, as images and ideas associated with the sublime are intertwined with descriptions of corrupt monks, animal manure, drunkenness, bawdy games, and garnished birds that cry 'Gees [geese] al hote, al hote!' as they fly— already cooked—into the mouths of the island's inhabitants.[59]

The short Middle Scots *eldritch* (uncanny) poems of the Bannatyne manuscript perhaps represent the most extreme manifestation of the comedy to be derived from the necessary excess of otherworld description.[60] Although collected in the second half of the sixteenth century, the poems appear to date from at least a century earlier and consist of short burlesque narratives that make free use of supernatural beings and motifs. One work, often known as *Lichtoun's Dreme*, recounts a series of journeys to fantastical realms prompted by overindulgence in 'gentill aill [ale]'.[61] Lichtoun imagines himself abducted and imprisoned by the 'King of Farye' in a palace made of 'mussill teith'.[62] He escapes and wanders through a variety of actual-world locations—before setting sail for the Earthly Paradise:

> Be we approchit inot þat port in hye
> We ware weill ware of Enoch and Elye
> Sittand, on ȝule evin, in ane fresch grene schwa   [wood
> Rostand straberris at ane fyre of snaw . . .[63]   [roasting

The poem evokes the tradition of Enoch and Elijah dwelling in the Earthly Paradise before collapsing the tableau into absurdity. In a set of texts where, in C. S. Lewis's words, 'the joke lies in the extravagance, the nonsensicality', the otherworld description provides ample grist to the comedic mill.[64]

---

[58] *Land of Cockaygne*, edited by Lucas, ll. 87–94.

[59] *Land of Cockaygne*, edited by Lucas, l. 104.

[60] Edinburgh, NLS Adv. MS 1.1.6, folios 101^r–102^r. For a more thorough examination of these poems, see Priscilla Bawcutt, 'Eldritch Comic Verse in Older Scots', in *Older Scots Literature*, edited by Sally Mapstone (Edinburgh: John Donald, 2005), pp. 292–313.

[61] *Lichtoun's Dreme*, in *The Bannatyne Manuscript*, edited by W. Tod Ritchie, 4 vols, STS, 2nd Ser., 22, 23, 26; 3rd Ser., 5 (Edinburgh: William Blackwood, 1928–1934), II (1928), pp. 268–71 (l. 90).

[62] *Lichtoun's Dreme*, ll. 6–10.   [63] *Lichtoun's Dreme*, ll. 39–42.

[64] C. S. Lewis, *English Literature in the Sixteenth Century Excluding Drama* (Oxford: Clarendon Press, 1944), p. 70.

OTHERWORLD EXCESS AND THE PERILS
OF DESIRE

The interest medieval writers often evince in human limitation is particularly pronounced in accounts where the mismatch between human nature and otherworld supernature is acute. The extremes of joy, beauty, wealth, and sensory stimulation that many such realms offer produce narrative treatments that may stress peril in the same breath as they express delight. Although the otherworld realm often appears to be what a human being would consider the 'land of heart's desire', the initial and active pursuit of desire is usually the prerogative of the otherworld being, a convention that seems to emphasize the limited potency of human will. Humans may not, in the ordinary course of things, actively seek out the joys of a supernatural realm. Sir Thopas proves himself comically ill-informed about the nature of otherworld narratives when he sets out to find an 'elf-queene'.[65] (Indeed, in a neat inversion of the convention, the text partly attributes Thopas's ultimate escape from the land to his 'fair berynge', the very quality that makes human protagonists of other narratives attractive to elf queens in the first place.)[66] Visiting the happy otherworld may seem to be the ultimate exercise in wish-fulfilment, where moral constraints are removed and humans may fulfil their desires without negative consequences. The paradigmatic instance of this fulfilment is the convention that human beings can indulge their sexual desires freely in the otherworld.

Marie de France's *Lais* deploy the idea at various points, while several Irish narratives insist on the possibility of sinless sex in an explicitly prelapsarian otherworld. The latter point is made in *Immram Brain*, in *Echtrae Chonnlai* (The Adventure of Connla), and in *Tochmarc Étaíne* (The Wooing of Étaín), where Midir tries to convince Étaín to accompany him back to his *síd* by means of the sort of detailed lyrical description employed elsewhere by otherworld women. He describes a land where there 'is neither mine nor thine', where people are eternally youthful, and where there are:

> Stately folk without blemish,
> conception without sin, without lust.
> We see everyone on every side,
> and no one seeth us.

---

[65] Chaucer, 'Sir Thopas', edited by Benson, ll. 798–9.
[66] Chaucer, 'Sir Thopas', edited by Benson, l. 832.

It is the darkness of Adam's transgression
that hath prevented us from being counted.[67]

The passage seems to owe something to Augustine's influential notion of lustless sex in a prelapsarian world[68] and recalls Manannán's assertion in *Immram Brain* that otherworld beings are, in some sense, unfallen. It is noteworthy that this sort of explicitly Christian rationalization of other-world behaviours does not tend to appear in later romance material, which typically has no recourse to frameworks of belief outside the text when presenting such conduct. The unglossed presentation of these behaviours in romance ensures that there is no rationalizing refuge for the audience; it presents human gratification at its most absolute and, therefore, the consequences at their most dramatic.

Of course, those narratives that leave aside the moral framework of Christianity at the entrance to the otherworld or in the encounter with an otherworld being often build up their own system of rules and guidelines to replace those they have discarded. A range of texts, including works like *Lanval* and *Melusine*, feature otherworld beings who impose taboos on their actual-world lovers.[69] These taboos may seem random but, from the point of view of sustaining narrative interest, they make sense.[70] A realm of completely unfettered sexual experience is not as interesting as a world where actions have consequences, and a plot needs complications to justify its existence. Gains in the otherworld are usually accompanied by losses or restrictions in the actual world. In *Immram Brain*, the sensual and sexual delights in which the hero and his company indulge in the otherworld appear to bind the hero and exact a price. The company is warned against touching the earth of Ireland on its return there and the only member of the group who does, Nechtán, turns to ashes immediately. This final alienation from their homeland, through their immersion in the other-world, is highlighted by the formal qualities of the narrative. Throughout the text, most descriptive passages (which generally focus on otherworldly

---

[67] 'daine delgnaide cen ón. / combart cen pecadh cen chol. / Atchiam cach for cach leath. / ₇ nícon aice nech. / teimel imorbuis Adaim / dodonarcheil ar araim.' 'Tochmarc Étaíne', edited by Osborn Bergin and R. I. Best, *Ériu*, 12 (1938), 137–96 (p. 180).

[68] Augustine of Hippo, *Concerning the City of God Against the Pagans*, translated by Henry Bettenson (Harmondsworth: Penguin, 1972), Book XIV, cpt 26, pp. 590–2.

[69] For a fuller account, see Wade, *Fairies*, pp. 109–45. These taboos in French and English romances have often been connected to the similar concept of the *geis* (taboo), widespread in Irish narrative. See further, John Revell Reinhard, *The Survival of Geis in Mediaeval Romance* (Halle: Max Niemeyer, 1933).

[70] For a fuller discussion of this view of romance taboos, see my paper: 'Fairy Lovers: Sexuality, Order and Narrative in Medieval Romance', in *Sexual Culture in Late-Medieval Britain*, edited by Robert Rouse and Cory Rushton (Cambridge: D.S. Brewer, 2014), pp. 99–110.

joy) are in verse, while the narrative portions are in prose. This fits well with the association the text establishes between music and the otherworld in its opening lines, where Bran is lulled to sleep by sweet music before coming upon the silver bough that presages his journey westwards.[71] Indeed, otherworld beings speak in verse and humans are restricted to prose until the final lines of the text, where Bran himself, after witnessing Nechtán's death, speaks one quatrain in mourning for him. This versification of human speech is apt coming at the point in the text where Bran and his companions have realized their otherworld experience has separated them permanently from the human world. Having fully partaken in the pleasures of the Land of Women, they are faced with the realization that it is essentially impossible to return home again.

In *Lanval*, the descriptive richness that, on one level, renders the unfamiliar otherworld landscape more tangible may also be directed at establishing a very clear defamiliarization of the narrative's context. So far, this recalls the Irish texts, like *Immram Brain*, which also feature lengthy descriptions of otherworld locations; however, *Lanval*'s engagement with the motif is more complex than this and must be situated within the overall structure of the narrative.[72] With his mistress's love and her generosity, Lanval lacks for nothing and this presents a problem: perfect bliss is no catalyst for narrative. The presentation of the fairy's pavilion has already gestured towards this—it is described at length and in loving detail, but it is static; in contrast to the paradigmatic landscape of romance, there are no opportunities here for onward exploration, and the necessary conditions for further plot development are lacking. The bliss of the fairy's bower is, formally and materially, a narrative dead end. Romance typically enacts a process of loss and recovery, or quest and reward. The satisfaction of the happy ending is in proportion to the perils and hardships endured to achieve it. In this respect, Lanval's happiness in the bower is not the happiness of the conventional romance ending. Lanval's perfect bliss with his fairy lover threatens to

---

[71] The narrative function of this item mirrors that of the more famous golden bough that provides Aeneas with access to the underworld in Book 6 of Virgil's epic. It is not improbable that the motif in the Latin poem lies behind that of the Irish text. Early medieval Ireland was no exception to the widespread popularity of Virgil's poem, and the existence of an early twelfth-century vernacular adaptation (*Imtheachta Aeniasa*) suggests that the work might have found a particularly wide audience in that island: see further, Erich Poppe, 'Imtheachta Aeniasa: Virgil's "Aeneid" in Medieval Ireland', *Classics Ireland*, 11 (2004), 74–94.

[72] For further discussion of this motif, see Cooper, *English Romance in Time*, Chapter 4; Carolyne Larrington, 'The Fairy Mistress: A Medieval Literary Fantasy', in *Writing and Fantasy*, edited by Ceri Sullivan and Barbara White, Longman Cross-Currents Series, (Harlow: Longman, 1999), 32–47.

short-circuit the narrative, placing the happy ending so close to the opening that it becomes banal.

This is where the taboo comes in. The fairy mandates Lanval to keep their liaison secret and never to mention her to others. On the most obvious level, this enjoinder reanimates the narrative, and Lanval's eventual violation of the taboo provides the necessary complication for the onward movement of the plot. Yet, the taboo itself is curious, primarily because it bears no relation to the situation at hand. It seems completely gratuitous and appears to have no clear moral or ethical import. It is difficult to escape the feeling that the imposition of the taboo is a piece of poetic expedience, a rather clumsy *deus ex machina* introduced to solve a plot problem of the poet's own making. However, the persistence with which authors engage with these sorts of taboos and the quality of the texts they produce argue against such an interpretation. As Wade has stressed, the caprice and arbitrariness of fairies in romance creates an ideal space for literary experimentation, a sort of literary laboratory.[73] When considered in the overall context of the otherworld plot, taboos reflect and probe some of the problems and opportunities presented by the tertiary world. Just as the otherworld often provides a means of stepping outside the human world in order to return to it with a greater degree of understanding, otherworld taboos may not only construct a space apart from conventional morality, but they can also enable a further stage of ethical engagement. The taboos are defined by their illogic and arbitrariness and, as such, draw attention to themselves in a way that foregrounds and emphasizes the machinery of the plot. Such an exposition can have what might be considered 'ethical' dimensions. It queries unproblematic and unfettered wish-fulfilment, but does so in narratological, rather than ideological, terms. It highlights the fact that completely fulfilled desire imposes a limit on narrative. In this respect, the treatment of the otherworld lover in a romance like *Lanval* is distinct from its treatment in texts like *Immram Brain* and *Tochmarc Étaíne*. Though never rationalizing or explaining the fairy's morality in terms of Christian ideas like prelapsarian behaviours, texts like *Lanval* still use the motif to produce plots that highlight distinctly non-transgressive orthodox ideas.

The ethical dimension of this literary experimentation is even clearer when we consider how the experience of narrative stasis affects the human protagonist of the romance. The human's peril is not explicitly moral, but, in romance terms, it is real and acute. It might be characterized in terms of a certain diminution on the level of both the plot and the individual, a

---

[73] Wade, *Fairies*, pp. 3–6.

potential curtailing of the narrative action that mirrors a stunting of the personal growth so fundamental to romance. Complete fulfilment without effort, self-denial, or sacrifice diminishes the hero of romance. Breaching the taboo provides the means, not only to reanimate the plot, but to test the human protagonist. Lanval's sufferings when he realizes that his taboo-breach has lost him his love are described at great length in all versions of the story. The necessity of some sort of personal sacrifice as a prelude to fulfilled desire is articulated particularly emphatically in the very similar narrative of *Graelent*. Here the fairy only forgives the protagonist for breaking the taboo when he nearly dies in the attempt to follow her across a turbulent river.[74] This gesture of self-sacrifice leads to fulfilment of a more complete kind than the initial one. Their relationship is healed by the gesture and the fairy takes Graelent definitively into the otherworld.

Like *Graelent*, *Lanval* also ends with the hero's disappearance into the otherworld. The treatment of this final episode in these two texts usually attributed to Marie is worth considering further. The narrative shape of both *Lanval* and *Graelent* asserts the value that should be placed on fulfilled desire, while also recognizing the limitations and problems that attend it in the human world. These romances avoid the twin poles of puritanical anxiety and sensual fantasy by stressing this world is not the natural place for unfettered gratification, but that another one might be. The echo of religious thinking is obvious and is most pronounced at the end of *Lanval* and *Graelent* when removal to the otherworld is figured in terms very reminiscent of death. Human life and the progress of narrative are drawn together particularly clearly in Thomas Chestre's version of *Lanval*; definitive abandonment of this world is the point where this narrative breaks down, where the reach of words ends, and silence takes over:

> Thus Launfal, wythouten fable,
> That noble knyght of the Rounde Table,
> Was take ynto Fayrye;
> Seththe saw hym yn thys lond noman,   [Since then
> Ne no more of hym telle y ne can
> For sothe, wythoute lye.[75]   [truth

This land to which Lanval departs is, presumably, the Olyroun with which Triamour has been associated earlier in the narrative. The association with

[74] *Graelent*, in *Eleven Old French Narrative Lays*, edited Glyn S. Burgess and Leslie C. Brook (Cambridge: D. S. Brewer, 2007), pp. 349–412 (ll. 680–731).
[75] Thomas Chestre, *Sir Launfal*, ll. 1033–8.

death is made even more explicit in *Graelent*. At the close of the poem we are offered a title for the story, the *Death of Graelant*, even though a few lines earlier it is noted that the hero lives on in the otherworld.[76] Death is the ultimate experience of stasis and, as such, definitive removal to the otherworld provides both a natural correlative for it and an arena where complete fulfilment of desire no longer limits the hero, because trial and ensuing personal growth are no longer a condition for happy human existence.

The anxiety authors can exhibit about the attractions of the otherworld is by no means limited to sexual desire. Availability and consumption of food and drink is a particular concern of otherworld narratives (though it has elicited considerably less scholarly comment than the theme of sexuality).[77] In some texts the two themes are intertwined. The otherworld woman of *Echtrae Chonnlai* lists 'everlasting feasts without service'[78] as one of the qualities of her island home and Midir uses the metaphor of drink to describe the merits and seductive qualities of his kingdom to Étaín: 'Though choice you deem the ale of Inis Fáil [i.e. Ireland], / More intoxicating is the ale of Tír Már [i.e. the otherworld]'.[79] Both otherworld beings are trying to seduce their interlocutor. The notion that food might be available 'without service', or without requiring any effort in preparation, is also a feature of other early Irish texts, such as the first recension of *Tochmarc Becfhola* (The Wooing of Becfola), where the hero travels with an otherworld woman to a deserted island and is supplied with food as soon as he reaches out his hands.[80] Carey has linked this motif to the prelapsarian connotations of these beings and these worlds in Irish narratives—in the same way the inhabitants of the otherworld experience the lustless sex associated with Eden, they are also free of any postlapsarian necessity to labour for their food.[81] Marie's *Lanval* uses the metaphor of food to express the sexual fulfilment the knight finds with the otherworld

---

[76] '.I. lai en firent li Breton; Graalant Muer l'apele l'on.' *Graelent*, edited by Burgess and Brook, ll. 734, 755–6.

[77] An exception is the treatment of consumption in Pleij, *Dreaming of Cockaigne*, pp. 89–162. This discussion focuses primarily on textual evidence from the Low Countries.

[78] 'fleda búana cen frithgnam', *Echtrae Chonnlai*, edited by Kim McCone, in *Echtrae Chonnlai and the Beginnings of Vernacular Narrative Writing in Ireland* (Maynooth: Maynooth Monographs, 2000), pp. 121–3, section 3.

[79] 'Cidh caín lib coirm Insi Fail, / is mescu cuirm Thiri Mair', 'Tochmarc Étaíne', edited by Bergin and Best, p. 180.

[80] 'Tochmarc Becfhola', edited by Máire Bhreathnach, *Ériu*, 35 (1984), 59–91 (p. 74). Later romance texts like *Partonope of Blois* may make a similar point less explicitly in depicting otherworld feasts served by invisible hands (*Partonope of Blois*, edited by A. Trampe Bödtker, EETS, e.s., 109 (1912), ll. 1002–1105).

[81] For comment on this motif and its prelapsarian connotations, see John Carey, 'Rhetoric of *Echtrae Chonlai*', 46.

lady: 'There was one dish in abundance that pleased the knight particularly, for he often kissed his beloved and embraced her closely'[82]—a way of putting things that is less like an erotic approach to food than a gastronomic approach to sex. The most obvious reasons for this emphasis on consumption are practical. The need to obtain a regular supply of food in the course of a long journey through unfamiliar territory almost becomes a leitmotif in *Immram Máele Dúin* (The Voyage of Máel Dúin) and provides the motivation for more than one island sojourn.[83] The availability of food and drink is the first quality of the eponymous realm mentioned in *The Land of Cokaygne*: 'In Cokaigne is met and drink, / With-vte care, how and swink [distress and labour]'.[84] The association of the otherworld with an endless supply of food is taken to its extreme in the late Middle Irish satire *Aislinge Meic Conglinne* (MacConglinne's Vision). The text recounts how a king of the Eóganachta dynasty, Cathal mac Finguine, was freed from the demon of gluttony by Aniér MacConglinne, who had a vision of an island across the ocean made entirely of food:

> The fort we reached was beautiful,
> With works of custards thick,
> Beyond the loch.
> New butter was the bridge in front,
> The rubble dyke was wheaten white,
> Bacon the palisade.[85]

The sheer excess of the vision, which piles image after image of food and drink upon each other, disgusts the king sufficiently to cure him of gluttony and, as MacConglinne finishes his speech, the demon is driven out of him.

There also appears to be a good deal of symbolism attached to consumption and non-consumption of otherworld food and drink. Ingesting something from the otherworld tends to commit the human to that realm

---

[82] 'Un entremés i ot plener, / Que mut pleiseit al chevalier: / Kar s'amie baisout sovent / E acolot estreitement', Marie, *Lanval*, p. 62 (ll. 185–8); translation from *The Lays of Marie de France*, translated by Glyn Burgess and Keith Busby (Harmondsworth: Penguin, 1986), p. 36.

[83] *The Voyage of Mael Duin*, edited by H. P. A. Oskamp (Groningen: Wolters-Noordhoff, 1970).

[84] *Land of Cockaygne*, edited by Lucas, ll. 17–18.

[85] 'Coem in dúnad ráncumar / co n-a ráthaib ro-brechtán / resin loch anall; / ba h-imm úr a erdrochat, / a chaisel ba gel-chruithnecht, / a shondach ba sall.' *Aislinge Meic Con Glinne*, edited by Kenneth Hurlstone Jackson (Dublin: Dublin Institute for Advanced Studies, 1990), ll. 443–8; translation from *Aislinge Meic Conglinne, The Vision of MacConglinne, a Middle-Irish wonder tale*, edited by Kuno Meyer (London: David Nutt, 1892), p. 36. For a consideration of this text that places it within the context of contemporary discourse on vice, see Scott James Gwara, 'Gluttony, Lust and Penance in the B-text of *Aislinge Meic Conglinne*', *Celtica*, 20 (1988), 53–72.

in the same manner as sexual congress with an otherworld being does. In Chrétien's *Erec et Enide*, humans who eat fruit from King Evrain's garden are unable to return from that realm. In *Echtrae Chonnlai*, it is his consumption of the otherworld apple that precipitates Connla's complete rejection of the human world. Rather more awareness of such dangers is displayed by a twelfth-century peasant who, in William of Newburgh's account, stumbles upon a fairy hall but takes care not to drink from the cup the inhabitants offer him.[86] A particularly well-known episode of this sort occurs in the *Navigatio Sancti Brendani Abbatis*. The mismatch between human limitation and otherworld abundance is a particular concern in this text. Indeed, the very premise of the narrative requires that the author perform a delicate balancing act between conveying the protagonist's desire to see God's wonders in the ocean and the risk of pride—craving inappropriate levels of knowledge and the experience of wonders for the sake of sheer novelty. After all, the voyage itself might be considered somewhat frivolous, a product of a rather unsaintly curiosity on Brendan's part, rather than sincere devotion. Indeed, at least one later commentator dismissed the Brendan legend on the grounds that the voyage displayed an adventurous and irresponsible spirit unbecoming of a saintly abbot.[87] As if mindful of such inbuilt problems, the author repeatedly presents situations that absolve Brendan, in particular, of any accusations of hubris. Although he recounts a voyage that might seem like a high point of human endeavour (and this is certainly one of the most prevalent modern interpretations of the Brendan legend), the author is at pains to stress the limitation of even the holiest of fallen human beings and to point out that Brendan himself accepts his own limitation and concomitant dependence on God. The eventual arrival of Brendan and his crew in the Land of Promise represents only a provisional end to their quest, since they are still alive in their mortal bodies and so lack the strength to bear the intense beauty and joy of that place.

A similar point about human fallibility in the face of otherworldly abundance is made earlier in the text in the monks' encounter with a mysterious island where they are given food and drink.[88] The island

---

[86] William, *History of English Affairs*, pp. 120–1.

[87] David, 'Hic poeta qui Brendani vitam vult describere', pp. 112–15.

[88] *Navigatio Sancti Brendani Abbatis from Early Latin Manuscripts*, edited by Carl Selmer (South Bend, IN: University of Notre Dame Press, 1959; repr. Dublin: Four Courts Press, 1989), Chapter 6, pp. 12–15. There is an English translation based on this edition by J. J. O'Meara: *The Voyage of St Brendan: Journey to the Promised Land* (Dublin: Dolmen Press, 1976). On the large body of scholarship treating the Brendan legend, see Glyn S. Burgess and Clara Strijbosch, *The Legend of St Brendan: A Critical Bibliography* (Dublin: Royal Irish Academy, 2000).

supplies the sort of food (loaves and fish) appropriate to the monastic voyagers; however, in this text at least, the danger does not lie in the food. Rather, the hall in which the monks eat is adorned with objects made from precious metal, and the temptation to avail themselves of these unprotected and, apparently, ownerless riches proves too much for one member of the company. He steals a silver bridle bit from the dwelling and attempts to take it with him from the island. However, his theft is exposed and he dies almost immediately. He is then buried on the island in a gesture that reads like a variation on the conventional idea of being forever bound to the otherworld by partaking in its delights. Both here, and in the final encounter with the Land of Promise, the *Navigatio* makes a clear symbolic link between untamed desire and death, suggesting that the excesses of otherworldly spaces are often too much for fallen mortals to bear.

The dangers of eating otherworld food are also highlighted in the late medieval romance *The Turke and Sir Gawain*. Sir Gawain and the Turk pass through the side of a hill before reaching a beautiful, deserted castle where a rich feast is laid out:

> A bord was spred within that place: [table
> All manner of meates and drinkes there was
> For groomes that might it againe. [men; take
> Sir Gawaine wold have fallen to that fare,
> The Turke bad him leave for care; [fear
> Then waxt he unfaine.[89] [displeased

There is a very similar episode in *Thomas of Erceldoune* where Thomas and the otherworld lady come upon a rich feast during their journey through the mountain and the fairy urges him not to take any food.[90] She warns him that the devil will take him if he partakes in this meal:

> He pressede to pulle frowte with his hande, [fruit
> Als mane for fude þat was nere faynt;
> Scho sayd, 'Thomas! þou late þame stande,
> Or ells þe fende the will atteynt. [sieze
> If þou it plokk, sothely to saye,
> Thi saule gose to þe fyre of helle;

[89] *The Turke and Sir Gawain*, in *Sir Gawain: Eleven Romances and Tales*, edited by Thomas Hahn (Kalamazoo, MI: Medieval Institute Publications, 1995), pp. 340–58, ll. 83–8.
[90] The similarities between this incident and that in *The Turke* have led E. B. Lyle to suggest that *The Turke* is the source of this motif in *Thomas*, 'The *Turk and Gawain* as a Source of *Thomas of Erceldoune*', *Forum for Modern Language Studies*, 6 (1970), 98–102.

It commes neuer owte or domesdaye,   [before
Bot þer in payne ay for to duelle.[91]

The motif acknowledges the temptations that arise from the excesses of
the otherworld. The overwhelming hunger of the human protagonist
points up his limitations as he enters into a world where he will encounter
temptations to pleasure and indulgence for which the human world has
left him entirely unprepared.

Although the beautiful otherworld might seem like the epitome of all
that a human being could desire, it is far from being alluring in all the texts
in which it appears. The impression made by the lengthy description of
the beauty of the otherworld in *Sir Orfeo* is swiftly undermined by the
description of the horrors within the fairy palace that follows. The otherworld journey of Guy of Warwick's son Reinbrun that occurs towards the
end of the romance of *Guy* in several versions includes an extended
exploration of the undesirability of otherworld beauty.[92] On leaving the
court of the Amiral, Reinbrun and Harrawde come to an almost deserted
country in which there is a castle. The lady of the castle informs them that
her husband, Amys de la Mountaine, an ally of Guy, has been abducted by
an elf-king, and Reinbrun vows to return him to her. From this point
onwards, the structure of the Reinbrun episode parallels the action of *Sir
Orfeo* rather closely: Reinbrun journeys through a dark forest before
coming to an opening in a hill,[93] he enters and rides through for half a
mile before seeing light, and he emerges into a beautiful country and crosses
a perilous stream before making his way to a jewel-encrusted castle where he
finds Amys imprisoned in a chamber. Reinbrun convinces Amys to return
with him to the human world. When the fairy king attempts to block
their escape, Reinbrun dispatches the fairy king in a more thoroughly

[91] *Thomas of Erceldoune*, edited by Murray, ll. 185–92.

[92] As Alison Wiggins has observed, the *Reinbrun* episode is a largely self-contained
narrative and is, perhaps, better described as a sequel to *Guy* rather than as an episode within
it. Indeed, in the copy of the text in the Auchinleck MS, the episode is presented as a
separate text. On fol. 167r, the scribe has written 'Explicit' at the end of the copy of the
stanzaic *Guy of Warwick* that precedes it. The *Reinbrun* narrative begins beneath with a
decorated initial after a miniature depicting an episode from the text that follows. Alison
Wiggins, 'The Manuscripts and Texts of the Middle English *Guy of Warwick*', in *Guy of
Warwick: Icon and Ancestor,* edited by Alison Wiggins and Rosalind Field, Studies in
Medieval Romance, 4 (Cambridge: D. S. Brewer, 2007), pp. 61–80 (p. 63). The *Reinbrun*
episode is edited in *The Romance of Guy of Warwick,* edited by Julius Zupitza, EETS, e.s.,
42, 49, 59 (1-vol. repr., 1966) III, pp. 631–74.

[93] Interestingly, the fifteenth-century Irish translation of *Guy* preserved in Trinity
College Dublin MS 1298/2 translates this into the Irish concept of the *síd* and refers to
the English text's elf-king as the king of the *síd* throughout. 'Stair Gui', in 'The Irish Lives of
Guy of Warwick and Bevis of Hampton', edited by F. N. Robinson, *Zeitschrift für Celtische
Philologie,* 6 (1908), 9–180, 273–338, 556 (p. 103).

conventional manner than Orfeo did—with the edge of his sword rather than with the music of a harp. He grants the elf-king mercy on the condition that he releases all his prisoners and rides out of the otherworld to reunite Amys with his wife. The episode asserts the superiority of human ties over the seductive beauty of the otherworld.

The otherworld of the *Reinbrun* episode is described in lavish terms; all the details of a paradisal landscape are supplied: green meadows, flowers, spices, bejewelled marble buildings, and birdsong by day and by night. Furthermore, Amys informs Reinbrun that humans may dwell in the palace without aging.[94] The elf-king's realm has all the attributes that render fairy kingdoms irresistible in a wide range of texts, yet here beauty and deathlessness have no allure. Although scholars have generally treated the *Reinbrun* episode as an independent romance, imperfectly integrated into *Guy of Warwick*, this episode appears to present some clear points of comparison with the final action of *Guy*. Whereas Guy forsakes his wife in pursuit of Heaven, his son retrieves a husband from a paradise-like location to reunite him with his wife. Apart from the obvious fact that the otherworld that lurks behind the conclusion of *Guy* is the kingdom of God, while the realm at the centre of the *Reinbrun* episode is the rather more ambiguous one of the fairies, the parallels between the episodes would seem to stress the basic goodness of human marriage and to highlight the centrality of free will to human experience. When the romance is taken as a whole, *Reinbrun*'s endorsement of the affective bond between spouses qualifies any anti-marriage message that might be derived from the narrative of his father's career. The beauty and life-giving virtues of the land of the elf-king are by no means inferior to those of, say, the Land of Women, but Amys is kept there by enchantment rather than by his own choice. The narrative is structured around the inversion of a series of otherworld conventions, Amys is constrained by the fairy realm rather than liberated by it, and sexual desire pulls him away from the otherworld rather than towards it.

MAPPING GENDER

A traditional definition of the value of fiction is that it allows its audience to imagine being other than what they are. It is common to find other-world narratives—these fictions within fictions—concerned with the interest and challenges of 'difference'. Other spaces within the

---

[94] *Reinbrun*, edited by Zupitza, ll. 86–91.

actual world certainly allow the audience to imagine a reality and an experience far removed from that of their own lives, but no realm supplies this opportunity in such an extreme and complete manner as the other-world. Otherworld narratives can emphasize the problem of difference, by presenting it at its most acute, and it is unsurprising that such narratives are quite frequently interested in issues of gender. Unsurprisingly, the 'other' of the narrative otherworld is usually female, though on rare occasions, such as in Marie de France's *Yonec* or in *Sir Degaré*, it may be male. The Land of Women of *Immram Brain* is an early and explicit instance of the tendency to map the male–female binary onto the actual–otherworld divide. The otherworld lady in *Echtrae Chonnlai* describes her home as a beautiful land inhabited only by women and girls.[95] The idea is still alive and well in late medieval texts like *The Isle of Ladies*.[96] In his description of Ireland, Gerald of Wales describes a type of northern Mount Athos, an island in a lake in Munster where no female creature, whether human or animal, may enter. The location is given a supernatural gloss by the assertion that any female who arrives there will die immediately.[97] Of course, the notion of a single-sex realm is not an innovation of medieval accounts: Strabo, for instance, tells of a fantastic island in the mouth of the Loire where only women may live. Nonetheless, the idea seems to have been a particularly powerful one for medieval authors, perhaps reinforced by the well-developed symbolism that attached to other gendered spaces, such as the cloister or the *hortus conclusus*.

The island of women across the ocean in *Immram Brain* is associated with femininity from the beginning of the text. When Bran comes upon a branch of silver with white blossoms and returns with it to his hall, a woman 'in strange raiment' appears among the company. The text recounts the song she then sings, most of which describes the beauty and properties of her island in the west. The fact that the land is inhabited only by women is noted in the nineteenth quatrain:

> Many shaped Emne by the sea
> Whether it be near, whether it be far,

---

[95] *Echtrae Chonnlai*, edited by McCone, p. 123, section 15. For a discussion of the role of women in Irish otherworld narratives, see Karin E. Olsen, 'Female Voices from the Otherworld: The Role of Women in the Early Irish *Echtraí*', in *Airy Nothings: Imagining the Otherworld of Faerie from the Middle Ages to the Age of Reason: Essays in Honour of Alasdair A. MacDonald*, edited by Karin E. Olsen and Jan R. Veenstra (Leiden and Boston, MA: Brill, 2014), pp. 57–74.

[96] *The Isle of Ladies or the Ile of Pleasaunce*, edited by Anthony Jenkins, Garland Medieval Texts, 2 (New York and London: Garland Publishing, 1980).

[97] Gerald, *Topographia*, II: 4, pp. 80–1.

In which are many thousands of motley women
Which the clear sea encircles.[98]

The image of the encircling sea emphasizes the boundedness of the island, reflecting the association of sealed space with a single-gender society. The final lines are an injunction to Bran: 'Begin a voyage across the clear sea / If perchance thou mayst reach the land of women.'[99] *Immram Máele Dúin*, a lengthier and somewhat later narrative than *Immram Brain*, also describes a stay on an Island of Women.[100] However, in this text it is merely one in a long series of island stops, rather than the ultimate destination of the journey. *Máel Dúin*'s Island of Women also appears to be more explicitly threatening. Presented with the possibility of attaining eternal youth and unstinting sexual pleasure, the company find it difficult to leave in order to continue their journey. Indeed, when they do attempt to sail away, the queen of the island draws them back in with a magical clew. They only manage to escape on the second attempt, and then only after cutting off the hand of a crew member in order to detach him from the queen's clew.[101]

Spaces can also be gendered in less explicit ways. Marie de France's *Guigemar* is a case in point—there is no 'land of women' in this text, but the spaces of the human world and the otherworld are associated with male and female experiences respectively.[102] At the beginning of the *lai*, Guigemar is established as a brave knight, but one who is impervious to love. He boards a mysterious deserted ship made of ebony and gold and with sails of silk, and is carried away on it before he can disembark. The lengthy description Marie devotes to this vessel recalls the long account of the pavilion in *Lanval* and suggests a similar motivation in establishing a thoroughly otherworldly context. The land where the ship finally docks is not, as Corinne Saunders notes, explicitly otherworldly, but the long description of the ship that takes the hero there provides an interpretative

---

[98] 'Emnæ ildelbach fri rían, / bésu ocus, bésu chían, / i fil ilmíli brecc mban; / immus-timchella muir glan', *Immram Brain*, edited by Mac Mathúna, p. 36.

[99] 'tinscan imram tar muir glan / dús in-rísta Tír na mBan', *Immram Brain*, edited by Mac Mathúna, p. 38.

[100] There are two versions of this tale, one in prose and a shorter one in verse. Both date from the Old Irish period and the verse version seems particularly heavily informed by monastic ideology. My comments here are limited to the more well-known prose version. For a brief account of the verse version, see Thomas Owen Clancy, 'Subversion at Sea: Structure, Style and Intent in the *Immrama*', in *The Otherworld Voyage in Early Irish Literature*, edited by Jonathan Wooding (Dublin: Four Courts, 2000), pp. 194–225 (pp. 208–9).

[101] *Voyage of Mael Dúin*, edited by Oskamp, pp. 134–5.

[102] Marie, *Guigemar*, pp. 3–25 (p. 9); translated by Burgess and Busby, p. 46.

cue lacking in the account of the land itself.[103] The plot of this *lai* is predicated upon problems of access, understanding, and interpretation. Guigemar's untouchable heart provides an emotional analogue to the heroine's physical imprisonment by her husband. The supernatural journey between these gendered worlds, the encounter with the 'other', is the means by which the hero and heroine are liberated from these restraints. Guigemar's heart is opened to love and the lady is freed from the prison her husband has built for her.

Marie's *Yonec* also maps the separate physical and psychological experiences of male and female onto clearly bounded spaces, though in this text, the origins of hero and heroine in the otherworld and the actual world are reversed from their positions in *Guigemar*. This text is far more explicit in its evocation of the otherworld than *Guigemar*, and it explores a similar set of themes. Space is the organizing principle of the narrative; it produces each of the plot's complications. The enclosure of the *malmariée* parallels her lover's bounded otherworld within the hillside. Where he accesses her prison through a window, she follows him back to his realm through an opening in a hill. The difficulty of moving between such spaces is expressed in very tangible terms; the knight is mortally wounded on the spikes with which the jealous husband has lined the tower window and the lady risks her life in leaping from her tower in pursuit of her wounded lover. These problems of access give spatial expression to the problems the relationship faces. When the lady finally reaches her lover's otherworld realm, she is presented with a series of interpretative difficulties.[104] The land contains forests, enclosures, a harbour with over three hundred boats, and a walled city of silver, yet, despite the numerous signs of habitation, the lady encounters no one in her passage through the city. More mysterious still is the unknown sleeping knight whom she sees on entering the palace. It is not until she enters a third room that she finds her lover on a golden bed. The description supplies a great deal of potentially significant but unexplained detail, similar in manner to the graveyard scene in *Amadas et Ydoine*. In the hands of the usually concise Marie, such an apparent excess of description and signification becomes even more resonant and mysterious. The reciprocal movement between clearly bounded spaces within the text underscores the mutual self-giving necessary for the union of the lovers and transforms the actual–other binary into something approaching a dialectical framework. However, a full reconciliation between the realms of the human and supernatural lovers proves impossible within the text. The otherworld lover dies and his lady returns

---

[103] Saunders, *Magic and the Supernatural*, p. 183.
[104] Marie de France, *Yonec*, in *Lais*, edited by Ewert, pp. 82–96 (ll. 360–92).

to her kingdom, where she bears his son, who becomes king of the fairy realm. Their final reunion is placed beyond the reach of the narrative, but the last lines gesture towards this meeting in recounting how, when the lady dies, she is laid in the tomb of the otherworld knight.[105] This is the first enclosed space in *Yonec* that unites the two lovers rather than dividing or confounding them.

Partonope of Blois offers some obvious points of comparison with these two texts by Marie.[106] This very popular French romance appears to be roughly contemporary with Marie's work, but there is no English translation before the fifteenth century. The English text is very long (over 12,000 lines) and particularly rich in description. As in *Guigemar*, the young protagonist boards an unmanned vessel that takes him to a mysterious realm in which there is a great city.[107] As in *Yonec*, the otherworld city is eerily deserted. Although the city is brightly lit, Partonope can see that there is still night-time darkness on the sea across which he had sailed.[108] We receive a lengthy account of the city's appearance as Partonope makes his way through it. It has walls checkered with black marble and crystal, and the houses within are decorated with gold embellishments.[109] The slow pace of the description, as seen through Partonope's confused human eyes, and the number of interpretative dead ends its provides, recalls the account of the lady's journey through the city of her otherworld lover in *Yonec*. Partonope attempts to understand his surroundings and rationalize what is happening to him on several occasions. He guesses that the vessel he boards is 'a Shyppe of ffayre / Or thynge made be Enchauntemente' and immediately prays to God that the devil be prevented from taking his soul.[110] When he arrives at the city, he guesses he is 'in fayre' but is also cautious for fear that what he sees may be the 'develles werke' and mere 'fantasye'.[111] Torches guide him to a bedchamber, and it is only when he is in bed that he encounters a living being. A woman, later revealed to be Melior, the Empress of Byzantium, arrives and climbs into bed with him. She requires him to stay with her for two and a half years, visiting her only at night and never beholding her. After that time has elapsed, she promises him that they will be married. There appear to be no other visible inhabitants in the vast city. Melior's realm is not a land of women, but the fact that she is the only individual

[105] Marie, *Yonec*, ll. 547–8. [106] *Partonope*, edited by Bödtker.
[107] The similarity of these two incidents is also discussed by Helen Cooper in *The English Romance in Time*, p. 130.
[108] *Partonope*, edited by Bödtker, l. 847.
[109] *Partonope*, edited by Bödtker, ll. 880–1.
[110] *Partonope*, edited by Bödtker, ll. 743–7.
[111] *Partonope*, edited by Bödtker, ll. 887–8, 1061.

with whom Partonope has any direct dealings there associates it with the feminine. A. C. Spearing has suggested that Partonope's solitary journey over the sea, through the city and castle, and finally to the darkened bedchamber 'corresponds to the quest into the 'depths of "female sexuality"'.[112] Such a correspondence would be less apparent if Melior's realm were not an other-world that tests and often confounds Partonope's powers of interpretation.

DEATH AND DEATHLESSNESS

In a text like *Yonec*, the final fulfilment of desire is only found in death, and the association of desire and death recurs frequently in otherworld narratives. Achieving personal immortality, freedom from moral con-straint, superabundant beauty, atemporality, and perfect joy requires a break with what is finite and mutable, a break most evident in death. The crossing of a significant physical boundary into a realm that does not appear to be subject to the rules and vicissitudes of the actual world could hardly fail to evoke the notion of the afterlife. Indeed, as we shall see in Chapter 2, the line between more 'secular' otherworlds and the afterlife of Christian belief is often blurred in medieval narratives. Furthermore, as scholars such as Patch have demonstrated, the underworld of classical mythology provides a backdrop to more than one medieval otherworld account. Some of the otherworlds of romance are described in terms that seem to evoke the afterlife. The *locus classicus* is Gorre in Chrétien's *Chevalier de la Charette* (Knight of the Cart), from where we are told no one has ever returned. The abode of Morgan in the Old French *Lancelot* is described similarly as the *Vals Sanz Retour*, while both Orfeo and Graelent initially imagine the fairy kingdom to be paradise. The persistent associ-ation of the otherworld with death may, in part, be due to the lingering influence of the afterlife locations of the pagan past, but the connection of the otherworld with death also seems to flow naturally from the nature and narrative functions of otherworld accounts. From a narratological point of view, the way death shifts narrative expectations has a parallel in how the otherworld encounter plays fast and loose with the rules of the fictional world.

The epistemological limit that death represents echoes that of the otherworld boundary. Both the otherworld and death present an imagina-tive problem; they are experiences that cannot, in the usual course of events, be related or fully articulated by those who encounter them, much

---

[112] Spearing, *Medieval Poet as Voyeur*, p. 144.

less understood by those who have not. Crossing the boundary between the actual world and the otherworld signals a shift in expectations more complete than in any other physical realm. That such a realm might be completely unrecognizable to human beings inevitably chimes with the associations and imaginative resonances of the ultimate human boundary and state-change, death. The nature of the boundaries that most frequently separate the actual world from the otherworld contributes to this effect. As demonstrated in *Pearl*, water crossings may symbolize the boundary between the living and the dead.[113] Cave entrances to the otherworld have clear echoes of the grave, and no appeal to Celtic mythology is needed to demonstrate the associations of such a place with the afterlife—the example of Aeneas' journey to the underworld through the cave at Lake Avernus was readily available to medieval audiences.[114]

The *Gawain*-poet makes ample use of the imaginative associations of comparable topographical features. *Sir Gawain and the Green Knight* seems to be heading for an otherworld denouement almost until the last possible moment. The description of the Green Knight as appearing to be 'fayryȝe' sets up such expectations at an early stage in the narrative.[115] The stream Gawain encounters at the Green Chapel seems to be invested with symbolic significance, the audience is informed that it 'blubred þerinne as hit boyled hade', and it would be natural to assume that it presents the same sort of significant physical barrier as the river in a narrative like *Reinbrun*.[116] The fact that the nearby hill also has 'a hole on þe ende and on ayþer side' further evokes the context of an otherworld entrance— hollow hills are not apt to serve any other function in medieval romance.[117] Indeed, the description of this hollow hill seems to have made a particular impression on the illustrator of the sole surviving manuscript. In his depiction of the encounter at the Green Chapel, Gawain, the Green Knight, and their surroundings seem to melt into an undifferentiated sea of green and brown paint, yet the hollow hill, on the bottom right of the page, is emphatically rendered in dense colour.[118] Gawain's assumption that he will meet his death there can be seen as

---

[113] *Pearl*, in *The Poems of the Pearl Manuscript*, edited by Malcolm Andrew and Ronald Waldron (Exeter: Exeter University Press, 2002), pp. 53–110 (ll. 323–4).

[114] Virgil, *Aeneid*, translated by Frederick Ahl (Oxford: Oxford University Press, 2007), Book 6, ll. 237–9.

[115] *Sir Gawain and the Green Knight*, edited by J. R. R. Tolkien and E. V. Gordon, 2nd edn, revised by Norman Davis (Oxford: Clarendon Press, 1967), l. 240.

[116] *Gawain*, edited by Tolkien and Gordon, l. 2174.

[117] *Gawain*, edited by Tolkien and Gordon, l. 2180.

[118] The image is on fol. 129v of the manuscript and is reproduced in A. S. G. Edwards, 'The Manuscript: British Library MS Cotton Nero A. x', in *Companion to the Gawain-Poet*, edited by Brewer and Gibson, pp. 197–220 (p. 216).

informed by, and informing, an otherworldly horizon of expectations within the narrative. Yet, as so often in the poem, the interpretative attempts of both Gawain and the poem's audience are frustrated. Not only is the Green Knight revealed to be identical with the (seemingly) real-world Bertilak, but whatever physical and metaphysical significance the conventions of otherworld description would encourage the audience to attach to the 'boiling' waters of the river are dissolved with an almost flippant lightness of touch as the Green Knight merely hops over it as he approaches Gawain.[119] The hillside opening is never mentioned again—that too seems to be a red herring.

However, there may be more to this than first meets the eye. This is not the only point in *Sir Gawain and the Green Knight* where we encounter a cluster of motifs and features typically associated with otherworld locations. The initial description of the castle of Hautdesert and the environment that surrounds it also hints at the location's potential otherworldliness, though this is never made explicit. On the most obvious level, the elegance and architectural sophistication of the castle seem rather out of place in the wilderness in which Gawain is travelling. Indeed, the castle is described in the sort of superlative terms usually associated with fairy possessions in romance: it is 'þe comlokest [most beautiful] þat euer knyȝt aȝte'.[120] The poet's account of how it 'schemered and schon' through the trees echoes the light-emitting qualities of explicitly fairy castles.[121] We have had earlier hints that Gawain might be moving towards an otherworldly location when he passes raging streams guarded by foes before he reaches Hautdesert.[122] Taken in isolation, these too seem ultimately to be natural, rather than supernatural, barriers, but, when we place them alongside the similar motifs in the description of the Green Chapel, apparent red herrings begin to look like something more significant. A recent suggestion by Richard North may provide the key.[123] He draws attention to the verbal and topographical similarity in how both Hautdesert and the Green Chapel are initially introduced: the castle is situated above 'a launde [clearing], on a lawe [mound]', while the Green Chapel is 'a lyttel on a launde, a lawe as hit were'.[124] North suggests that that the two locations are, in fact, one and the same, with the Green

[119] *Gawain*, edited by Tolkien and Gordon, ll. 2231–2.

[120] *Gawain*, edited by Tolkien and Gordon, l. 767.

[121] *Gawain*, edited by Tolkien and Gordon, l. 772.

[122] *Gawain*, edited by Tolkien and Gordon, ll. 715–17.

[123] Richard North, 'Morgan le Fay and the Fairy Mound in *Sir Gawain and the Green Knight*', in *Airy Nothings*, edited by Olsen and Veenstra, pp. 75–98.

[124] *Gawain*, edited by Tolkien and Gordon, ll. 765, 2171.

Chapel being the 'true form' of the castle.[125] The presence of features closely associated with the otherworld in both locations bears out this point. As we have seen, such motifs have a conventionality that would make it hard for a romance audience to miss or readily dismiss their implications.

The consistent association of the otherworld with death in the medieval imagination may also derive from a consciousness that death is something that breaks the constraints of linear time. As Simone de Beauvoir put it in *The Coming of Age*: 'death transforms life into a destiny: in a way it preserves it by giving it the absolute dimension... Death does away with time'.[126] The idea that death gives 'dimension' to life suggests that it is a concept most readily expressed in spatial rather than temporal terms.[127] As such, the encounter with otherworld spaces is an effective means of addressing the subject. Although 'secular' otherworld narratives tend not to depict lands where human time is replaced by eternity, a characteristic feature of these realms is their heterochronia, their distortion of normal temporality. In most instances, human characters stay in the otherworld for what they think is a short period, only to discover that centuries have passed in the real world. The journey to the otherworld from which the hero does not return may also give structure to medieval otherworld accounts, most notably in afterlife narratives and in romances where the otherworld is the final destination of the protagonist. In such texts, the point at which the temporally bound narrative ends (the material boundary of the text) coincides with the entry into the otherworld.

Texts which end with the protagonist being carried beyond the reach of the actual world inevitably evoke the idea of death even if their explicit engagement with the concept of the end of life is highly variable. The departure of Arthur to Avalon can be read as symbolic of the passage to the afterlife, even if the fact of the king's death would become a source of contention in the actual world. Texts which transport the protagonist

---

[125] North, 'Morgan le Fay and the Fairy Mound', p. 76. North develops his reading by drawing comparisons with other Middle English and French romances. His paper also considers the implications for the wider thematic concerns of the poem of identifying the two locations with each other.

[126] Simone de Beauvoir, *The Coming of Age*, translated by Patrick O'Brian (New York: Putnam, 1972), p. 539.

[127] A prominent medieval example of such thinking is the Hereford World Map, which appears to identify the limits of human geography with the end of mortal life. On this large *mappa mundi*, the circle of the earth is bounded by four ligatures, each bearing a letter of the word MORS (death). Reproduced as the (unpaginated) frontispiece in P. D. A. Harvey, *Mappa Mundi: The Hereford World Map* (London: British Library, 2006). Naomi Reed Kline provides extensive discussion of the interaction of time and space in the Hereford map in *Maps of Medieval Thought: The Hereford Paradigm* (Woodbridge: Boydell, 2001). See, in particular, Chapter 3, 'The Frame as Time', pp. 49–84.

beyond the reach of the actual world at their close rarely make any attempt to follow the hero there. In the case of Lanval, the mistreatment and misunderstanding he endures in the actual world make his final departure from it seem like his vindication and appears to map a pattern more typical of hagiography onto a resolutely secular story. Even before the fairy enters the scene, the narrative insists that Lanval is too good for the actual world. In the very first episode of Marie's text, the jealousy of the other knights and courtiers deprives Lanval of any reward for his faithful service to the king and precipitates his penury. As the text progresses, his isolation increases, culminating in his initial inability to raise bail before his trial: 'Lanval was alone and forlorn, having no relation or friend there'.[128] In Marie's version (though not in the Middle English versions), this sense that Lanval is out of place within the world of the Arthurian court is deepened by the assertion that he is also, quite literally, a foreigner, he is a 'man from abroad'.[129] This detail helps explain why Lanval seems to have no friends to help him in his predicament, but it also draws a parallel between him and his mistress, who is similarly, though more absolutely, alien to Arthur's realm. Lanval's predicament can only be resolved by shifting the scale by which authority is measured in the world he inhabits. The encounter with the otherworld introduces an authority higher than that of human royalty. The knight has the appearance of a suffering saint, and his departure to the fairy otherworld becomes a reward for his patient endurance and situates him in a context more befitting his beauty, generosity, and loyalty.

Narratives structured around the idea of exile-and-return, where the otherworld does not constitute the end point of the plot but a place of quest or adventure from which the protagonist may re-emerge into the actual world, would not seem to map the otherworld onto death in quite such explicit terms, and yet their engagement with the theme is frequent. Otherworlds, both secular and religious, may supply visitors with prophecies or tokens of their final end. In certain versions of the Alexander legend, the conqueror receives a prophecy and token of his death from the inhabitants of the Earthly Paradise, mapping a spatial limit to Alexander's conquests onto the temporal limit of his human life.[130] As this particular example suggests, death is still an obvious theme in exile-and-return narratives because the otherworld is such an absolute geographical and narrative limit. In fact, the otherworld has particular utility for authors of

---

[128] 'Lanval fu sul e esgaré, / N'i aveit parent në ami', Marie, *Lanval*, ll. 398–9; translated by Burgess and Busby, p. 78.

[129] 'humme d'autre païs', Marie, *Lanval*, l. 429; translated by Burgess and Busby, p. 78.

[130] Discussed further in Chapter 3.

romance, a genre that rarely allows for the death of the questing hero. In such texts, the otherworld visit is perhaps the closest a hero may come to leaving the real world entirely and functions as a surrogate for the role played by death in other genres.

Another, and related, theme of otherworld accounts that facilitates an engagement with the notion of death is the recurrent emphasis on human impotence in the face of the supernatural. The hero might reasonably be expected to exert some degree of influence over his fate when encountering threats in the actual world—indeed, it is a prerequisite for taking on the role of hero in the first place—but human agency diminishes significantly when faced with the otherworld. This is largely due to the fact that encountering the supernatural introduces an entirely new scale of power and authority into the narrative, against which the human hero cannot usually hope to measure himself. The otherworld allows the author, quite literally, to have the best of both worlds—to test his hero to the limit without diminishing his heroism. Like the encounter with death, entrance to the otherworld is rarely willed, at least initially, by the human who travels there. The luckier humans who go there are, almost irresistibly, seduced; the less fortunate are abducted. The Orpheus legend presents a particularly influential example of the latter kind of narrative, where the realm to which the human is taken is the underworld of the dead. On the face of it, the most famous Middle English adaptation of this story, *Sir Orfeo*, seems to avoid making death as central a concern as it is in other versions: Orfeo's wife is not poisoned and she is abducted to a fairy kingdom that cannot easily be identified with the underworld of the myth. Indeed, the poem seems to explicitly deny the power and finality of death, allowing Heurodis to be rescued rather than lost forever as she is in the standard version of the story.[131] Yet, *Sir Orfeo* also emphasizes the limits of human agency in the face of the supernatural, and this makes the picture more complex. The actions of the fairy king in the Middle English poem highlight the human hero's limitations at every turn. The abduction of Heurodis takes place despite Orfeo's prior knowledge of its occurrence and the efforts he makes to prevent it. All his military might does not prevent her being taken from him. Most versions of the myth allow Orpheus to discover the entrance to the underworld through his own agency, but in *Sir Orfeo* the hero's encounter with the fairy kingdom comes about by pure chance. When his wife is abducted, he does not go in search of her but retreats to the forest to live the life of a hermit. The fact that Orfeo's rescue of his wife comes as a result of good fortune (or providence) is one of the most

---

[131] On medieval engagement with the classical tradition of Orpheus, see J. B. Friedman, *Orpheus in the Middle Ages* (Cambridge, MA: Harvard University Press, 1970).

notable points of divergence from the standard version of the story. Although the final outcome in the medieval romance is a happy one, the barriers to its attainment are far less clearly and systematically surmountable than in texts that adhere to the better-known versions of the tale. For instance, in Robert Henryson's fifteenth-century take on the story, Orpheus passes the time between his wife's death and his entry into Hades in a flurry of activity.[132] He begs Phebus for aid, and then proceeds, quite literally, to search heaven and earth for his lost wife, before finally finding her in Hades. Yet, in their randomness, inexorability, and seeming inescapability, the fairy king's actions in *Sir Orfeo* can, in many ways, be mapped more readily onto the reality of death than the action of Pluto in Henryson's more mainstream version of the plot. While the latter is more overtly about death, the applicability of the former to the fact of dying may, in fact, be more complete.

Several of the seeming oddities of *Sir Orfeo* make more sense if we assume the poet is attempting a serious exploration of the mystery of death through his treatment of the fairy kingdom and its denizens. The transformation of Hades into a seemingly beautiful fairy kingdom in this romance underscores its emphasis on the uncanny and the intractable. It provides a neat inversion of the convention of the fairy otherworld offering eternal youth to humans who remain there. The range of motifs that fairy otherworlds share with Paradise makes this youth-giving quality seem rather more natural than it ought to be, and the *Orfeo*-poet seems to play on this, depicting a realm where human beings exist in pain at worst and in a sort of limbo at best, where they appear to be undead rather than immortal. The ambiguity of the fairy otherworld serves the author's interest in disorientation and loss more fully than a more conventional, and hence more rationalized, realm of the dead. *Sir Orfeo* does not narrow the otherworld's meaning so as to allow it to signify only death. Rather, the *Orfeo*-poet's overdetermined otherworld description 'courts chaos' and in so doing approaches the most universal of human experiences in a way that draws out that experience's full violence and unfathomability. In a culture where there was no shortage of explicit treatments of death, the otherworld of *Orfeo* also, potentially, does death more justice than an overt treatment. The fairy kingdom resists all attempts at a totalizing interpretation, meaning the audience cannot stabilize their experience by anchoring it in, say, a religious framework. It also makes no appeal to standard images of death that might have grown tame by familiarity.

---

[132] *Orpheus and Eurydice*, in *The Poems of Robert Henryson*, edited by Robert L. Kindrick (Kalamazoo, MI: Medieval Institute Publications, 1997), pp. 187–222.

The Anglo-Norman *Amadas et Ydoine* is, as we have seen, another poem that 'courts chaos', but there are other respects in which it bears comparison to *Sir Orfeo*.[133] This poem also seems to map the notion of the fairy otherworld onto the realm of the dead, though it transpires that the heroine has been transported to neither, but has merely been under an enchantment. *Amadas et Ydoine* takes place within the actual world, but awareness of alternative realms of experience—the afterlife, the otherworld, and, ultimately, the separate subjectivities of its hero and heroine—drives the narrative and thematic interests of the romance. One day when out riding, Ydoine is carried off by a mysterious supernatural knight, causing the rest of her company to give chase. The knight relinquishes the lady before vanishing into thin air. The riders return to the city with great rejoicing, at which point the narrative pauses to reflect on Ydoine's beauty: 'The Countess no longer felt any anguish or torment, but was so healthy and cured and so attractive that in all the world at that time, no other woman so beautiful could be found—unless she was a fairy'.[134] The use of 'fee' as a term of praise rapidly takes on a more sinister ring when Ydoine suddenly falls ill that evening. In contrast to the ambiguous outcome of Heurodis's illness in *Orfeo*, it is stated from the outset that Ydoine will die; she lingers in anguish for some time before succumbing. Before she dies she attempts to dampen Amadas's love for her, and so dissuade him from committing suicide, by telling him she has lead a deeply immoral life. The way Ydoine's illness and death are portrayed suggests that the mysterious knight has laid a spell on her and, having been foiled in his attempt to abduct her to the otherworld, has removed her from the human world by another means. The comparison of Ydoine to a fairy prefigures this by suggesting that she has, or has taken on, some of the qualities appropriate to the paramour of a supernatural being and that her encounter, like Heurodis's, has rendered her unable to remain in the human world.

Indeed, in contemplating his lover's death, Amadas explicitly compares death to an abductor. The rhetorical emphasis is on the finality of death, its randomness and how it separates people so definitively from each other: 'Death has taken [her] away and led her out of this world. God! What a wicked destiny, for me to be left behind, wretched and sad! Our love is

[133] The range and nature of the similarities between the two texts are discussed in Cartlidge, 'Sir Orfeo in the Otherworld', 217–18.

[134] 'Que la contesse mais ne sent / Mal ne angousse ne torment, / Ains est si saine et si garie / Et de si grant biauté garnie / Qu'en tout le mont a icel jor, / De façon, de fresce coulor, / Ne fu ausi bele trouvee, / Se ne fu figure de fee ...' *Amadas*, edited by Reinhard, ll. 4691–8; translated by Arthur, p. 89.

sundered'.[135] The living and the dead are described as 'ces deus ordres' (these two orders).[136] In this anguished contemplation, Amadas imagines his separation from Ydoine in terms of unbridgeable spaces. The sense of estrangement is deepened, in the eyes of the audience, by the deception that Ydoine has practised on her lover in order to ensure he does not kill himself from grief. The gap between the subjectivities of two human beings is given spatial representation in the distance between the human world and that to which Amadas believes Ydoine has been taken. Indeed, the text also links this estrangement to the difficulty of comprehension that inheres in gender difference. When given seemingly inarguable proof of Ydoine's faithlessness by the mysterious knight, Amadas concludes that women operate by an entirely different standard of loyalty to men. Men and women can also be seen as 'deus ordres', as incomprehensible to each other as the living and the dead, or the actual and the otherworld. This rather hopeless view is, of course, not the romance's final word on the problem of difference. Like Orfeo, it is not Amadas's active attempt to be reunited with his lady that prompts the happy outcome. Rather, her recovery is made possible through his desire for her good, as exemplified by the prayers he vows to say for her soul, and to believe good of her, as evidenced by his insistence on her virtue in the face of all evidence to the contrary. These acts of will, made without hope of success, prove efficacious in mediating the boundaries between the multiple pairs of opposing orders in the narrative: male and female, living and dead, Heaven and Hell, actual and otherworld.

The otherworld, then, is a highly adaptable vehicle for the expression of absolutes and extremes. The concern of otherworld descriptions with excess is partly a function of the 'otherness' of the motif itself, the necessity of detailed and hyperbolic rhetoric when describing what is beyond human experience and human language. This rhetoric can sometimes be pressed to the point where it seems comical and overinflated, but in most cases authors use otherworlds as a means of giving spatial expression to extremes of human experience and to radical difference. This translates into an interest in indescribable or transcendent states, such as death, and into an engagement with fundamental human differences, such as gender. It should be stressed that this interest is often of a very contingent kind. Otherworld spaces are not easily reducible to any single concept, however profound that concept might be. Otherworlds heighten every facet of

---

[135] 'Par la mort qui l'en a ravie / Et hors de cest siecle menee. / Dix! com mauvaise destinee / De moi qui sui si aprés vous / Remés caitis et dolerous, / Et nostre amors est departie.' *Amadas*, edited by Reinhard, ll. 5468–73; translated by Arthur, p. 100.

[136] *Amadas*, edited by Reinhard, l. 5375.

earthly reality, presenting wish-fulfilling abundance that can both delight and confound limited, fallen human beings. The surplus of the otherworld account is a necessary surplus, as necessary to the text as the surplus represented by fiction in the actual world, and the seriousness authors brought to the otherworld encounter could be as limited or as absolute as the seriousness of fiction itself.

2

Otherworlds and the Afterlife

As we have seen, otherworld narratives are natural vehicles for exploring the theme of death. Yet, despite this, there are good reasons to be cautious about connecting the sort of realms we have been discussing so far too readily with descriptions of the Christian afterlife.[1] There are a variety of perspectives from which the afterlife could look very different from most of the realms we have been considering. Places like Heaven and Hell draw considerable, and usually consistent, meaning from belief systems external to the text. They commanded belief in the culture as a whole, while realms such as Avalon might command credulity no greater than the suspension of disbelief brought by a particular audience, or audience member, to an individual literary text. Spaces such as Heaven or Hell were not without their mystery, but their place within the salvific economy was more or less clear. The place of somewhere like a fairy kingdom in such an order is ambiguous.[2] The starting point of this book, that otherworlds are first and foremost imaginative spheres, is less clearly applicable to the afterlife. However, it is not entirely redundant. While narratives treating the afterlife certainly constitute a 'special case' in the study of otherworld locations, there are strong arguments against completely divorcing their study from that of realms like fairyland. It is not unusual for descriptions of the afterlife to draw upon the same body of motifs that characterize otherworld locations that have no obvious

[1] On medieval visions of the afterlife, see the classic account by Peter Dinzelbacher, *Vision und Visionsliteratur im Mittelalter* (Stuttgart: Hiersemann, 1981). In Anglophone scholarship, Carol Zaleski's study, *Otherworld Journeys: Accounts of Near-Death Experiences in Medieval and Modern Times* (Oxford: Oxford University Press, 1987), provides a good review of medieval vision literature. A helpful overview of key primary and secondary literature relating to medieval accounts of the afterlife is Robert Easting, *Visions of the Other World in Middle English*, Annotated Bibliographies of Old and Middle English Literature, 3 (Woodbridge: D. S. Brewer, 1997). On the Middle English tradition specifically, see F. A. Foster, 'Legends of the Afterlife', in *A Manual of the Writings in Middle English, 1050–1500*, edited by J. Burke Severs (Hamden, CT: Archon Books 1970), II, 452–7, 645–9.

[2] Chera A. Cole stresses the overlap between fairy realms and afterlife locations, but also the ultimately ambiguous status of these places on the scale of rewards and punishment in ' "Fairy" in Middle English Romance' (PhD dissertation, University of St Andrew's, 2013), pp. 123–61.

eschatological dimension. In fact, the author of an afterlife account could be forgiven for thinking he was making more appropriate use of such motifs than a writer of romance, since many of these motifs, as we will see, have their most obvious source in the Bible. Furthermore, afterlife spaces often raise similar issues and inhabit narrative frameworks analogous to otherworld realms that have a less obvious eschatological import.

Given the ambiguities of the modern term 'otherworld', in this chapter I will use 'afterlife' to refer to Heaven, Hell, Purgatory, and the Earthly Paradise, reserving 'otherworld' for the sorts of fairy realms we discussed in Chapter 1. In what follows, I will look at three narratives that illuminate some of the ways in which overlap or cross-pollination between otherworld accounts and afterlife accounts could occur. The first is the *Tractatus de Purgatorio Sancti Patricii*. The fortunes of this text in the centuries after its original composition in the 1180s illustrate how readily a text about the afterlife might be adapted to look remarkably like the sort of otherworld quest that we associate with romance.[3] The second is the *Navigatio Sancti Brendani Abbatis*, another Latin text set in Ireland that appears to emanate from a monastic milieu. The *Tractatus* and the *Navigatio* were exceptionally well known and widely circulated, but my final narrative case study, *Eachtra Thaidhg Mhic Céin* (The Adventure of Tadhg Mac Céin) survives only in a single manuscript and has received little attention from scholars.[4] *Eachtra Thaidhg*'s afterlife topography is a striking blend of conventional eschatological material and pure invention. Despite being of a later date, the narrative is in very much the same tradition as the Brendan legend—a text with a pious purpose and framework that still depicts otherworld islands that usually have no source in Christian belief. Finally, I will return to the question of the supposed 'Celtic' sources of otherworld accounts that I discussed in the Introduction. The impact of biblical accounts of afterlife locations, particularly descriptions from the Book of Revelation, has an immediate bearing on this issue.

But before considering the points where otherworld and afterlife readily and naturally intersect, it is worth pausing to consider the ways in which their relationship could also be more uneasy. Orthodoxy can certainly be a

---

[3] *Saint Patrick's Purgatory*, edited by Robert Easting, EETS, o.s., 298 (1991). This edition of Middle English versions of the text includes an edition of the Latin *Tractatus* at pp. 121–54. For a modern English translation, see *Saint Patrick's Purgatory*, translated by J. M. Picard and Yolande de Pontfarcy (Dublin: Four Courts Press, 1985).

[4] Edited and translated as the *Voyage of Tadhg Mac Cein*, in *Silva Gadelica: A Collection of Tales in Irish*, edited and translated by Standish H. O'Grady, 2 vols (London: Williams and Norgate, 1892), I (text), pp. 342–59; II (trans.), pp. 385–401.

sticking point, but certain otherworld accounts seem to have attracted more sustained criticism on these grounds than others. Despite its popularity, medieval responses to the *Tractatus de Purgatorio Sancti Patricii* often express doubt about whether the afterlife really could be accessed via a cave at Lough Derg in Ireland.[5] Some also doubted the *Tractatus*'s account of purged souls spending time in the Earthly Paradise before entering Heaven. This objection seems rooted in the doctrinal developments that took place in the century or so after the *Tractatus* was composed. Vincent of Beauvais tells us that the *Tractatus* was rejected by many readers because it employed a fourfold division of the afterlife.[6] A fourfold scheme usually offers two 'middle places', between Heaven and Hell, for souls who are not entirely evil and not entirely good. In the case of the *Tractatus*, these intermediate places are Purgatory itself and the Earthly Paradise. The text is very clear in stating that souls must pass through both realms before entering Heaven.[7] During the Middle Ages, these two divisions were gradually resolved into a more clearly conceptualized single space: Purgatory. Both the First Council of Lyon in 1245 and the Second Council in 1274 stated that souls needed only to pass through Purgatory, not through any further location, before entering Heaven.[8] The resulting threefold division of the afterlife commanded common assent until the Reformation. A text like the *Tractatus* was, therefore, at variance with orthodox eschatology from the late thirteenth century onwards, yet this disquiet did not seem to lessen the general appetite for the narrative.[9] Although the popularity of the original Latin *Tractatus* appears to have peaked in the thirteenth century, the rate of production of manuscripts and the production of translations and adaptations in the later Middle Ages was still considerable.

Another similarly popular text, the Brendan legend, also seems to have attracted opprobrium, most of it directed at its more fantastical components.[10] Some of this is predictable enough: the author of the *Navigatio*

---

[5] Easting, 'Purgatory and the Earthly Paradise', pp. 23–48.

[6] Vincent, *Speculum Historiale*, p. 789. Quoted and discussed in Easting, 'Purgatory and the Earthly Paradise', p. 44.

[7] *Tractatus*, edited by Easting, p. 144; translated by Picard, p. 69. The idea that souls might pass through the Earthly Paradise before entering Heaven is found as early as Origen and in writers such as Bede and Hildegard of Bingen; see further, Easting, 'Purgatory and the Earthly Paradise', pp. 44–5.

[8] Easting, 'Purgatory and the Earthly Paradise', p. 44.

[9] On this paradox, see Easting, 'Purgatory and the Earthly Paradise', 44, and Watkins, 'Doctrine, Politics and Purgation', 235.

[10] Scepticism was expressed by Vincent of Beauvais and Gerald of Wales among others. See further, Joseph Dunn, 'The Brendan Problem', *The Catholic Historical Review*, 6 (1921), 395–477 (pp. 465–7).

gives an account of the fate of angels who remained neutral during Lucifer's rebellion and he also depicts Judas enjoying a day of respite from Hell. Neither idea squared well with orthodox theology. In the late twelfth or early thirteenth century, one reader of the Brendan legend, who appears to have been named 'David', copied a particularly long and biting response to it into Oxford Lincoln College MS 27 on fol. 2v.[11] This response takes the form of fifty-four lines of pentadecasyllabic Latin verse.[12] The poem describes the *Navigatio* as an indictment on Saint Brendan.[13] It protests that a true saint would never abandon so many of the monks under his care to sail in search of what he will find, in any case, in Heaven.[14] It highlights the fabulous nature of the saint's purported exploits as evidence for the untruthfulness of the text. In criticizing the account of the neutral angels, the poem accuses the author of the *Navigatio* of articulating positions inimical to faith.[15] Not only does the Lincoln 27 poem call into question the text's fantastical narrative, it also deplores its depiction of the promised land of the saints: 'O how lean or unhappy is the hope of the Irishmen, for whom after this life the entire reward for their works will be a bare land and pebbles and the flowers of trees'.[16] It is a strange point on which to take issue with the *Navigatio*, since the text's depiction of the Earthly Paradise appears to be a relatively mainstream treatment. Indeed, the Lincoln poem's condemnation seems to be based on a misreading of the text itself. At no point does the Brendan narrative state that the Promised Land of the Saints is an 'entire reward', rather, the text is emphatic in its assertion that the land is only a temporary staging post for the saints before the Last Judgement—a view common and relatively uncontested for much of the Middle Ages and still very much part of the mainstream at the

---

[11] In his catalogue, Henry O. Coxe suggests that this manuscript is largely of twelfth century date. The nature of the other contents would suggest a Cistercian context. There is, therefore, some possibility that the attitude exhibited in the poem could be a function of the twelfth-century drive for reform of the Irish Church, in which the Cistercians were heavily involved. Henry O. Coxe, *Catalogus codicum MSS. qui in collegiis aulisque Oxoniensibus hodie adservantur*, 2 vols (Oxford: Oxford University Press, 1852), I, Catalogus Codicum MSS Collegii Lincolniensis, pp. 26–7.

[12] David Howlett believes that these are not the original work of this writer, but are an imperfect redaction of an earlier text; see David, 'Hic poeta qui Brendani vitam vult describere', pp. 112–15.

[13] David, 'Hic poeta qui Brendani vitam vult describere', l. 2.

[14] David, 'Hic poeta qui Brendani vitam vult describere', ll. 10–11.

[15] David, 'Hic poeta qui Brendani vitam vult describere', l. 26.

[16] 'O quam macra uel infelix spes est Hibernensium / Quibus post hanc uitam erit tota merces operum / Terra nuda et lapilli atque flores arborum'. David, 'Hic poeta qui Brendani vitam vult describere', ll. 37–9.

time Lincoln 27 was written.[17] Furthermore, the Brendan narrative takes its description of the land from the Book of Revelation 21, itself ultimately derived from Ezechiel.

The Lincoln poem's attitude to the *Navigatio*'s account of Paradise is a good example of the diversity of opinion that could exist regarding certain afterlife locations in the central Middle Ages. Treatments of two locations, in particular, can tend to blur the distinction between afterlife and otherworld. For many centuries, neither Purgatory nor the Earthly Paradise occupied the same sort of well-defined doctrinal and theological framework as Heaven and Hell. As we have seen, it was not until the second half of the thirteenth century that the notion of Purgatory was given a precise doctrinal formulation. The Earthly Paradise was many things to medieval Christians: the Eden of prelapsarian humanity, a walled-off paradise located in, but inaccessible from, the contemporary world, and, in some renditions, the future location of the New Jerusalem. The fact that Purgatory and, particularly, the Earthly Paradise feature more frequently in literary works may reflect how much more ambiguous their status was than that of Heaven or Hell in the period. Such ambiguity could be imaginatively stimulating and, potentially, left considerable room for narrative manoeuvre.[18]

There is another quality of Purgatory and the Earthly Paradise that leaves particular scope for overlap with otherworld accounts. In contrast with descriptions of Heaven and Hell, the Earthly Paradise was usually treated as a physical location on earth.[19] It is a well-established feature of medieval *mappae mundi*, and geographers and travel writers consistently affirm its location on the far eastern edge of the world. Purgatory is less frequently pinpointed, but routinely placed on or under the earth. From an early point it was assumed that purgation after death could occur in locations that were, in some sense, contiguous with the mortal world.[20] Gregory the Great's *Dialogi*, for instance, recounts how living people visited bathhouses only to encounter souls who were being purged of sin after their death. The eleventh-century Irish text, *Immram Curaig Ua*

---

[17] This belief is discussed in Jean Delumeau, *The History of Paradise: The Garden of Eden in Myth and Tradition*, translated by Matthew O'Connell (New York: Continuum, 1995), pp. 23–38.

[18] For an overview of literary treatments of Heaven, see the essays collected in Carolyn Muessig and Ad Putter, eds., *Envisaging Heaven in the Middle Ages*, (London: Routledge, 2007). On depictions of Hell, see D. D. R. Owen, *The Vision of Hell: Infernal Journeys in Medieval French Literature* (New York: Barnes & Noble, 1971).

[19] Patch makes this distinction in treating 'The Literature of Visions' and 'Journeys to Paradise' in separate chapters in his study (Patch, *The Other World*, pp. 80–133, 134–74). However, he treats the *Tractatus de Purgatorio Sancti Patricii* in the chapter on 'visions'.

[20] See the discussion in Watkins, 'Doctrine, Politics and Purgation'.

Corra (Voyage of the Húi Corra), depicts a penitential voyage into the Atlantic where the sailors encounter dead souls awaiting the Last Judgement and, in some cases, being purged of their sins.[21] The *Tractatus* places Purgatory just under the earth, but physically accessible from an entry point in Ireland. Significantly, its protagonist does not die and is able to return to the world of the living. The location of the entrance in a cave on an island in Lough Derg (just north of the modern-day border between counties Donegal and Fermanagh) is one of the few places in Ireland to regularly appear on medieval world maps. By contrast, there was no tradition of Heaven being accessible to living, corporeal human beings. Hell, though often placed in a pit at the centre of the earth,[22] was also not typically experienced in anything other than vision form.[23] On leaving Purgatory, Owein sees Hell beneath a river a great distance below him— the clear implication of the *Tractatus* is that this is not a realm from which living beings could hope to return. The physically locatable quality of both the Earthly Paradise and Purgatory must surely have enhanced the parallels with realms like fairyland, which are most typically reached by a physical journey rather than experienced in a vision or dream. The possibility that these two places might be physically contiguous with the contemporary world aligns them with the sort of otherworld spaces through which knights and heroes journey. Both still draw out themes such as desire, knowledge, mortality, and authority, while depictions of the Earthly Paradise draw on a very similar range of images to, say, the fairy kingdom in *Sir Orfeo*. We will return to the particular reasons for that at the end of this chapter.

The relatively ambiguous status of Purgatory and the Earthly Paradise allows writers who depict them freer reign. The fact that these two different types of otherworld share imagery gives authors considerable scope to explore the overlap between them. Although afterlife spaces certainly have distinctive qualities, conceptualizing the otherworld as an imaginative field may, ultimately, enable rather than frustrate comparative work. Approaching the relationship between otherworld and afterlife in terms of shared motifs and themes allows the points of congruity to be

[21] 'The Voyage of the Húi Corra', edited and translated by Whitley Stokes, *Revue Celtique*, 14 (1893), 22–69 (pp. 46–7).
[22] The author of the *Tractatus* makes this point at the opening of his work. *Tractatus*, edited by Easting, p. 122; translated by Picard, p. 45.
[23] There are exceptions of course; for instance, the Middle English text *The Adulterous Falmouth Squire* relates how a clerk praying at his father's grave is approached by man robed in white, who 'led him to a comly hille; / The Erthe opened, and in thay yode' (195–6) and then brings him to visit his father, who is unambiguously in Hell. *The Adulterous Falmouth Squire*, in *Political, Religious, and Love Poems*, edited by F. J. Furnivall, EETS, o.s., 15 (1866), pp. 93–102.

acknowledged while simultaneously giving the pitfalls of complete identification a wide berth.

OWEIN IN THE OTHERWORLD

The *Tractatus de Purgatorio Sancti Patricii* is a natural text with which to
begin. Its probable Cistercian provenance and serious tone belies its overlap
with the otherworlds of romance. If the high number of surviving manuscripts is anything to go by, this narrative was one of the most widely
disseminated texts of the Middle Ages.[24] The most complete list of *Tractatus*
manuscripts yet published is in R. L. Hayes's *Manuscript Sources for the
History of Irish Civilisation* and it enumerates over one hundred manuscripts
of the Latin text distributed throughout the collections of almost every major
library in Europe.[25] However, Easting estimates that the total number of
copies of the Latin text is actually around 170 and suggests an even higher
number of copies of vernacular adaptations that survive in over thirty
languages.[26] Chroniclers like Matthew Paris and Caesarius of Heisterbach
also drew on the story in their works. It dates from the early 1180s, making it
a key text for historians tracing the developments in the doctrine of post-
mortem purgation associated with the twelfth and thirteenth centuries. In
The Birth of Purgatory, Jacques Le Goff notes that the *Tractatus* is the first
major text to use 'purgatory' as a noun.[27] The text has not attracted the same
degree of attention from literary scholars.

   On the face of it, an account of Purgatory might not seem like the most
promising point of comparison with fairy realms. There is little to distinguish the imagery of purgation from that of damnation in most medieval

---

[24] *Patrick's Purgatory*, edited by Easting, p. xvii.

[25] R. L. Hayes, *The Manuscript Sources for the History of Irish Civilisation*, 14 vols
(Boston: G. K. Hall, 1965–1975). Professor Easting informs me that the fullest list was
compiled in Dr Peter De Wilde's doctoral thesis: Peter de Wilde, *Le Purgatoire de saint
Patrice: Origines et naissance d'un genre litteraire au XIIe siècle* (unpublished doctoral thesis,
University of Antwerp, 2000), pp. 174–94.

[26] Some copies post-date the original date of composition by only a few years: Ghent,
Bibliothèque de l'Université, MS 289 (662), for instance, dates from the end of the twelfth
century and, as Carl Watkins has noted, the unusually high survival rate of twelfth- and
thirteenth-century manuscripts in general may suggest that the popularity of the text was
both immediate and widespread (Watkins, 'Doctrine, Politics and Purgation', 235).

[27] Jacques Le Goff, *The Birth of Purgatory*, translated by Arthur Goldhammer (London:
Scolar Press, 1984), pp. 193–201. For a critique of Le Goff's reading of the *Tractatus*, see
Robert Easting, 'Purgatory and the Earthly Paradise in the *Tractatus de Purgatorio Sancti
Patricii*', *Cîteaux: Commentarii Cistercienses*, 37 (1986), 23–48. Easting queries Le Goff's
'"nominalist" proposition that Purgatory as a distinct state of place between Heaven and
Hell did not really exist in the imagining ("l'imaginaire") of Western Christendom until the
noun *purgatorium* came into use.' (p. 25).

accounts and, as we have seen, the beauty of fairy kingdoms is one of their most immediately obvious characteristics (even if they tend to have a threatening dimension too). However, it is important to bear two key features of the *Tractatus* in mind. Firstly, despite the title it is usually given, the text is an account of a journey through Purgatory *and* through the Earthly Paradise. The latter is also described in a great deal of detail. Secondly, the text recounts a journey undertaken in the flesh, rather than in the spirit, from an entrance that could be pinpointed in the actual world. It is categorically *not* an afterlife vision, of the sort described in the *Visio Tnugdali*, with which the *Tractatus* is often coupled. The peculiarity of this, often overlooked, dimension to the *Tractatus* is stressed by Robert Easting, who points out that '[t]here is no comparable collection of medieval other-world experiences tied to a specific geographical place believed to be an otherworld entrance'.[28] What we know of medieval responses to this narrative, some reported in the text itself and others reflected in the many adaptations of the narrative, suggests medieval audiences put more store by this aspect of the *Tractatus* than we tend to do today.

The author of the *Tractatus* identifies himself as 'H. of Saltrey' ('frater .H., monachorum de Saltereia minimus'), but this is usually rendered as 'Henry'.[29] He appears to have been a Cistercian monk of the monastery of Saltrey (or Sawtry) in Huntingdonshire. His text is composed of several different parts, but it was the central narrative section of the *Tractatus* that, unsurprisingly, became the most widely adapted and disseminated part of the text. The *Tractatus* relates how the purgatory at Lough Derg was revealed to Saint Patrick and then moves on to the central narrative of how an Irish knight, Owein, resolves to enter the purgatory in order to make reparation for his sins. He undertakes fifteen days of prayer and preparation before being sealed into the cave on an island in Lough Derg. After a long journey in darkness, he emerges into a twilight plain in which stands a hall of great size and beauty. There he encounters fifteen men robed in white who advise him to call on Christ to deliver him from any difficulty he might encounter on his journey. When the men depart, Owein hears a great noise and he is seized by a swarm of devils that carry him into

---

[28] Easting, *Visions of the Otherworld*, p. 44.

[29] 'brother H. the least of the monks of Saltry' (*Tractatus*, edited by Easting, p. 121; translated by Picard p. 43). Most scholarship has ascribed this expansion of 'H' to 'Henry' to Matthew Paris, but this appears to be specious, and the identification of 'H' as 'Henry' may go back no further than the fifteenth century. For discussion of the issue, see *Saint Patrick's Purgatory*, edited by Easting, p. 236n. Robert Easting argues convincingly that there is every reason to believe that Owein was an historical figure: 'Owein at Saint Patrick's Purgatory', *Medium Aevum*, 55 (1986), 159–75.

Purgatory. Ten separate torments are enumerated and the demons attempt to subject Owein to each. On every occasion, he is delivered as soon as he remembers to call on Christ. Eventually, he reaches a huge stinking river, over which rises a narrow slippery bridge. He is told that the Hell of the eternally lost is beneath that river. Placing his trust in God, Owein discovers that the bridge widens as he makes his way across. On the other side he is admitted to the Earthly Paradise and greeted by a great throng of people. A group of bishops guide him to the foot of a mountain, on the top of which is the blazing gold entrance to the Celestial Paradise. Each day the inhabitants of the Earthly Paradise are fed with heavenly food which falls from the gate. Because he is still alive, Owein is permitted to go no further. He returns by the way he came and this time the demons flee before him. On returning to the world, he travels to Jerusalem as a crusader. He considers becoming a monk, but in the end resolves to remain a knight.

Entrance to a supernatural realm through a cave is entirely conventional in a range of otherworld descriptions. As we have seen, some of the clearest signposts of the presence of an otherworld realm in literary texts are the distinctive boundaries between the actual world and the otherworld: water barriers, the bottoms of lakes, hillsides, or cave entrances feature frequently.[30] Since they are often the first signal of the presence of such a realm, and since they are a particularly small group, these motifs play a key role in shaping audience expectations of the narrative. Not only does Henry describe a cave entrance, but that cave is located on an island accessible only by crossing a water barrier. There is a certain geographical aptness to the idea of someone entering Purgatory from Ireland and finishing in the Earthly Paradise. As Sara V. Torres has recently observed, an entry point in Ireland positions Purgatory's entrance on an island on the extreme western periphery of the earth, while Eden or the Earthly Paradise was generally placed in the extreme east and usually depicted as an island.[31]

There are good reasons to believe that medieval readers were very conscious of the *Tractatus's* exceptionality in recounting an in-the-body

---

[30] On the, sometimes similar, sometimes differing ways in which the afterlife, in particular, was entered, see Peter Dinzelbacher, 'The Way to the Other World in Medieval Literature and Art', *Folklore*, 97 (1986), 70–87.

[31] Sara V. Torres, 'Journeying to the World's End? Imagining the Anglo-Irish frontier in Ramon de Perellós's Pilgrimage to St Patrick's Purgatory', in *Mapping Medieval Geographies: Geographical Encounters in the Latin West and Beyond, 300–1600*, edited by Keith D. Lilley (Cambridge: Cambridge University Press, 2013), pp. 300–24 (pp. 315–16). For further discussion of geographical connections between Ireland and the Earthly Paradise, see Chapter 4 of the present volume.

journey through afterlife locations. The special nature of the experience is repeatedly highlighted in the text itself. Indeed, Henry cites Owein's testimony as proof of the tradition that certain afterlife realms were also physical realms:

> Furthermore this account confirms what is believed by some, namely that hell is under the earth or rather at the bottom of a cavity in the earth, like a dungeon or a prison of darkness. It also shows that there is a paradise on earth towards the east where the souls of the faithful, freed from the purgatorial punishments, are said to stay for some time in bliss.[32]

Since the text's geography places Purgatory and the Earthly Paradise immediately beneath or on the surface of the earth, Owein is allowed access to both, but he is excluded from Heaven and Hell as long as he is still alive and in his body. During his walk across the test bridge, we are told that if he falls into Hell far beneath, he will die and be lost there. Although it is not made explicit in the text, the upward trajectory of the bridge Owein crosses between Purgatory and the Earthly Paradise may suggest that he is returning to the surface of the earth at this point. All this would fit with the usual placement of the Earthly Paradise on the earth's surface, though it would also suggest his journey was of enormous length.[33]

The text's particularly pronounced concern with establishing its own basis in fact underlines how unusual and potentially problematic the notion of a near-contemporary bodily experience of Purgatory must have seemed in the late twelfth century. The sizeable portions of the *Tractatus*, which precede and follow Owein's story, are largely devoted to what may be loosely termed 'authenticating material'. The relatively cohesive central narrative is set in an elaborate frame of anecdotes, theological digressions, and personal recollections. Henry had no intention of creating a text that might be considered in any way fictional; rather, he is at great pains to establish the narrative's historicity and authenticity. The visit to Lough Derg is not located in some hazy long-ago time, but in 'our age', during the reign of King Stephen only a quarter of a century earlier.[34] The author also provides ample context for the text's central figures,

---

[32] 'Et quidem infernus subtus terram uel infra terre concauitatem quasi carcer et ergastulum tenebrarum a quibusdam esse creditur, narratione ista nichilominus asseritur. Et quod paradysus in oriente et in terra sit, narratio ista ostendit, ubi fidelium anime, a penis purgatoriis liberate, dicuntur aliquandiu morari iocunde.' *Tractatus*, edited by Easting, ll. 52–6; translated by Picard, p. 45.

[33] Easting notes that Owein's journey takes him first north-east and then south-east from Ireland, 'a route suitable for taking him to the orient where the Earthly Paradise is situated', 'Purgatory and the Earthly Paradise', p. 30.

[34] *Tractatus*, edited by Easting, l. 206.

detailing Gilbert's origins and his activities in Ireland with great precision.
The text opens by noting how the authority of Gregory, Augustine, and a
long visionary tradition confirms, and is confirmed by, Owein's experience.
When Owein's story concludes, we are given a detailed account of the
narrative's provenance, detailing how the story made its way across the Irish
Sea through the monk Gilbert. Henry claimed to have heard the story from
Gilbert himself at a large assembly. Of course, texts that claim to relate
visionary experiences also make ample use of such provenance accounts and
analogies to anticipate and rebut objections to their truth, but the nature of
the objections to the *Tractatus* are of a very specific kind. Henry relates how
Gilbert was challenged by a man who refused to believe these things actually
happened. It is clear from Gilbert's response that the source of the objection
is the physical nature of the experience:

> There are people who say that when they enter the hall at the beginning they
> fall into ecstasy and they see all these things in their minds. But the knight
> denied adamantly that this had happened in his case; on the contrary, he
> testified very consistently that he had seen these things with his own bodily
> eyes and that he had endured the torments in the flesh.[35]

Visions, which are treated with scepticism in many other accounts, would
seem to be considerably more credible than the physical experience related
here. Gilbert elaborates by citing the example of a monk of his acquaint-
ance who was abducted by devils and suffered real bodily wounds as
evidence that the pains of Purgatory might really be experienced before
death and in the flesh. Not content, or perhaps fearing his readers might
not be content, with this proof, Henry recounts how he sought further
testimonies in order to be even more certain. Four further authorities are
consulted, with three confirming the story and supplying further authenticating anecdotes of their own. The first of these is an abbot who gives a
straightforward confirmation of the existence of the Purgatory at Lough
Derg. A bishop named Florentanius also confirms that the Purgatory
exists, before relating a story about a nearby hermit who is visited and
tempted by devils each night. The bishop's chaplain then supplies a story
about devils who stole bread, cheese, flour, and butter from an unchari-
able peasant. Henry concludes with a tale of another hermit who is
tempted to unchastity by devils. They leave an abandoned baby girl at
his cell for him to take in and she grows into a very beautiful young

---

[35] 'Sunt quidam...qui dicunt quod aulam intrantes primo fiunt in extasi et hec omnia
in spiritu uidere. Quod omnino sibi miles ita contigisse contradicit, sed corporeis oculis
uidisse et corporaliter hec pertulisse constantissime "testatur"'. *Tractatus*, edited by Easting,
ll. 1100–4; translated by Picard, p. 73.

woman. On the face of it, it is hard to see the immediate relevance of these three stories to authenticating the central narrative of the *Tractatus*. They are certainly all exempla which warn against the temptations and powers of demons, yet Henry introduces the accounts as evidence he has gathered 'to be even more certain' of Owein's testimony.[36] The only clear thematic link between the anecdotes is the fact that the devils have abilities that suggest they can be part of, and can interact with, the material world: the devils who tempt the hermit are clearly visible, the thieving devils can carry away foodstuffs, and the final story features devils who appear to be able to abduct a baby and leave her near a hermit's cell. The authenticating material appears to be intended to address doubts specific to this text's physical, rather than visionary, experience of the supernatural.

The apparent effects of Owein's physical experience of the afterlife, as reflected in numerous vernacular adaptations, are quite paradoxical. The 'real' quality of this otherworld journey is instrumental in enabling a shift in the narrative's status from an ostensibly factual history to the more 'fictive' mode of romance.[37] Another facet of the *Tractatus*'s otherworld account that has been underemphasized by modern scholars, with the notable exception of Easting,[38] may also have aided the process. As noted at the outset, the more infernal qualities of Purgatory accounts have little in common with secular otherworld descriptions, but the *Tractatus* recounts a journey that takes Owein, not merely through Purgatory, but also through the Earthly Paradise. Indeed, it represents a particularly extensive account of that realm.[39] Although modern scholarship tends to focus on the Purgatory account to the neglect of the Earthly Paradise, medieval reception did not necessarily reflect this emphasis. For instance, Cambridge University Library MS Ee. 6. 11, a manuscript of an Anglo-Norman adaptation of Owein's journey, contains an explicit in the same scribal hand as the rest of the text which calls the narrative 'liber de gaudio

---

[36] *Tractatus*, edited by Easting, l. 1131.

[37] Ad Putter provides an excursus on the links between afterlife visions and romance across a wide range of texts, including the *Tractatus*, in 'The Influence of Visions of the Otherworld', pp. 237–51.

[38] In his 1986 article on Le Goff's analysis of the *Tractatus*, Easting stresses the importance of the Earthly Paradise in the narrative and states that 'Le Goff's omission of the Earthly Paradise from his consideration of the *Tractatus*'s division of the other world is untenable' (Easting, 'Purgatory and the Earthly Paradise', p. 42).

[39] Easting, 'Purgatory and the Earthly Paradise', p. 42.

paradisi terrestris'.[40] Although the narrative was more commonly known by some variation of the title 'Saint Patrick's Purgatory', the focus of the text could also be located in its Earthly Paradise account. Revising the somewhat anachronistic scholarly emphasis on the text's account of Purgatory is necessary to any full understanding of the *Tractatus*. Such a shift in focus also goes some way towards illuminating the points of similarity that a medieval audience may have discerned between the *Tractatus* afterlife account and otherworlds. As we will see in the section of this chapter entitled 'Biblical Sources and 'Celtic' Otherworlds', the various biblical accounts of the Earthly Paradise had a clear influence on secular otherworld descriptions, and the description in the *Tractatus* draws on the same range of images: fruitful trees, flowers, unceasing light, and melodious song.

No genre is more thoroughly associated with wonders and marvels than romance, and most medieval depictions of otherworld realms occur in texts operating in this mode. The stress on the physical nature of the journey is one of several facets of the *Tractatus*'s widely disseminated core narrative that affiliate it with the emerging genre of romance. The physical nature of the journey also fits with another characteristic of the *Tractatus* that would appear to lend itself to romance adaptation: its explicitly chivalric ethos. Almost all the descriptions of Owein are couched in terms that emphasize his knightly calling:

> The knight, who had in his breast a manly heart, does not fear the danger that he was told had engulfed others. And the man who, armed with an iron sword, had taken part in the battles of men, now armed with faith, hope, and justice, confident in God's mercy and stronger than iron, hurls himself boldly into a battle with demons.[41]

---

[40] CUL MS Ee. 6. 11, p. 37. It might be objected that, since this appellation is placed at the end of the text, it merely reflects the fact that the experience of the Earthly Paradise constitutes the final section of the narrative. However, the use of the term 'liber' suggests that the entirety of the preceding text is being described, particularly since neither the text nor the layout of the manuscript suggest any break of the sort that might lead to a description of the text being composed of more than one 'liber'. The manuscript appears to be composed of three originally distinct booklets of different sizes and in different scribal hands which were later bound together. The Saint Patrick's Purgatory text occupies a fourteen-folio booklet (of which the final, presumably blank, page is now missing) of its own between pp. 13–37 of the manuscript as a whole.

[41] 'Miles autem uirilem in pectore gerens animum, quod alios audiuit absorbuisse, periculum non formidat. Et qui quondam ferro munitus pugnis interfuit hominum, modo, ferro, durior, fide, spe et iusticia, de Dei misericordia presumens, ornatus, confidenter ad pugnam prorumpit demonum.' *Tractatus*, edited by Easting, ll. 246–51; translated by Picard, pp. 52–3.

Indeed, Henry continually draws parallels between Owein's journey and knightly duty. The journey into Purgatory is described as a novel act of chivalry and the metaphor is picked up again after Owein has received the counsel of the fifteen men:

> Thus instructed for a new kind of chivalry, the knight, who in the past had bravely fought men, is now ready to give battle bravely to demons. Shielded by Christ's arms he waits to see which of the demons will first challenge him to a fight.[42]

The passage is followed by an elaborate description of how each item of the knight's arms corresponds to a particular virtue. Throughout the text, Henry generally refers to Owein by the title 'miles' rather than by his given name; he is 'uerus miles Christi' and his acts of faith are represented as the arms of spiritual chivalry.[43] Christ himself is twice depicted as a lord watching and protecting Owein from his battlements. These qualities mark the *Tractatus* out from the text with which it is most often associated, the *Visio Tnugdali*.[44] The *Tractatus* and the *Visio* are not infrequently found together in manuscripts and both claim Ireland as their ultimate origin but, significantly, the points where the two differ tend to ensure that the *Visio* is adapted into romance rather less persistently than the *Tractatus*. Aside from the obvious factor—the *Tractatus*'s distinctive in-the-body otherworld journey—Owein journeys alone throughout his time in Purgatory.[45] There is no analogue in the *Tractatus* for the angelic being who guides and interprets Tnugdal's hellish experience in the *Visio*, and Owein bears a closer resemblance to the solitary, questing hero of

[42] 'Miles itaque, ad noui generis militiam instructus, qui quondam uiriliter oppugnabat homines, iam presto est uiriliter certare contra demones. Armis igitur Christi munitus exspectat quis eum demonum ad certamen primo prouocet.' *Tractatus*, edited by Easting, ll. 295–9; translated by Picard, p. 54. The chivalric appeal of the location is evident in the number of accounts of medieval knights who visited there, including George Grissaphan (1353), Louis of France (*c*.1360), Ramon de Perellós (1379), and Laurence Rathold of Pászthó (1411). In an entry from 1497, the Irish *Annals of Ulster* also appear to highlight the military or chivalric dimension of the *Tractatus* when they refer briefly to 'sdair an Ridire ocus a seinlebraibh eile' ('the History of the Knight and other old books') when describing the sources of evidence for the location of the entrance to Purgatory in Lough Derg. *Annala Uladh: The Annals of Ulster*, edited and translated by W. M. Hennessy and B. MacCarthy, 4 vols (Dublin: Thom, 1887–1901), iii (1895), pp. 416–17. For a discussion of the particular attraction of the Purgatory to men from a military background, see D. R. French, 'Ritual, Gender and Power Strategies: Male Pilgrimage to Saint Patrick's Purgatory', *Religion*, 24 (1994), 103–15.

[43] *Tractatus*, edited by Easting, ll. 335, 345.

[44] *Visio Tnugdali: Lateinisch und Altdeutsch*, edited by Albrecht Wagner (Erlangen: Deichert, 1882). The Latin text is translated as *The Vision of Tnugdal*, by Jean-Michel Picard, with an introduction by Yolande de Ponfarcy (Dublin: Four Courts, 1989).

[45] He is, of course, afforded the guidance of the bishops when he enters the Earthly Paradise.

romance as a result. Although the *Tractatus* is deeply concerned with the idea of surrender to divine will, Owein is allowed more agency than Tnugdal insofar as the impetus for him to continue his journey is primarily his own. In the company of the angel, Tnugdal is a rather more reluctant penitent than Owein and, on several occasions, has to be cajoled into undertaking the punishments he merits. Tnugdal's deliverance from the tortures he endures is dependent on forces outside his control. In the *Tractatus*, the relationship between passivity and activity is rendered more complex by the knight's talismanic use of the name of Christ. The fact that the name of Christ operates like a magic charm is very much in the tradition of romance.[46] The power to be delivered lies within the exercise of Owein's own will, although each time the rescue is the work of God's hand rather than the knight's own skill and physical prowess. Owein's use of Christ's name is a test of trust and an injunction not to despair in the face of overwhelming suffering and, like many talismans in romance, the efficacy of Christ's name in the *Tractatus* is tied to the hero's exercise of courage and virtue.

The number and extent of the adaptations that the *Tractatus* undergoes throughout the Middle Ages provide a large body of evidence for how it was read and interpreted. Insofar as this process has been acknowledged by scholars, it has been generally viewed as a function of a movement from a clerical to a lay context for the text. There are five Anglo-Norman verse versions of the narrative.[47] The most famous is *Espurgatoire Seint Patriz*, the adaptation attributed to Marie de France, which survives in a single thirteenth-century manuscript (Paris B.N. Fr. 25407).[48] Its apparently early date means it may provide some interesting indications of the near-contemporary reception of the *Tractatus* and how rapidly the text was adapted into vernacular form. Curley suggests that Marie's text may date from as early as 1190, less than a decade after the *Tractatus*'s original composition.[49] Marie states that she has translated the text into 'romanz' for the religious edification of the 'laie gent' (layfolk).[50] She describes the story of Owein as an *aventure*, the same term she uses in the lays that are also attributed to her, but there is little evidence that she has systematically toned down the piety of her source. Certainly Marie compares the monastic life less favourably to Owein's journey and she also emphasizes

---

[46] This point is further developed by Edward Foster in *Sir Owain*, in *Three Purgatory Poems*, edited by Edward E. Foster (Kalamazoo, MI: Medieval Institute Publications, 2004), pp. 109–78 (p. 116).

[47] Easting, *Visions of the Other World*, p. 48.

[48] Marie de France, *Saint Patrick's Purgatory*, edited by Michael J. Curley (New York: Garland, 1993), p. 33.

[49] Marie, *Patrick's Purgatory*, p. 11.   [50] Marie, *Patrick's Purgatory*, ll. 2298–3000.

Owein's decision to remain a knight. Such details gesture towards the new audience for whom Marie intended her poem, but they do not suggest an alteration or even a dilution of the religious ideology that pervades the *Tractatus*. As Laura Ashe notes, Marie 'has not suppressed the piety of her source, but rather its strongly Cistercian institutionalism, its organised religiosity, and its clerical politics'.[51] In Marie's text, knightly *aventure* and explicit, undiluted piety are two sides of the same coin.

The Anglo-Norman version in Cambridge University Library MS Ee. 6. 11 appears to be independent of any other French version of the story. The manuscript in which it is preserved is East Anglian and has been dated to the second half of the thirteenth century.[52] It includes a conventional declaration that the redactor has translated the text as he found it, which, in this instance, seems to reflect a high degree of fidelity to its source.[53] The poem contains several turns of phrase which suggest that it was adapted directly from a Latin text of the *Tractatus*, rather than another vernacular version.[54] Nonetheless, the Cambridge text also contains several alterations to the Latin. Like many vernacular and some Latin adaptations of the *Tractatus*, it omits all the prefatory and introductory material except those passages which pertain to Saint Patrick. The Cambridge poem also dispenses with the authenticating material that Henry assembles at the conclusion of his work. Unlike both the *Tractatus* and Marie's text, the Cambridge poem states that Owein did, in fact, take the habit on returning from the Holy Land.[55] Like Marie's poem, the Cambridge text casts itself as 'un aventure'[56] and follows the Latin original in referring to Owein as 'un chevalier' throughout. Examination of the Cambridge text reinforces the impression given by Marie's poem that readers of the *Tractatus* saw the elements of a knightly *aventure* in Owein's otherworld journey.

The situation in Middle English is similar. Three complete verse redactions of the *Tractatus* survive in Middle English.[57] The earliest is the use of the Owein story as the *South English Legendary*'s entry for 'Saint

---

[51] Laura Ashe, *Fiction and History in Medieval England, 1066–1200* (Cambridge: Cambridge University Press, 2007), p. 200.

[52] *Étude sur le Purgatoire de Saint Patrice accompagnée du texte latin d'Utrecht et du texte anglo-normand de Cambridge*, edited by C. M. Van der Zanden (Amsterdam: H. J. Paris, 1927), p. 89.

[53] *Étude*, edited by Van der Zanden, ll. 21–4.

[54] *Étude*, edited by Van der Zanden, p. 150.

[55] *Étude*, edited by Van der Zanden, ll. 1788–9.

[56] *Étude*, edited by Van der Zanden, l. 3.

[57] For a full account, see Robert Easting, 'Middle English Translations of the *Tractatus de Purgatorio Sancti Patricii*', in *The Medieval Translator II*, edited by Roger Ellis (London: Queen Mary and Westfield College, 1991), pp. 151–75.

Patrick'.[58] This version survives in around twenty manuscripts and is primarily responsible for making the *Tractatus* the afterlife encounter with the widest circulation in Middle English.[59] A second version in octosyllabic couplets is preserved in two fifteenth-century manuscripts, Yale MS 365 ('The Book of Brome') and British Library MS Cotton Caligula A. ii.[60] There is also a Middle English tail-rhyme version preserved in the Auchinleck manuscript.[61] Robert Easting has suggested that a text very similar to the Cambridge Anglo-Norman metrical version of the *Tractatus* was the model for this English version.[62] The verse form of the tail-rhyme stanza associates it with popular romance.[63] Once again, the authenticating material and the homiletic digressions of the Latin text are omitted in the vernacular adaptation. The Auchinleck text also omits the account of the ritual untaken before admission to the purgatory, although neither the Cotton nor the Yale texts do so. However, no major incident in the narrative itself is omitted and alteration of individual events is surprisingly minimal. Edward Foster has argued, in *Sir Owayne*, 'tract has become romance';[64] however, as we have seen, this transition is by no means a complete reorientation of the text since the original text has narrative and thematic affinities with romance. The piety of the original is retained in all the adaptations and sometimes elements of it are deepened. The editor of the Cambridge Anglo-Norman version, C. M. Van der Zanden, discerns a Marian emphasis in that text which is absent in the original.[65] A peculiarity of the Auchinleck text is that it repeatedly refers to Owein as 'Seynt Owain' while he is in the Earthly Paradise.[66] There is no precedent for this in any of the other surviving vernacular versions and certainly none in the *Tractatus*. The Auchinleck version is also unique in having the monks at Lough Derg witness the newly purified knight emerging from the cave shining like fire.[67] This (literally) glowing portrait of the knight does not feature in the *Tractatus* or in the Anglo-Norman redactions and smacks more of hagiography than of romance.

[58] Robert Easting discusses the ways in which this text has been adapted from its source in 'The South English Legendary "St Patrick" as Translation', *Leeds Studies in English*, n.s., 21 (1990), 119–40.

[59] Easting, *Visions of the Other World*, p. 48.

[60] This version is edited in parallel from these two manuscripts in *Saint Patrick's Purgatory*, edited by Easting, pp. 36–75.

[61] The Auchinleck text is edited in *Saint Patrick's Purgatory*, edited by Easting, pp. 3–34. A fragment of this version also survives as a paste-down in BL MS Lansdowne 383.

[62] *Patrick's Purgatory*, edited by Easting, p. xlvi.

[63] *Patrick's Purgatory*, edited by Easting, p. lvi.

[64] *Sir Owain*, edited by Foster, p. 118.

[65] *Étude*, edited by Van der Zanden, p. 153.

[66] *Owayne Miles* (Auchinleck), edited by Easting, ll. 892, 1123, 1186.

[67] *Owayne Miles* (Auchinleck), edited by Easting, ll. 192–3.

Another development in the narrative that occurs in certain vernacular versions is an elaboration in the *Tractatus*'s description of afterlife geography and the addition of further characteristic features of otherworld description. This tendency is pronounced in the most romance-like of the adaptations, the Auchinleck text, but it is also discernible elsewhere. The Cambridge poem in Anglo-Norman alters the *Tractatus*'s narrow slippery bridge over the river of Hell to a crossing that is 'trenchant cum un rasur' (sharp as a razor).[68] The Auchinleck version follows suit. This variation on the bridge motif unavoidably recalls the sword bridge over the perilous stream that Lancelot must cross to reach the otherworldly Gorre in Chrétien's *Chevalier de la Charette*. Such an alteration might suggest a tendency towards sensationalism, were it not for the fact that elsewhere the author draws back from translating some of the *Tractatus*'s more gruesome moments. It is more likely that the change reflects the parallel the adaptor discerned between the bridge episode in the *Tractatus* and an analogous motif in more secular material. Key to this parallel is the status of the bridge as a point of access to an otherworld location.

Elaboration of the *Tractatus* in romance-style adaptations is most pronounced in treatments of the visit to the Earthly Paradise. An Anglo-Norman version preserved in British Library, Harley MS 273 depicts Owein arriving at the walls of Paradise and seeing a gate encrusted with gemstones as in the *Tractatus*. The text then departs from the Latin original to give a catalogue of the stones:

> ... jaspers and crystals,
> Sardonyx and alabandica,
> Topaz and cornelians,
> Beryls, sapphires, and carbuncles
> Adamants, emeralds, onyx.[69]

This seems like yet another instance of the density of description which, as we have seen, is typically brought to bear on otherworld locations of every kind. The Auchinleck version features a description of the gold walls of Paradise and goes into even more detail than the Harley text in describing them:

> Jaspers, topes, and cristal,   [topaz
> Margarites and coral,   [pearls

---

[68] *Étude*, edited by Van der Zanden, l. 1116.

[69] ... jaspes e cristals, / Sardoines et alabandines, / Topaces e cornelines, / Berils, safirs e charbocles, / Adamantz, smaraudes, onicles.' *Le Purgatoire de Saint Patrice: des manuscrits Harléien 273 et Fonds français 2198*, edited by Johan Vising (Göteborg: W. Zachrisson, 1916), ll. 618–22.

And riche saferstones,   [sapphire stones
Ribes and salidoines,   [rubies; chelidonius?
Onicles and causteloines,   [onyx; chalcedony
And diamaunce for the nones.
In tabernacles thai wer ywrought,
Richer might it be nought,
With pilers gent and small;   [splendid
Arches ybent with charbukelston,   [carbuncle
Knottes of rede gold theropon,
And pinacles of cristal.[70]

It seems clear that the Auchinleck text of the story responds to the Saint Patrick's Purgatory material most enthusiastically at the points where the narrative's afterlife topography most clearly overlaps with features typically associated with the otherworlds of romance writing. It expands considerably on all Anglo-Norman versions of the Earthly Paradise episode and, as Easting notes, it is in the Earthly Paradise section that the redactor of the Auchinleck text has added most copiously to his source.[71] From the point Owein passes through the gates of Paradise to when he is greeted by the bishops, this poet devotes one hundred and forty-three lines to a description of this realm, nearly one eighth of the entire text. He adds a more detailed account of the inhabitants of the Earthly Paradise, includes a description of the four rivers of Paradise, and dwells at some length on the singing and music making of the people there.[72] Although the primary additions to this section are descriptive rather than narrative, one interesting exception is a unique episode in which the wounded knight, whose clothes have been tattered by his experiences in Purgatory, is healed in the Earthly Paradise:

A cloth of gold him was ybrought,
In what maner he nist nought,   [did not know
Tho God him hadde ysent.
That cloth he dede on him there,   [put on
And alle woundes hole were,
That er then was forbrent.[73]   [burned

---

[70] *Owayne Miles* (Auchinleck), edited by Easting, ll. 781–92.

[71] *Patrick's Purgatory*, edited by Easting, p. liv.

[72] There are close connections between much of the added material and descriptions in Genesis 2. 8–17, Ezechiel 28. 13–15, Isaiah 51. 3, and Revelation 21. 11–25. The influence of these passages on medieval accounts of the otherworld and the afterlife is discussed in the next section of this chapter.

[73] *Owayne Miles* (Auchinleck), edited by Easting, ll. 763–8.

Paradise is an obvious place of healing, but this addition also recalls the more general association of otherworld locations with relief from wounds.

The *Tractatus de Purgatorio Sancti Patricii* has a chameleon-like quality that allows it to be located within a number of generic traditions with relative ease. It proved a highly adaptable and frequently adapted text. The atypicality of Owein's afterlife journey is a primary factor in stimulating the particular gravitation of this narrative towards romance. The special nature of the text's 'real' experience of the afterlife has not been sufficiently stressed and not only facilitates adaptation into romance, but also gives it a particularly affinity with otherworld accounts.

BIBLICAL SOURCES AND 'CELTIC' OTHERWORLDS

The catalogues of gems that appear in the vernacular adaptations of the *Tractatus* have a very obvious model. This way of describing the Earthly Paradise owes a good deal to biblical models, most particularly the account of the New Jerusalem in the Book of Revelation 21. Although the *Tractatus* sheds its homiletic and theological trappings in its vernacular adaptations, a good deal of biblical imagery absent from the Latin text is included in the account of the Earthly Paradise in these versions. In fact, the extent of dependence on the biblical material is greatest in the 'most fully developed' version of the 'romance element inherent in the structure of the tale of Owein', the Auchinleck text.[74] On the face of it, this seems rather surprising, but it is worth bearing in mind that this imagery is used extensively in romance, where it is most typically associated with the otherworld, not the afterlife. *Sir Orfeo*'s account of fairyland, as we shall see, is a case in point.

The extent to which the vernacular adaptations of the *Tractatus* draw on biblical imagery raises a larger set of issues concerning the relationship between depictions of otherworlds and the afterlife. It brings us back to the question raised at the start of this book about the extent to which it is worth exploring the pre-medieval roots for medieval otherworld motifs. Identifying the precise sources of otherworld imagery is perhaps most clearly relevant in the context of the afterlife. The notion that depictions of otherworlds might contain relics, however fragmentary, of past pre-Christian belief underpinned much early scholarly discussion of these spaces. Watkins' work on the idea of the supernatural has demonstrated

---

[74] *Patrick's Purgatory*, edited by Easting, p. lvi.

how implausible such a state of affairs is and how, even if such 'pagan survivals' are embedded in medieval texts, they would likely have held none of their original significance for writer or audience.[75] Of course, Watkins' study focuses on the twelfth century, and it is logical to assume that the further back we go the more probable the conscious literary use of such survivals and their recognition by audiences becomes. The idea has been particularly persistent in respect of texts with a Celtic provenance (real or supposed). Not a little ink has been spilled on the influence of the 'Celtic land of the dead', for instance, but the few features of that realm are known from classical accounts are difficult to detect in medieval texts that have been through multiple retellings in a thoroughly Christianized context.[76] Rather than trying to speculate about exactly where these ideas ultimately came from, it might be more fruitful to consider with what works or authorities medieval authors and audiences would be most likely to connect them. Of course, knowledge of imagery derived from folk belief or other 'literary' texts might vary from audience to audience and, in the case of folk belief, such knowledge is also notoriously difficult to prove. Imagery derived from the Bible does not present these problems and can certainly be thought of as commanding almost universal recognition. The evidence we have for biblical imagery in otherworld narratives is quite considerable and tends to undercut the assumptions that have been made in the past about the influence of Celtic language literatures.

While not denying that Irish and Welsh otherworld descriptions can have their own distinctiveness, an instructive case study through which to explore the supposed Celticity, as opposed to biblical Latinity, of otherworld imagery is the *Tractatus*. The apparent cultural provenance of this text unavoidably raises the issue of the status of Celtic otherworld accounts as sources. Like the *Visio Tnugdali* before it, the wide circulation of the *Tractatus* demonstrates how narratives with Irish origins (or, at least, those that existed in Latin versions) could spread around Britain and Europe in the central Middle Ages. According to Henry of Saltry's account, the original protagonist of the tale, the Irish knight Owein, was assigned to the English monk Gilbert as a translator during his time in Ireland. Gilbert then recounted the narrative to Henry. Assuming we can take this line of transmission at face value, the text provides a particularly detailed record of how narrative transmission might take place between medieval Ireland and England. Might a text like the *Tractatus* provide the sort of conduit through which distinctively Celtic ideas about afterlife and otherworld locations could spread to the wider world? The *Tractatus* is

---

[75] Watkins, *History and the Supernatural*, pp. 68–106.

[76] See further my discussion of the usefulness of these classical accounts in Chapter 4.

almost a roll call of conventional otherworld motifs and themes. Its relatively early position in the tradition and its wide dissemination suggest that it might have been influential in forming and cementing audience expectations of literary otherworlds. Yet, on close re-examination, this text seems to be an object lesson in how firmly rooted in Judaeo-Christian tradition medieval descriptions of supernatural realms can be. Some of the *Tractatus*'s features could be described as 'Irish', but the motifs used in its description of the afterlife are not among them.

The sources for the *Tractatus*'s imagery are almost exclusively of a mainstream sort, particularly biblical texts and widely read Apocrypha. Some Irish texts, such as the *Vision of Laisrén* (late ninth or early tenth century) and the *Vision of Adamnán* (tenth to eleventh century), bear striking resemblances to the *Tractatus*, but, like many of the afterlife descriptions in medieval Irish literature, they too have a lot of material in common with early Christian texts which were popular throughout Europe. The perilous test bridge which appears in both the *Vision of Adamnán* and in the *Tractatus* seems to originate in Gregory the Great's *Dialogi*,[77] and the detail of many of the torments enumerated in the *Tractatus* may be traced to the fourth-century *Visio Sancti Pauli* which also exerts influence on *Vision of Laisrén* and the *Vision of Adamnán*.[78] Although the *Tractatus*'s approach, particularly its bodily journey into the afterlife, is very original, the imagery of the afterlife realms, particularly the descriptions of the Earthly Paradise and of the torments of Purgatory, is standard fare. Indeed, it could not be otherwise, since such texts derived their authority from their very conventionality; it would be all too easy to question the reliability of a witness who sketched a particularly novel otherworldly topography far removed from that related in the great bulk of vision literature that had preceded it.[79] Henry himself appeals to such authorities early on in the *Tractatus*, listing 'rivers, flames, bridges, ships,

---

[77] For a discussion of the wider religious symbolism of bridges and how it is reflected in the motif of the perilous otherworld bridge, see Peter Dinzelbacher and Harald Kleinschmidt, 'Seelenbrücke und Brückenbau im mittelalterlichen England', *Numen*, 31 (1984), 242–87. The test bridge also appears in the *Visio Tnugdali*.

[78] Theodore Silverstein, *Visio Sancti Pauli: The History of the Apocalypse in Latin Together with Nine Texts*, Studies and Documents, 4 (London: Christophers, 1935). This Latin text derives from a Greek work which in turn was inspired by 2 Corinthians 12:1–5 where St Paul describes a man who was caught up into Paradise. It was much copied and translated throughout the Middle Ages.

[79] Robert Easting, 'Access to Heaven in Medieval Visions of the Otherworld', in *Envisaging Heaven in the Middle Ages*, edited by Carolyn Muessig and Ad Putter (London: Routledge, 2007), pp. 75–90 (p. 77). For a more general discussion of this idea, see Barbara Newman, 'What Did it Mean to Say "I Saw"? The Clash between Theory and Practice in Medieval Visionary Culture', *Speculum*, 80 (2005), 1–43.

houses, woodlands, fields, flowers' as features of the otherworld typically reported by visionaries.[80]

Certain motifs frequent in otherworld descriptions clearly reflect biblical accounts, particularly descriptions of Eden. A few key passages from the Old and New Testaments are worth highlighting. The first is from the Book of Ezechiel:

> Thou wast in the pleasures of the paradise of God: every precious stone was thy covering: the sardius, the topaz, and the jasper, the chrysolite, and the onyx, and the beryl, the sapphire, and the carbuncle, and the emerald: gold the work of thy beauty: and thy pipes were prepared in the day that thou wast created. Thou wast a cherub stretched out, and protecting, and I set thee in the holy mountain of God, thou hast walked in the midst of the stones of fire. Thou wast perfect in thy ways from the day of thy creation, until iniquity was found in thee.[81]

This passage fleshes out and reinforces imagery found in Genesis 2. 8–17, wherein Eden is established as a fertile garden out of which flow four rivers. The association of certain otherworld accounts with sweet music and song also finds a biblical mirror in Isaiah 51. 3, where such sounds are, once again, associated with Eden. The Book of Ezechiel also relates a vision of the restored temple that draws upon Edenic imagery. This passage hints at the sort of distortion of typical seasonal changes and the healing properties that are often associated with otherworlds in medieval romance:

> And by the torrent on the banks thereof on both sides shall grow all trees that bear fruit: their leaf shall not fall off, and their fruit shall not fail: every month shall they bring forth firstfruits, because the waters thereof shall issue out of the sanctuary: and the fruits thereof shall be for food, and the leaves thereof for medicine.[82]

---

[80] 'flumina, flammas, pontes, naues, domos et nemora, prata, flores'. *Tractatus de Purgatorio Sancti Patricii*, in *Patrick's Purgatory*, edited by Easting, pp. 121–54, l. 29. All translations are taken from *Saint Patrick's Purgatory*, translated by J.-M. Picard and Yolande de Pontfarcy (Dublin: Four Courts Press, 1985), p. 44.

[81] 'In deliciis paradisi Dei fuisti; omnis lapis pretiosus operimentum tuum: sardius, topazius, et jaspis, chrysolithus, et onyx, et berillus, sapphirus, et carbunculus, et smaragdus, aurum, opus decoris tui: et foramina tua, in die, qua conditus es, praeparata sunt. Tu cherub extentus, et protegens; et posui te in monte sancto Dei, in medio lapidum ignitorum ambulasti. Perfectus in viis tuis a die conditionis tuae, donec inventa est iniquitas in te.' (Ezechiel 28. 13–15). All biblical quotations are taken from the Vulgate Bible: *Biblia Sacra Vulgatae Editionis Sixti V Pontificis Maximi Jussu Recognita et Clementis VIII Auctoritate Edita* (London: David Nutt, 1868). English translations are from the Douay-Rheims translation of the Vulgate Bible: *The Holy Bible Translated from the Latin Vulgate* (Baltimore, MD: John Murphy, 1914). Names of biblical books are rendered as in this translation.

[82] 'Et super torrentem orietur in ripis eius, ex utraque parte omne lignum pomiferum: non defluet folium ex eo, et non deficiet fructus ejus: per singulos menses afferet primitiva,

Of course, perhaps the single most notable biblical description of a marvellous country is that of the New Jerusalem in the Book of Revelation, which builds on the imagery of Eden from the Old Testament tradition. The New Jerusalem is described as:

> Having the glory of God, and the light thereof was like to a precious stone, as to the jasper stone, even as crystal. And it had a wall great and high ... And the building of the wall thereof was of jasper stone: but the city itself pure gold, like to clear glass. And the foundations of the wall of the city were adorned with all manner of precious stones. The first foundation was jasper: the second, sapphire: the third, a chalcedony: the fourth, an emerald: The fifth, sardonyx: the sixth, sardius: the seventh, chrysolite: the eighth, beryl: the ninth, a topaz: the tenth, a chrysoprasus: the eleventh, a jacinth: the twelfth, an amethyst. And the twelve gates are twelve pearls, one to each: and every several gate was of one several pearls. And the street of the city was pure gold, as if it were transparent glass ... And the city hath no need of the sun, nor of the moon, to shine in it. For the glory of God hath enlightened it, and the Lamb is the lamp thereof. And the nations shall walk in the light of it: and the kings of the earth shall bring their glory and honour into it. And the gates thereof shall not be shut by day: for there shall be no night there.[83]

The key visual features here are the ubiquity of precious stones and the (somewhat counter-intuitive) simile 'pure gold, like to clear glass' which is echoed in numerous otherworld depictions that emphasize the quantity of gold and the presence of crystal. The catalogue of precious stones is also a feature of descriptions of such realms. Finally, the absence of darkness or of night is a characteristic component of many otherworld accounts, whose light sources not infrequently take the form of large jewels.

The source of narrative imagery takes on a high degree of importance when that source is as culturally central a text as the Bible. The specific point of reference within the Bible is perhaps of less fixed significance. In a

---

quia aquae ejus de sanctuario egredientur; et erunt fructus ejus in cibum, et folia ejus ad medicinam' (Ezechiel 47. 12).

[83] 'Habentem claritatem Dei, et lumen ejus simile lapidi pretioso tamquam lapidi jaspidis, sicut crystallum. Et habebat murum magnum et altum ... Et erat structura muri ejus ex lapide jaspide; ipsa vero civitas, aurum mundum simile vitro mundo. Et fundamenta muri civitatis, omni lapide pretioso ornata. Fundamentum primum, jaspis; secundum sapphirus; tertium, chalcedonius; quartum, smaragdus; quintum, sardonyx sextum, sardius; septimum, chrysolithus; octavum, berillus; nonum, topazius; decimum, chrysoprasus; undecimum, hyacinthus; duodecimum, amethystus. Et duodecim portae, duodecim margaritae sunt, per singulas; et singulae portae erant ex singulis margaritis; et platea civitatis aurum mundum, tanquam vitrum perlucidum ... Et civitas non eget sole, neque luna ut luceant in ea, nam claritas Dei illuminavit eam, et lucerna ejus est Agnus. Et ambulabunt gentes in lumine ejus; et reges terrae afferent gloriam suam et honorem in illam. Et portae ejus non claudentur per diem; nox enim non erit illic' (Revelation 21. 11–12, 18–21, 23–25).

further example of how imaginative considerations might be the primary driving force behind these depictions, medieval writers often mix imagery redolent of Eden and New Jerusalem descriptions quite freely in their otherworld accounts. Although both can be described as 'Paradise', the New Jerusalem and Eden are, in theological terms, rather different concepts: one is earthly, the other is celestial. One is the place of humanity's beginning and the other is its possible destination.[84] However, the rigidity of medieval concepts of Paradise can be overstated. Allegorical, typological, historical, and eschatological interpretations of biblical accounts of Eden and the New Jerusalem were available to medieval Christians and 'the relationship of literal and spiritual truth was most variously interpreted in art and literature'.[85] Indeed, '[t]he teaching of the Church on Paradise provided writers and artists . . . with a range of alternatives, rather than a straightforward choice between literal and spiritual truth, between history and exegesis. Above all, it provided for the simultaneous holding of beliefs which to later ages might seem mutually exclusive'.[86] Furthermore, this overlap in the imagery between these two distinct realms is not without biblical precedent. As the passages quoted above make clear, the author of the Book of Revelation is clearly influenced by the imagery of Eden, particularly the imagery used in the Book of Ezechiel, in developing his account of the New Jerusalem. It is not difficult to see how these accounts might have been considered a contiguous imaginative field, with shared imagery and thematic concerns.

Of course, suggesting that otherworld motifs might have evoked biblical contexts is not to suggest that the Bible is necessarily the immediate source of this sort of imagery when it is used by medieval authors. These images are so widespread that authors could easily have encountered them in multiple texts, and the fact that the Judaeo-Christian tradition regarding the appearance of Paradise is representative of more widely dispersed ideas has been clearly established by Patch, among others.[87] Furthermore, the demands of the narrative need to be taken into account. An author who has set himself the task of describing a realm that is more than natural, a realm that is beautiful, wondrous, and joyous, is very likely to

---

[84] Yet, even these distinctions are not always firm ones. For instance, writers sometimes identify Eden as the place where souls will wait for Judgement Day (the *Navigatio Sancti Brendani* is a prominent example of this).

[85] Derek Pearsall and Elizabeth Salter, *Landscapes and Seasons of the Medieval World* (London: Elek, 1973), p. 60.

[86] Pearsall and Salter, *Landscapes and Seasons*, p. 59. There is further discussion of medieval attitudes to notions of Paradise in Delumeau, *History of Paradise*, esp. cpts 1–3.

[87] See, in particular, the account of oriental and classical analogues in Patch, *Other World*, pp. 7–26.

draw upon images that are associated with these ideas in his culture. Put another way, it would be surprising if precious gems, fertile plains, fruits, sweet music, gold, year-round summer, and day-long light did *not* form the core of such descriptions.

A particularly notable instance of biblical imagery informing the portrayal and interpretation of an otherworld occurs in *Sir Orfeo*. The otherworld of this Middle English poem has been subjected to more thorough scrutiny than that of many other texts. Taking their cue from the text's self-identification as a Breton Lay, many scholars have suggested Celtic origins for its more outlandish supernatural components, notably its uncanny fairy realm.[88] Yet, there is nothing in surviving Celtic language literatures quite like this realm, and medieval Irish or Welsh otherworld accounts bear no closer a resemblance to it than English or French descriptions of such places. Indeed, when the structure and details of the description are considered, it becomes clear that the features of the fairy kingdom in *Orfeo* owe rather more to the Bible than to any supposed Celtic or folkloric roots. Even if it could be demonstrated that the *Orfeo* author drew upon such sources, it seems highly unlikely that the tale's audience would have made such connections, particularly when biblical associations were obvious and available. The *Orfeo*-poet's initial description of the fairy otherworld is worth examining closely. After passing through a hollow hill in pursuit of the fairy hunt, Orfeo sees a beautiful, bright country, with smooth green plains. The text lingers over the description of the fairy palace:

Amidde þe lond a castel he siȝe,	
Riche & real & wonder heiȝe.	
Al þe vt-mast wal	[outermost
Was clere & schine as cristal;	
An hundred tours þer were about,	
Degiselich and bataild stout;	[Wonderful
Þe butras com out of þe diche	
Of rede gold y-arched riche;	
Þe vousour was auowed al	[vaulting; decorated
Of ich maner diuers aumal.	[enamel

[88] For some influential arguments for *Orfeo*'s Celticity, see George Kittredge, '*Sir Orfeo*', *The American Journal of Philology*, 7 (1886), 176–202; Bruce Mitchell, 'The Faery World of *Sir Orfeo*', *Neophilologus*, 48 (1964), 156–9; Patrizia Grimaldi, 'Sir Orfeo as Celtic Folk-Hero, Christian Pilgrim, and Medieval King', in *Allegory, Myth, and Symbol*, edited by Morton W. Bloomfield (Cambridge, MA: Harvard University Press, 1981), pp. 147–61; Dorena Allen, 'Orpheus and Orfeo: The Dead and the Taken', *Medium Aevum*, 33 (1964), 102–11. There is a full-length exploration of possible Celtic sources by Marie-Thérèse Brouland: *Sir Orfeo: le substrat celtique du lai breton anglais* (Paris: Didier Érudition, 1990).

Wiþ-in þer wer wide wones,   [streets
Al of precious stones;
Þe werst piler on to biholde
Was al of burnist gold.
Al þat lond was euer liȝt,
For when it schuld be þerk & niȝt,   [dark
Þe riche stones liȝt gonne   [shone
As briȝt as doþ at none þe sonne.
No man may telle, no þenche in þouȝt,   [think
Þe riche werk þat þer was wrouȝt...[89]

As Ad Putter has demonstrated, the imagery of Revelation 21 lurks in the background of a number of romance depictions of castles and beautiful cities, whether or not they are explicitly otherworldly.[90] Nonetheless, the biblical account has not displaced Celtic material as the source for the *Orfeo* description most typically cited by scholars. The text's most influential editor, Alan Bliss, bypasses the biblical context and draws parallels with a series of medieval Irish texts. He suggests that the crystal walls are similar to those in the *Immram Máele Dúin* and the *Adventure of St Columba's Clerics*, while the bejewelled walls of the buildings are like those in *Serglige Con Culainn* (The Love Sickness of Cúchulainn) and *Eachtra Thaidhg Mhic Céin*.[91] Bliss also notes the resemblance between the *Orfeo* description and the account of the Earthly Paradise in Benedeit's Anglo-Norman adaptation of the *Navigatio Sancti Brendani* (though he feels that these details are more likely to be the innovations of the Anglo-Norman redactor than evidence of a putative 'Celtic' source).[92] However, none of these works represents the line of least resistance when tracing sources for the otherworld imagery in *Sir Orfeo*. All these elements can be more readily traced to the Bible.

On seeing this palace, Orfeo immediately assumes that it is the 'proude court of Paradis'.[93] He is not the only character in romance to mistake the otherworld for a manifestation of Heaven. There is a sort of 'logic of the superlative' at work in Orfeo's reaction, which leads him to try and rationalize the most beautiful place he has ever seen in heavenly terms.[94] Although he is ultimately proven wrong, his reaction reflects how far the visual detail of the fairy kingdom echoes specific features of scriptural

---

[89] *Sir Orfeo*, edited by Bliss, ll. 355–74.

[90] Putter, 'The Influence of Visions of the Otherworld', pp. 237–51.

[91] *Sir Orfeo*, edited by Bliss, p. xxxix. It should also be noted that the *Eachtra Thaidhg* is almost certainly of a later date than *Sir Orfeo*.

[92] *Sir Orfeo*, edited by Bliss, p. xxxix. Benedeit's debt to biblical accounts is detailed in the final section of this chapter below.

[93] *Sir Orfeo*, edited by Bliss, l. 376.   [94] Putter, 'Influence of Visions', p. 239.

accounts of Paradise. The influence of the description of the New Jerusalem from the Book of Revelation, quoted above, is particularly noticeable in the *Orfeo* description. The sheer size of the castle is the first point of similarity to the heavenly city (Revelation 21. 16–17), but more explicit comparisons are yet to come. The outer wall of the castle, which shines like crystal, recalls the shining New Jerusalem, where although the walls are of jasper, the city itself is 'like to clear glass' (Revelation 21. 11, 18). The use of precious stones and gold as building materials and as decoration in the castle supplies a further echo of the account of the New Jerusalem with its twelve foundations of precious stones, gateways made of pearls, and streets of gold (Revelation 21. 19–21). The final, and perhaps most striking, mirroring is the reference to the continual brightness of the surrounding country in *Sir Orfeo*, which parallels the absence of night in the biblical account (Revelation 21. 23–5). As if the parallels needed reinforcing, the *Orfeo*-poet's description follows precisely the same structure as the portrayal of the New Jerusalem in Revelation 21. In both texts the description begins with an account of the brightness of the castle/city and then proceeds to an account of its size, the precious materials from which it is constructed, and finally to the absence of night. The first point at which the account gestures towards a biblical book other than Revelation is in the lines 'No man may telle, no þenche in þou3t, / Þe riche werk þat þer was wrou3t'. Here, too, the biblical reference drives home the paradisal connotations of the scene. The verbal echo of Paul's comment on Heaven in 1 Corinthians 2. 9 is unmistakable: 'But, as it is written: That eye hath not seen, nor ear heard, neither hath it entered into the heart of man, what things God hath prepared for them that love him'.[95] The initial lengthy description of the fairy kingdom in *Sir Orfeo* would seem to be unambiguously paradisal. The structure and contents of that first sighting could not be much more explicit in their evocation of biblical accounts of Paradise.

Of course, Orfeo's subsequent experience of the realm, particularly of the interior of the palace, complicates this initial interpretation considerably, but recognizing the biblical allusions in the first impression of the fairy kingdom deepens the enigma and, indeed, the horror of what is to come. In identifying the place as Paradise, Orfeo is responding to the symbolically loaded imagery in the same manner as a medieval reader. However, like the protagonist of the *Tractatus*, who believes he is in Hell for much of his journey through Purgatory, and in Heaven for his journey through the Earthly Paradise, Orfeo's initial interpretative efforts are

---

[95] 'Sed sicut scriptum est: Quod oculus non vidit, nec auris audivit, nec in cor hominis ascendit, quae praeparavit Deus iis qui diligunt illum'.

misleading. The paradisal connotations rapidly evaporate when Orfeo is admitted to the fairy palace. There, he enters a hall filled with a host of people who, we are assured, seem dead but are not. Some are in various states of mutilation, while others bear the signs of sudden and early death as a result of childbirth, drowning, or choking.[96] It might be suggested that the author has merged the Earthly Paradise and the purgative or infernal regions into a single figure: the fairy palace. The richness of the description seems designed to stimulate the interpretative efforts of the audience, only for them to be thwarted. The evocation of biblical material, notably the descriptions of Revelation 21, in *Sir Orfeo* prompts expectations of order and clarity that are ultimately frustrated. The overall effect is rather disturbing. It is not just the shift from the beautiful to the horrific that produces this effect, but the sudden transformation of the paradisial into the infernal. *Sir Orfeo*'s otherworld owes much of its impact to the elaborate game of subterfuge that the text plays with the audience's interpretative faculties. This collapsing of the neat schematization of the afterlife, familiar from religious writing, results in an otherworld whose significations are so chaotic that it has been interpreted as a symbol of the unknowable.[97] The evocation of biblical accounts that would be immediately recognizable and resonant to the text's audience is key to any such effect. Because of its cultural centrality, imagery associated with the afterlife can be a potent artistic tool and the frequency and implications of its use in literary accounts of otherworld realms have not been adequately stressed.

In view of the well-documented contacts between medieval Ireland, Britain, and the Continent, it is perhaps unrealistic to assume narrowly native origins for the material that recurs in so many Irish otherworld descriptions. This does not mean that we should retreat entirely from pan-insular perspectives. It is no stretch to argue that Ireland and England were the 'two nations perhaps most productive of otherworld visions in the Middle Ages'.[98] The reasons for the emphasis on such material in the insular world are difficult to pin down, but the Celtic-language culture of the regions of the British Isles (at various degrees of chronological remove) cannot provide the full rationale. As we will see in Chapter 4, the eschatological implications of Western insular geography may have had a part to play.

[96] *Sir Orfeo*, edited by Bliss, ll. 391–400. The description of this scene in British Library, Harley MS 3810 is considerably less horrific. The remaining manuscript witness, Bodleian Library MS Ashmole 61, is much closer to the Auchinleck account. All three manuscripts are edited in parallel by Alan Bliss in his 1954 edition of the romance.
[97] See the arguments summarized at the beginning of Cartlidge, 'Sir Orfeo in the Otherworld', pp. 195–9.
[98] Easting, 'Purgatory and the Earthly Paradise', p. 24.

OTHERWORLDS IN THE OCEAN: SCRIPTURE AND SYNCRETISM

Two narrative texts associated with Ireland and depicting a sea journey provide particularly interesting evidence for how authors exploit the overlap between the imagery of the afterlife and the otherworld to a variety of ends. The first, and by far the most famous, is the *Navigatio Sancti Brendani Abbatis*. This text develops its deeply religious themes not only through a biblically derived description of Paradise, but also through accounts of fantastical islands. The second is the late medieval Irish narrative *Eachtra Thaidhg Mhic Céin*, which has received scant scholarly attention. This text supplies a particularly memorable example of the originality with which afterlife and otherworld motifs could be woven together.

Like the *Tractatus*, the account of the voyage of Brendan the Navigator has been described as a 'medieval best seller'.[99] The Latin text was read across Europe and it was translated and adapted into many vernaculars.[100] In both texts Ireland provides a starting point for the journey. The original version of the *Navigatio* is considerably older than the *Tractatus*; in its earliest form it may date from the eighth or ninth century.[101] The *Navigatio* presents several interesting points of contrast with the *Tractatus*. Owein is a lay hero, explicitly sinful and ignorant, while Brendan is a monk, and his personal sanctity and understanding of the ways of God are emphasized throughout the text. The *Tractatus* maps a vast subterranean space, whereas the *Navigatio* traces a journey through a similarly vast and mysterious ocean zone. Both journeys end where they began. However, the two-way journey described in the *Tractatus* is essentially a linear route towards the East and back again, whereas that of the *Navigatio* appears to be circular and the monks set out for the West.[102]

---

[99] John D. Anderson, 'The *Navigatio Brendani*: A Medieval Best Seller', *The Classical Journal*, 83 (1988), 315–22.

[100] There is an overview of the vernacular adaptations in Carl Selmer, 'The Vernacular Translations of the *Navigatio Sancti Brendani*: A Bibliographical Study', *Mediaeval Studies*, 18 (1956), 145–57.

[101] James Carney influentially argued for *c.*800 in his 'Review of *Navigatio Sancti Brendani Abbatis*, edited by Carl Selmer', *Medium Aevum*, 31 (1963), 37–44. More recently, David Dumville has suggested a date before 786: 'Two Approaches to the Dating of *Nauigatio Sancti Brendani*', *Studi Medievali*, 29 (1988), 87–102.

[102] This facet of the text is often overlooked by interpretations that see it as an account of a transatlantic voyage. See further, J. J. O'Meara, 'In the Wake of the Saint: The Brendan Voyage, an Epic Crossing of the Atlantic by Leather Boat', *Times Literary Supplement*, 14 July 1978; repr. in *The Otherworld Voyage in Early Irish Literature: An Anthology of Criticism*, edited by Jonathan Wooding (Dublin: Four Courts Press, 2000), pp. 109–12.

Ocean spaces seem to lend themselves to the multiplication of other-world experiences. In the *Navigatio*, the vast unmapped spaces of the Atlantic are peppered with fantastic islands and the movement across water from island to island, describing multiple thresholds to multiple otherworlds, stresses the episodic nature of the text. The multiplicity of the lands visited by Brendan makes the text highly resistant to overarching interpretations, particularly those of an allegorical nature, yet some under-pinning of consistent meaning is supplied by the liturgical calendar. As Helen Cooper puts it:

> In each of their seven years at sea they spend the periods around Easter and Christmas in the same series of places. . . . Their recurrent visits to the same places mark the cyclical time of the liturgical calendar, time measured as space, the unmeasured wastes of the Atlantic mapped like a calendar.[103]

Here religious meaning is supplied by an extra-textual source, but its application to particular locations is entirely contingent on the narrative at hand. For instance, liturgical time would seem to provide a compelling interpretation for the sojourn on Jasconius, the whale whom the monks initially mistake for an island. They spend Holy Saturday and Easter Sunday on the back of the creature—a time period which would seem apt, since there was a long-standing exegetical tradition that regarded Jonah's time in the belly of the whale as a figure for Christ's descent to the dead after the crucifixion.[104] However, other locations at which feasts are celebrated are not so easily allegorizable. The liturgical calendar would seem to map the familiar onto the unknown but, in doing so, tends to deepen, rather than lessen, the mystery of the vast Atlantic spaces.

As far as their outward characteristics are concerned, the fantastic Atlantic locations of the *Navigatio* would, for the most part, be equally at home in a text without explicit religious import. Their descriptions appear to depend on no authority external to the text. Only Brendan's final destination on his outward journey, the Promised Land of the Saints (*Terra Repromissionis Sanctorum*), which draws heavily on biblical and popular apocryphal material, falls into this category. The author of the *Navigatio* seems to be drawing on the tradition of the saints dwelling on earth for a thousand years before the end of the world.[105] However, it is worth noting that even though Brendan's westward voyage should, by the conventions of medieval geography, take the monks to the eastern edge of

---

[103] Cooper, *English Romance*, p. 125. On the allegorical dimension of the *Navigatio*, see Dorothy Ann Bray, 'Allegory in the *Navigatio Sancti Brendani*', *Viator*, 26 (1995), 1–10; repr. in *The Otherworld Voyage*, edited by Wooding, pp. 175–86.

[104] Bray, 'Allegory in the *Navigatio*', pp. 8–9.

[105] Delumeau, *History of Paradise*, p. 24.

Asia, no explicit identification is made between the site of Eden and the Promised Land of the Saints in the Latin text. Indeed, the description of the mysterious island on which Brendan and his crew eventually land is brief and rather lacking in specifics in the *Navigatio* and in many of its adaptations. A significant exception is the early twelfth-century Anglo-Norman adaptation by Benedeit, a cleric connected to the court of Henry I. His poem features by far the richest description of Brendan's destination in the insular tradition of the Brendan legend.[106] This enlarged account may be a manifestation of Benedeit's exploitation of the sea as what Sebastian Sobecki terms a 'locus of *merveilles*, often of a dramatic kind'.[107] As Sobecki demonstrates, the Anglo-Norman adaptation places far greater emphasis on the text's more fantastical elements and greatly expands the *Navigatio*'s account of events like the Battle of the Sea-Monsters. Such elaborations may reflect the interests and demands of Benedeit's courtly audience and a contemporary fascination with the marvellous in such circles.[108] This Anglo-Norman version omits the more explicitly monastic concerns of its source, but it more than makes up for them in homiletic digressions entirely lacking in the Latin original.

The *Navigatio* describes how Brendan and his crew reach the Promised Land of the Saints after travelling through dense fog. They explore the fruitful land for forty days, without finding the end of it. Eventually, they reach a river that bisects the island and are met by a young man who embraces them and tells them that they may go no further. He explains that this is the land they have been seeking and describes how it is always fruitful and is illuminated by the light of Christ. The young man urges them to take fruit and precious stones back with them. Although Benedeit's account of this episode is similar in its narrative outline, it is far lengthier and considerably richer on a descriptive and thematic level. The Anglo-Norman text is also a good deal clearer about the nature of the land: it unequivocally identifies Brendan's final destination as Eden and describes it in terms familiar from biblical accounts. High walls surround it, and it is covered in gemstones that Benedeit lists at length in the manner of Ezechiel 28 and Revelation 21.[109] The land emits a great

---

[106] Among the major Continental versions, only the Dutch adaptation (also from the twelfth century) rivals it for length and vivid detail. *De reis van Sente Brandane*, edited by H. P. A. Oskamp (Zutphen: Thieme, 1972).

[107] Sebastian I. Sobecki, 'From the *Désert Liquide* to the Sea of Romance: Benedeit's *Le Voyage de Saint Brendan* and the Irish *Immrama*', *Neophilologus*, 87 (2003), 193–207, (p. 203).

[108] As described by Watkins, *History and the Supernatural*, pp. 12–18.

[109] Benedeit, *The Anglo-Norman Voyage of St Brendan*, edited by Brian Merrilees and Ian Short (Manchester: Manchester University Press, 1979), ll. 1679–92. Translations are from Glyn S. Burgess, trans., 'The Anglo-Norman Version', in *The Voyage of St Brendan:*

light of its own and the garden itself is on the top of a high mountain of gold and marble. When Brendan and his monks land, they are met by a young man who takes them inside the first gate, quelling both a dragon and a whirling sword that guard it. Within is a fertile land of woods and meadows, filled with fruit and flowers, where the seasons never change (cf. Ezechiel 47:12). The episode mixes this sort of rich description with constant reminders of the limitations and exiled nature of humanity. Early in the description, Benedeit comments, 'such is that wall, set high above us, where our home ought to have been',[110] and, after a certain point, it transpires Brendan and his companions may go no further 'because they have insufficient knowledge'.[111] Although it is humanity's 'true home', the account stresses the monks' alienation from it. Indeed, the beauty of the place fast becomes more than they can bear: the melody of angel voices that fills the air is hard to endure because their mortal human nature is so limited. They return home, taking some stones from the place as 'tokens of hope'.[112]

The Anglo-Norman poet appears to have consciously heightened the set-piece nature of the description. Where his source gives the same, sparser description of the land twice—once in Barrindus's account at the beginning of the text and a second time on Brendan's own arrival—Benedeit omits the initial account and produces a final account that is considerably expanded and enriched. The result is that the goal of Brendan's quest has greater descriptive impact in the Anglo-Norman text than in its Latin source. The extent to which the expanded description looks to biblical accounts for its imagery and themes also enhances its imaginative resonance. As in other texts, lengthy description is necessary to bring about the sort of suspension of disbelief required to accept the claims of such a fantastical narrative. In a medieval context, biblical accounts might fairly provide the sort of authenticating material that could root the Brendan legend in reality. As such, Benedeit's lengthy description of the Earthly Paradise, though it is more fantastical and marvel-filled than that of his source, may be read as an attempt to enhance the believability of his text.

Since an encounter with the unknown is an inherent facet of otherworld descriptions, it would be strange if the theme of the acquisition of knowledge were not pervasive in such narratives. Knowledge becomes a

---

Representative Versions of the Legend in English Translation, edited by W. R. J. Barron and Glyn S. Burgess (Exeter: University of Exeter Press, 2002), pp. 65–102.

[110] 'Tels est li murs, si surplantez, / Qui doust estre de nus hantez'. Benedeit, *Voyage*, ll. 1701–2; translated by Burgess, p. 100.

[111] 'Quar poi estes a ço savant'. Benedeit, *Voyage*, l. 1788; translated by Burgess, p. 101.

[112] 'A enseignes de conforter'. Benedeit, *Voyage*, l. 1800; translated by Burgess, p. 102.

loaded theme when treated in an explicitly religious context. This is particularly true of the Brendan legend since its final destination is the place where human beings fell from grace because of their desire for knowledge. Knowledge is a key thematic concern of Benedeit's text and the adaptation features, as Glyn Burgess has highlighted, a rather nuanced treatment of the verb *savoir*.[113] The text strikes a balance between the knowledge that can be derived from the encounter with the fabulous and the limitations of the interpretative efforts of human beings. Like many texts depicting otherworld or afterlife realms, it is concerned with the extent and the limitations of human understanding and achievement. Corporeality (and attendant mortality) appears to place a limit on the monks' journey and so the exploration of knowledge and desire is linked to the theme of death. In Benedeit's text, the guide informs the monks that they will only be able to experience the Earthly Paradise fully when they return there in spiritual form after their death.[114] This sort of developed engagement with the twin themes of knowledge and death can only deepen the association of the Earthly Paradise with the narrative of the Fall in Genesis.

While the imaginative vitality of Benedeit's account of Brendan's destination makes its identity with Eden much more explicit than in the *Navigatio*, not all narrative accounts imagine afterlife realms that are so easily situated within medieval categories of belief. Some writers create realms that are more thoroughly syncretic, blending the material of Christian belief with that of legend. The rarely studied late medieval Irish text *Eachtra Thaidhg Mhic Céin*[115] demands attention for its creative mixing of material from a wide range of sources. This narrative is preserved in the large fifteenth-century miscellany, the 'Book of Lismore',[116] and, although it was edited and translated by Standish O'Grady over a century ago, references to it in subsequent scholarship have been few and brief.[117] What little linguistic analysis there has been has tended to place the text in the Early Modern Irish period, most likely in the fourteenth or fifteenth century.[118] *Eachtra Thaidhg* can be loosely divided into a frame

[113] Glyn Burgess, '*Savoir* and *Faire* in the Anglo-Norman *Voyage of St Brendan*', *French Studies*, 49 (1995), 257–74.

[114] Benedeit, *Voyage*, ll. 1793–7; translated by Burgess, p. 102.

[115] The pseudo-historical progenitor of the Ciannacht dynastic groups, see Chapter 4 of this volume.

[116] Also known as 'The Book of MacCarthy Reagh' (*Leabhar Mhic Cárthaigh Riabhaigh*). The late date of this manuscript itself is no evidence of the lateness of *Eachtra Thaidhg* since it contains a large number of earlier texts, notably the twelfth-century *Acallam na Senórach*.

[117] Prionsias MacCana discusses it very briefly in 'The Sinless Otherworld of *Immram Brain*', *Ériu*, 27 (1976), 95–115; repr. in *Otherworld Voyage*, edited by Wooding, pp. 52–72.

[118] MacCana, 'Sinless Otherworld', 103.

and core narrative. The story is set in the pre-Christian era in Ireland and the frame narrative relates how the legendary hero Tadhg undertakes a voyage to rescue his family after their abduction by pirates. The core narrative relates the experiences of Tadhg and his men on an island dubbed the 'world's fourth paradise' during the course of their journey.

These two principal narrative threads are so different in emphasis, subject matter, and tone that it is tempting to suggest that they are originally independent stories grafted together at a later date. On the other hand, some thematic continuity between frame text and core text is, perhaps, discernible: Tadhg voyages to save those persons most dear to him in life and in the course of that journey he (wholly unexpectedly) saves his soul. Whatever the structural merits of his work, there is little doubt that the author of this text is keenly aware of wider narrative traditions. The encounter with a series of islands while voyaging in the Atlantic appears to gesture towards the *immram* tradition. Tadhg's party reaches an island of gigantic sheep which recalls that explored by Máel Dúin's crew in the earlier, more famous narrative, and their ultimate destination is the sort of island of the blessed that, in various guises, appears in many of the tales usually classed as *immrama*. There are particular echoes of the island paradise encountered in a short episode in *Immram Curaig Ua Corra*. Like the paradise encountered by Tadhg and his crew, this realm also features a fortress, in both texts the voyagers are met and counselled by a beautiful woman, and in both texts they are met by a flock of birds on their departure from the island.[119] The author also draws on popular narratives such as *Lebor Gabála* (The Book of Invasions) in depicting an encounter with Noah's granddaughter Cessair, who features in that work as the leader of the first settlers in Ireland. Most significantly, the work functions as a gap-filler and sequel to the much earlier *Echtrae Chonnlai*, clarifying the reasons for Connla's departure across the sea, detailing his life after leaving his homeland, and revealing the identity of the woman that lured him away from his family.[120]

Eachtra Thaidhg also appears to be a sequel with a very specific agenda, namely the post-hoc Christianization of the earlier text. Take, for instance,

---

[119] *Voyage of the Hui Corra*, edited by Stokes, pp. 46–7.

[120] Drawing on linguistic evidence, Kim McCone posits that the original version of *Echtrae Chonnlai* may have been composed as early as the eighth century (*Echtrae Chonnlai*, edited by McCone, p. 63), but the fact that seven of the eight surviving manuscripts date from the fifteenth century suggests that it enjoyed a wide popularity in the period in which *Eachtra Thaidhg* appears to have been composed.

the speech of Cessair, who meets Tadhg and his crew when they land. She tells them that the island is called *Inisderglocha* and explains its nature:

> ... this precisely is the earth's fourth paradise: the others being inis Daleb in the world's southern, and inis Escandra in its boreal part (to the northward of 'the black watery isle'), Adam's paradise, and this island in which ye are now: the fourth land, I say, in which Adam's seed shall dwell—such of them as are righteous.[121]

It is tempting to suggest a source for some of this in earlier (safely lost) pagan material, but the probable late date of this work makes such an explanation more than usually implausible. There is certainly nothing like this 'four paradises' scheme anywhere else in medieval Irish literature, or other European literatures for that matter. *Eachtra Thaidhg* gives the identity of Connla's otherworldly lover as Venuisa, one of the four daughters of Adam:

> ... four daughters we are in the four mysterious magic countries [i.e. the four paradises] Venuisa, Letiusa, Aiusa, and Eliusa our names are, whom through the guilt of our mother's transgression suffers not to abide together in one place, yet for our virginity and for our purity that we have dedicated to God we are conveyed to these separate joyful domiciles.[122]

Just as there is no other source that enumerates four paradises, no other text discusses or names these daughters of Adam. It seems that in this detail, *Eachtra Thaidhg* matches its elaboration of earlier native legend with an extrapolation of Genesis itself. Nothing in this text contradicts the biblical account, yet the author adds to it freely and displays particular originality in doing so.

The blurring of the boundary between otherworld and the afterlife is also mirrored in the application of notions associated with Heaven itself to 'Inisderglocha'. Tadhg engages Connla and the woman in conversation and elicits this observation on their relationship:

> 'I had bestowed on him true affection's love', the girl explained, 'and therefore wrought to have him come to me in this land; where our delight, both of us, is to continue in looking at and in perpetual contemplation of

---

[121] 'is é so cethramad parrthas in talman do shunnrad .i. inis Daleb i ndeiscert in talman . ocus inis Ercandra i tuaiscert in talman .i. do'n leth i tuaidh do'n oilén dub uiscide . ocus parrthas Adaim ocus in tailén atáithíse in cethramad tír i náitrebait síol Adaim doneoch atá firénach díob'. *Tadhg*, edited and translated by O'Grady, I, p. 349, II, pp. 391–2.

[122] 'ár ceithri hingena atám isna ceithrib tírib diamra dráidechta....i. Ueniusa ocus Letiusa ocus Aliusa ocus Eleusa ár nanmanna. cionta imarbais ár máthar tucad orainn gan ár mbeith i naeininad . ocus is aire tucad sinn isna sosaidib suarcasa ar ár nóige ocus ar ár nionnracus do choisecramar do dhia', *Tadhg*, edited and translated by O'Grady, I, p. 350, II, p. 392.

one another: above and beyond which we pass not, to commit impurity or fleshly sin whatsoever.'[123]

The pagan Tadhg's response is to call the situation 'a beautiful and, at the same [time], a comical thing'.[124] Prionsias MacCana has argued that this represents 'a pious, puritanical, and somewhat extravagant exemplar of Christian love' which renders the otherworld 'a kind of wan prefiguration of Paradise clouded in Pre-Raphaelite sentimentality'.[125] Yet, *Eachtra Thaidhg*'s blending of Christian belief and narrative tradition may be more skilful and less 'wan' in its effects than this. The description of a continual gaze that gives mutual joy in a paradisal context seems a clear echo of the notion of the beatific vision. Indeed, the word used for 'look' in the text, *silled*, is also used elsewhere to describe the beatific vision—'in t-silleadh chonaigh'[126]—an experience medieval audiences are unlikely to have considered in any sense 'wan'. Indeed, this allusion to the Christian theology of Heaven accomplishes a good deal of work in the author's syncretizing scheme. In one stroke it absolves Connla and Veniusa from any 'impurity' that might have been inferred from the original *echtra*, while not diluting the intensity or delight of their mutual love. The function of these afterlife components in *Eachtra Thaidhg* may, in fact, be pseudo-mimetic. The more fantastic a literary world becomes, the more it risks undermining the audience's suspension of disbelief. The biblical and theological references in *Eachtra Thaidhg* buttress its author's elaborate fictive edifice. The narrative also reflects an enthusiastic engagement with earlier texts and a response to the imaginative stimulus they provide. The otherworld island of this text occupies a consciously blurry midpoint between the Paradise of Judaeo-Christian revelation and the fairy kingdoms of more 'fictive' creations. Its author appears to have created an entirely original, alternative geography and situated it within, and insulated it with, the established facts of revelation.

It is difficult to imagine that medieval readings of otherworld narratives would not have been substantially coloured by an overriding concern with a spiritual reality beyond this world. Conceptually, an otherworld location that is not explicitly the afterlife would seem to fall within the gap that

---

[123] 'tucassa grád carthanach do ar an ingen . ocus tucas chugam isin chríchsi é . ocus is é ár náibes ár ndís beith oc silled ocus oc sírdhécsain araile ocus ní dénmait col ná corbad eile acht sin'. *Tadhg*, edited and translated by O'Grady, I, p. 350, II, p. 393.

[124] 'is aebda ocus is ait sin'. *Tadhg*, edited and translated by O'Grady, I, p. 350, II, p. 393.

[125] MacCana, 'Sinless Otherworld', 61.

[126] *Instructio Pie Vivendi Et Superna Meditandi*, edited and translated by John McKechnie, 2 vols, ITS, 29, 29a (Dublin: Educational Company of Ireland, 1934–1946), I (1934), p. 228.

Watkins describes 'between normative and condemned belief and praxis, [where] there existed a substantial space in which extra-ecclesial ideas could flourish'.[127] This position is backed up by the attitudes of numerous chroniclers. It would seem that the general tendency of writers, when contemplating the meaning of realms that did not seem to reflect any category of Christian belief, is not to question the veracity of the accounts, or even the rightness of their world view, but to assume, like William of Newburgh did when reflecting on his account of the green children of Woolpit, that 'the frailty of our intelligence is quite incapable of unearthing this'.[128]

A striking passage in the romance of *Thomas of Erceldoune* does something rather unusual—it maps the relative location of these various worlds. Thomas travels in darkness through a hill for three days before his fairy guide directs his attention to the vista before him. He sees a bright landscape with roads leading in various directions. The lady explains that the first road goes to Heaven:

> 'Seese þou nowe ȝone faire waye,
> Þat lygges ouer ȝone heghe mountayne?—
> Ȝone es þe waye to heuene for aye,   [forever
> Whene synfull sawles are passede þer payne.[129]

She goes on to point out another route, which she says goes to the Earthly Paradise, another to Purgatory, and a further one to Hell. The final part of the scene she describes is her own fairy homeland.

> Seese þou ȝitt ȝone faire castelle,
> Þat standis ouer ȝone heghe hill?
> Of towne & towre, it beris þe belle;   [i.e. is the most beautiful
> In erthe es none lyke it vn-till.
> ffor sothe, Thomas, ȝone es myne awenne,   [my own
> And þe kynges of this countree.'[130]

Using the term 'otherworld' to refer to both the afterlife of Christian belief and realms like fairyland can lead us to overlook some of the nuance in this tableau. On the face of it, the *Thomas*-poet seems to bracket the fairy's realm with the four afterlife locations as places that are not-of-this-world.

---

[127] Watkins, *History and the Supernatural*, p. 87.

[128] 'quam utique nostri sensus tenuitas non sufficit indagare'. William, *History of English Affairs*, pp. 120–1.

[129] *Thomas of Erceldoune*, edited by Murray, ll. 201–4.

[130] *Thomas of Erceldoune*, edited by Murray, ll. 217–22. For a more recent overview of the romance and its context, see James Wade, 'Ungallant Knights', in *Heroes and Anti-Heroes in Medieval Romance*, edited by Neil Cartlidge (Cambridge: D. S. Brewer, 2012), pp. 201–18.

However, a clear distinction is also made. Thomas merely sees the routes leading to Heaven, Hell, Purgatory, and the Earthly Paradise, not the locations themselves. These are completely removed from view. Accessing Heaven comes with the sort of conditions we see in other texts: souls must first have passed 'þer payne' or have passed through death and probably Purgatory.[131] Purgatory is where souls must suffer with 'tene and traye' (pain and affliction), and Hell is the 'birnande fyre' from which it has already been stressed that no one can return.[132] Only the Earthly Paradise is described without a clear statement that someone still living, like Thomas, would find it a location to which access might be problematic or from which it might be impossible to return. By contrast, the fairy's realm is visible a short distance away and Thomas and the fairy reach the beautiful castle quickly. Thomas ultimately returns to the human world. Putter highlights how this very clear 'mapping' of fairyland places it somewhere between the human world and the afterlife—it is in some sense intermediate, not only physically, but perhaps ontologically as well.[133] As we have seen, it was possible for medieval writers to be more nuanced still—certain afterlife locations, particularly the Earthly Paradise, but also Purgatory, might be considered more proximate to and contiguous with the human world than Heaven and Hell.

---

[131] *Thomas of Erceldoune*, edited by Murray, l. 204.
[132] *Thomas of Erceldoune*, edited by Murray, ll. 211, 216, 187–92.
[133] Putter, 'Influence of Visions', p. 240. An extended reading of the intermediate status of fairyland and its position in romance topographies is supplied by Cole in '"Fairy" in Middle English Romance', pp. 144–61.

3

Supernatural Authorities

In the Victoria and Albert Museum in London, there is an artefact now known as the 'Luck of Edenhall' (see Figure 3.1).[1] This is a fourteenth-century glass cup that is elaborately decorated with gilding and enamel. It appears to be of Syrian design. Its precise origins are unknown, but it seems likely that it was brought back to England from the Crusades, eventually finding its way into the possession of the Musgrave family of Edenhall in Cumberland. It is called Edenhall's 'luck' because of a belief that the fortunes of the family would take a turn for the worse should the cup ever be broken. The cup has a particularly interesting backstory. According to a local tradition, which first seems to have been committed to writing in the eighteenth century, a group of fairies left the cup behind when they were suddenly disturbed at St Cuthbert's Well near Edenhall.[2] It is not unusual for medieval accounts of otherworld journeys to describe how certain objects were brought back from the realm of the supernatural and the Luck of Edenhall may provide evidence that such tales could be formulated to provide a compelling backstory for particularly unusual or ancient objects. However, the relationship between object and narrative can work in more than one direction and in more than one context. Such objects can also act as a sort of 'proof' of a narrative's veracity, lending authority to the stories that lie behind them. Association with otherworld objects can also enhance the prestige, and concomitant authority, of their owners.

The Luck of Edenhall, and the micro-mythology that goes with it, is an example of concern that recurs in otherworld narratives. Many authors take pains to include evidence that might make their accounts more plausible. We saw this in the last chapter, with the extensive authenticating material

---

[1] Museum no. C. 1–1959.

[2] For the earliest written notice of this story, see William Musgrave, 'The Luck of Edenhall', *The Gentleman's Magazine*, 61 (1791), 721–2. On the origins and design of the cup, see W. B. Honey, 'A Syrian Glass Goblet', *The Burlington Magazine*, 50 (1927), 286, 289, 291, 293–4, and Glyn Davies, 'New Light on the Luck of Edenhall', *The Burlington Magazine*, 52 (2010), 4–7.

Fig. 3.1. The Luck of Edenhall (© Victoria and Albert Museum, London)

that Henry of Saltry wove into the *Tractatus de Purgatorio Sancti Patricii*. Henry's supporting evidence takes the form of citation of religious author- ities and eyewitness testimonies of similar experiences, but tokens brought back from the otherworld are a particularly frequent mode of authentica- tion. William of Newburgh tells us of a drunken peasant who came across a fairy kingdom in a hollow hill and steals a cup 'of unknown material, unusual colour, and strange shape' from the otherworld feast.[3] In Gerald of Wales' account of Elidyr's journey to the fairy kingdom under the earth, the young boy also attempts to obtain tangible evidence of his experience.

---

[3] William, *History of English Affairs*, pp. 120–1.

At his mother's urging, he tries to bring a golden ball back from one of his visits. However, the fairies give chase and retrieve this object. At this point, the account shifts its attention to another source of validation: the authority that the boy's testimony derives from the priestly vocation he pursues in adult life.[4] Of course, such proofs do not have to take the form of a token brought from the otherworld to this one: Ralph of Coggeshall, for instance, cites the fact that one of the green children of Woolpit married and had offspring living at the time he was writing as an indication that his story was not mere fancy.[5]

The authorizing capacity of otherworld objects is not limited to the credibility their beauty or strangeness may lend to the story that lies behind them. Objects associated with otherworld encounters may, in turn, authorize power relations in the historical world. William of Newburgh states that the cup retrieved by the drunken peasant was given to Henry I, from whom it passed to David I of Scotland (presumably in his time as a dependant at Henry's court) before being given to Henry II by David's grandson, William, King of the Scots.[6] In William's account, the token performs two authorizing functions. On the most obvious level, the cup's royal ownership provides a further layer of credibility for the story— a sort of tacit endorsement of the marvellous nature of this artefact. The possession of an object of supposed supernatural origin by Henry I might also be considered a symbol of power in and of itself, since, although the item was not directly bestowed on him by the denizens of an otherworld, it suggests a reach for the king's actions that is more than ordinarily human. As we will see, otherworld narratives can have particularly close connections to kings and rulers, historical or fictional, in the actual world.

The inherent disparity in power between the human world and the otherworld provides a natural basis for addressing issues of authority. Although otherworld narratives tend to deal with issues of authority with great frequency, previous discussion of the role of authority in otherworld narratives has often been limited to Celtic-language texts. In these contexts, the prevalence of this theme has often been attributed to ancient beliefs about kingship, rather than the nature of the motif itself.[7]

---

[4] Gerald, *Itinerarium Kambriae*, I: 8, p. 78.

[5] Ralph of Coggeshall, *Chronicon*, pp. 117–21.

[6] William, *History of English Affairs*, pp. 120–1.

[7] This approach is summarized by Dan Wiley in his discussion of Irish king tales: 'Of particular importance are the many tales that deal with the King's relationship with the Otherworld, a relationship that can be either hostile or beneficial depending on the circumstances. Studies of these tales in conjunction with other sources have revealed important glimpses into the ideology of pre-Christian Irish kingship.' 'An Introduction to the Early Irish King Tales', in *Essays on the Early Irish King Tales*, edited by Dan M. Wiley (Dublin: Four Courts Press, 2008), pp. 13–67 (p. 22).

Otherworld narratives from Ireland feature a king or an heir to a kingdom as their human protagonist with striking frequency. In almost every case, the human in the narrative has close ties to historical kings. The particular relevance of the idea of the otherworld to such political texts has often been connected to the sacral nature of early Irish kingship.[8] Although otherworld narratives certainly gesture toward the king's capacity to provide a bridge between the two worlds, their continued popularity and use as vehicles for dynastic propaganda, long after such beliefs had lost anything other than a ceremonial potency, demands closer attention. The longevity of this connection seems to reflect the fact that the motif is particularly suited to the treatment of issues of authority, irrespective of beliefs like that of sacral kingship. The tendency to link kings and rulers to otherworld journeys, beings, or items also extends far beyond Celtic-language literatures. In this chapter, I will explore how treatments of authority in otherworld narratives are grounded in the possibilities presented by the literary motif itself. After all, the juxtaposition of actual-world authority with that of the otherworld provides a particularly loaded point of departure for a narrative, and historical rulers could still benefit from symbolic association with the marvellous even when a notion like sacral kingship had lost its cultic significance.

In his work on literary authority in medieval England, Larry Scanlon draws attention to the propensity of scholars to use the term 'authority' without interrogating the basis on which they do so.[9] Discussing the question of literary authority, he suggests that imagining authority as a 'binary structure' involving the straightforward deference of the present to the past is too limiting a perspective.[10] Authority, in his view, should be thought of as 'triangulated'—the relationship of the present to the past is not only deferential, but appropriative, ensuring that authority can be figured as 'an enabling past reproduced in the present'.[11] Although Scanlon applies this model of authority on the diachronic level of the present and the past and centres his discussion on how a text might engage with an authority that is prior and external to it, such a model could also be applied on a spatial level, reflecting the transfer of authority from the otherworld into the primary world of the narrative and, sometimes, into the actual world inhabited by the author and the audience. More often than not, otherworld beings serve this-worldly interests, despite not being

---

[8] For an account of Irish sacral kingship, see Bart Jaski, *Early Irish Kingship and Succession* (Dublin: Four Courts Press, 2000), pp. 57–88.

[9] Larry Scanlon, *Narrative, Authority and Power: The Medieval Exemplum and the Chaucerian Tradition* (Cambridge: Cambridge University Press, 1994), pp. 37–8.

[10] Scanlon, *Narrative, Authority and Power*, p. 37.

[11] Scanlon, *Narrative, Authority and Power*, p. 38.

bound by any power within it. The third term of comparison that the tertiary world supplies allows a high degree of flexibility in the treatment of different types and degrees of authority.

Although the construction of authority and power *within* the other-world narrative is my main concern, such internal operations can only be partially separated from the sort of external, historical (or pseudo-historical) evidence routinely used to authorize ideas, people, and places within a text. Indeed, the authorizing capacity of history in these narratives is matched, and sometimes surpassed, by the ability of such texts to authorize history. The royal heroes who travel to the otherworld in a range of Irish texts are often the progenitors of dynasties whose authority is confirmed and whose future fortunes are assured by the intervention of an otherworld being. The translation of authority from the otherworld to the actual world often takes the form of, or is symbolized by, a physical object. In *Baile in Scáil* (The Phantom's Frenzy) and *Echtrae Chormaic*,[12] Conn Cétcathach and his grandson Cormac Mac Airt are given cups that symbolize and aid their rule. Conn's cup is explicitly described as the cup of sovereignty.[13] Cormac's cup enables the king to distinguish truth from falsehood during his reign, and it returns to the otherworld on his death.[14] In the later narrative of *Echtra Thaidhg*, the emerald goblet given to Tadhg Mac Céin has the capacity to turn water into wine, but it will also provide him with a warning of his own death by leaving him shortly beforehand.

In a rather less direct but often very effective fashion, the imaginative attraction of the otherworld narrative may lend authority to a historical figure: the cult of Saint Brendan would surely have remained a local one had the account of his voyages not attained such popularity across medieval Europe. The *Navigatio* is too short on detail about the saint's life to be considered a conventional piece of hagiography, but its incident-packed narrative and rich evocations of fantastic Atlantic islands ensured it a wide influence that significantly raised the profile of its eponymous saint. Similarly, the fame of Saint Patrick's Purgatory as a pilgrimage site spread

---

[12] The term *echtra* in these titles is usually translated as 'adventure'. It has generally been accepted that a defining characteristic of tales designated *echtrae* is a journey to the other-world, though otherworld journeys in Irish occur in many other texts as well. On the question of the *echtrae* as a clearly defined genre, see Dumville, '*Echtrae* and *Immram*'. An in-depth study is Leonie Duignan, 'The *Echtrae* as an Early Irish Literary Genre' (PhD dissertation, National University of Ireland, Maynooth, 2010).

[13] *Baile in Scáil: The Phantom's Frenzy*, edited by Kevin Murray, ITS, 58 (Dublin: Brunswick Press, 2004).

[14] '*Echtra Cormaic Maic Airt*: The Adventure of Cormac Mac Airt', edited by Vernam Hull, *Papers of the Modern Language Association*, 64 (1949), 871–83 (p. 877). This edition is the second of the two Middle Irish recensions of this narrative.

throughout Christendom on account of the success of the *Tractatus*, which, despite its elaborately constructed truth-claims, owed much of its cultural impact to its descriptive vitality. The influence of otherworld narratives in (and on) the historical world is largely founded on the extent to which the singularity and authority of such realms are imaginatively realized within the text.

The following three case studies reflect the persistence with which otherworld realms feature in texts that explore notions of authority and the varied ways in which power relationships can be articulated through the narrative treatments of otherworld spaces. The first study draws together four Irish otherworld narratives that are not typically treated as a group, but which all use the otherworld encounter to bolster the claims of the same historical dynasty. For the second case study, I turn to the role played by Avalon in the Arthurian tradition and investigate the paradox whereby the engagement of a succession of narratives with this fantastical realm actually serves to deepen the relevance of Arthur to contemporary political reality. Finally, I consider Gilbert Hay's little-studied Scottish adaptation of the widely known story of Alexander the Great's journey to the Earthly Paradise. Although the various versions of the Alexander legend never allow their protagonist to enter the otherworld, the shift in the horizon of expectations within the text which the encounter brings about allows the narrative to deal directly with complex questions of the nature of authority and, most fundamentally, with the nature of being human.

KINGSHIP, RULERS, AND OTHERWORLD REALMS

Otherworld narratives from Ireland feature a king or an heir to a kingdom as their human protagonist with striking frequency. It is not unusual for the human in the narrative to have close ties (usually ties of blood) to an historical kingship. Among the most widely disseminated Irish engagements with kingship and the otherworld is a group of texts that recount the otherworld exploits of Conn Cétcathach (Conn of the Hundred Battles) and his descendants, the Dál Cuinn (Conn's Sept). Conn's status as the pseudo-historical ancestor of the Uí Néill dynasty[15] ensured that contemporary political concerns were central to the inception and development of accounts of his life and those of his children and grandchildren. The Uí Néill were the most powerful dynasty in Ireland from the seventh

---

[15] The closely related Connachta, Uí Maine, and Airgíalla group of dynasties also claimed Conn as their ancestor.

through to the eleventh century. Conn, his two sons, Connla and Art, and his grandson, Cormac mac Airt, are all protagonists of popular otherworld narratives: Conn visits the otherworld to be told the names of his successors in *Baile in Scáil*, Connla forsakes his family for the otherworld in *Echtrae Chonnlai*, Art embarks on a series of otherworld adventures in *Echtrae Airt meic Cuinn*,[16] and Cormac visits the Land of Promise in *Echtrae Chormaic*.

The texts in this group are likely to be rather earlier in date than most of the surviving otherworld narratives from, for instance, medieval England; however, all were copied and adapted until the end of the Middle Ages. Indeed, most of the manuscripts in which they survive date from the fourteenth or fifteenth century, suggesting that these texts retained an audience for many years after their original composition and remained very much part of the Irish cultural imagination. *Echtrae Chonnlai* may be the earliest of the group (its most recent editor, Kim McCone, argues for an original date of composition in the eighth century[17]), but seven of the eight surviving manuscripts of the text date from the fifteenth century or later. Scholars generally agree that *Baile in Scáil* dates from the ninth century,[18] that *Echtrae Chormaic* dates from the twelfth century but may incorporate earlier elements,[19] and that, while *Echtrae Airt* survives only in a fifteenth-century copy, it is likely to have been composed significantly earlier.[20] Although these four texts are certainly the products of different periods, the close ties of these narratives to the Dál Cuinn suggest considerable congruence between them.[21]

---

[16] 'Echtra Airt meic Cuinn: The Adventures of Art Son of Conn', edited and translated by R. I. Best, *Ériu*, 3 (1907), 149–73.

[17] *Echtrae Chonnlai*, edited by McCone, p. 41.

[18] However, it is preserved in two fifteenth-century manuscripts: Oxford, Bodleian Library, Rawlinson MS B 512 and an incomplete version in British Library, Harley MS 5280. The version of the *Baile* that has survived appears to be an eleventh-century redaction, but it has long been recognized that the core of the narrative dates to the middle of the ninth century. See Kevin Murray, 'The Manuscript Tradition of *Baile Chuinn Chetchathaig* and its Relationship with *Baile in Scáil*', in *The Kingship and Landscape of Tara*, edited by Edel Bhreathnach (Dublin: Four Courts Press, 2005), pp. 69–72 (p. 70).

[19] 'Echtra Cormaic maic Airt', edited by Hull, 872–3.

[20] A tale of this title is included in a list of narratives that may go back to the tenth century. A narrative with the title *Echtrae Chormaic* also appears in this list. On the dating of the list, see Prionsias MacCana, *The Learned Tales of Medieval Ireland* (Dublin: Dublin Institute for Advanced Studies, 1980), pp. 81–4. See also, Rudolph Thurneysen, *Die irische Helden- und Königsage bis zum siebzehnten Jahrhundert* (Halle: Max Niemeyer, 1921), pp. 21–4, and, more recently, Gregory Toner, 'Reconstructing the Earliest Irish Tale Lists', *Éigse*, 32 (2000), 88–120. The evidence these lists provide for the corpus of medieval Irish *echtrae* is discussed in Duignan, 'The *Echtrae*', pp. 2–6.

[21] It seems likely that authors and adaptors were aware of earlier texts in this group: the author of the second recension of *Echtrae Chormaic* makes explicit reference to *Baile in Scáil*. See Kevin Patrick Murray, '*Baile in Scáil* and *Echtrae Chormaic*', in *Ogma: Essays*

In *Echtrae Chormaic*, Cormac travels to the otherworld to retrieve his son, daughter, and wife. *Echtrae Airt Meic Cuinn* incorporates two otherworld journeys. The first is Conn's journey in a coracle to a marvellous island where he is served by invisible hands. The second is Art's own journey that takes him first to a beautiful island inhabited by women and then to a place called the Land of Wonders. In a rare instance of a human exerting control over a marvellous location, Art takes possession of this island and its treasure, and rescues the maiden Delbchaem, who returns with him to Ireland as his wife. In both texts the journey to the otherworld has a tangible impact in the world of Irish politics. As we have seen, Cormac brings a cup from the otherworld that helps him distinguish truth from falsehood. He is also granted possession of a beautiful branch, which produces soothing music and enables men to forget their sorrows. The two gifts are very appropriate for a king. The truth-telling cup guarantees the justice of his judgements and the branch brings peace in times of turbulence. Art's return with Delbchaem precipitates the banishment of his father's evil second wife from Ireland and the consequent return of fertility to the land. He also brings back the riches he looted from the otherworld.[22] These stories share certain details that suggest close connections between the Dál Cuinn *echtrae* as a group. For instance, *Echtrae Chormaic* begins with Cormac being approached by an otherworld warrior when he is guarding the ramparts of Tara at sunrise. *Baile in Scáil* places Conn in the same place at the same time of day when he is approached by a horseman from the otherworld. In both *Echtrae Chormaic* and *Baile in Scáil*, the otherworld is accessed through a great mist, not through the more typical hillside or water barrier. Both otherworld dwellings described in *Echtrae Airt* feature roofs thatched with bird's wings, a detail that also features in *Echtrae Chormaic*.

The politics of *Baile in Scáil* are particularly overt. This text elucidates its symbolism precisely and would seem to provide a clear link with the beliefs of a prehistoric pagan past. Its plot may be summarized briefly. One morning as Conn and his men are guarding the ramparts of Tara against supernatural beings, a mist descends all around and they hear a horse approaching. After making three casts with his spear at them, the horseman invites Conn to come to his home. They come to a plain in which they see a golden tree and a house; within is a young woman on a crystal chair, a golden cup, a silver vat of red ale, and, seated on a throne, a beautiful man described as a *scál* (phantom) who identifies

in Celtic Studies in Honour of Próinséas Ní Chatháin, edited by Michael Richter and J.-M. Picard (Dublin: Four Courts Press, 2001), pp. 195–9.

[22] Duignan, 'The *Echtrae*', pp. 152–3.

himself as Lugh. The phantom informs Conn he has come to tell him the length of his reign and those of his successors at Tara. The text identifies the woman as the 'sovereignty of Ireland' and she offers Conn the rib of a gigantic ox and the rib of a boar to eat. She then distributes ale and asks repeatedly to whom she should give the drinking cup, receiving the name and a short biography of a descendant of Conn in response from the phantom each time. Conn's poet, Cessamn, notes the names in *ogham* script on four staves of yew.

The depth of this text's investment in medieval Irish politics is obvious even from this short summary of the text's narrative core; as Kevin Murray notes, the original work is very clearly intended as 'a propaganda document for the Uí Néill'.[23] However, summarizing the narrative alone elides the fact that the king lists are proportionately the most significant component of the work. For instance, they take up eight and a half of the ten manuscript pages devoted to the only complete surviving copy of the text.[24] The ways in which *Baile in Scáil* was apparently expanded and revised over time also highlight its continued political relevance. Most scholars agree that the text as we have it represents a revised and updated version of an earlier narrative.[25] The text has linguistic features that date to the late Old Irish period in the ninth century, but various other linguistic and textual details point to an early eleventh century date.[26] In particular, the king list gives a recognizable account of Irish rulers right up to Brían Bóruma (Brian Boru), who died in 1014.[27] The fact that the text seems to have been revised and updated in the years following Brían Bóruma's ascendency may help illuminate why the *Baile* might have seemed particularly interesting to a redactor working in the first decades of the eleventh century. There can be little doubt that the eleventh-century redactor had the same pronounced Uí Néill loyalties as the original author(s) of the text. From 1002 to his death in 1014, Brían Bóruma, a member of the Dál Cais dynasty, became the first man in several centuries to break Uí Néill political dominance in Ireland.[28] As Máire Herbert has noted, it seems likely that this moment of crisis for the Uí Néill prompted

---

[23] *Baile*, edited by Murray, p. 29. The otherworld narrative followed by a long set of prophecies is a structure that also appears much later in a very different context in the romance of *Thomas of Erceldoune*.

[24] Oxford, Bodleian Library, MS Rawlinson B 512, ff. 101ra–105vb.

[25] These additions and some other elements in the text suggest that, in the eleventh century, *Baile in Scáil* was significantly revised by someone with close ties to the Cenél nEóghain branch of the Uí Néill, *Baile*, edited by Murray, pp. 29–30.

[26] Baile, edited by Murray, pp. 4–5.

[27] *Baile*, edited by Murray, p. 47 (para 57).

[28] *Baile*, edited by Murray, pp. 29–30.

re-engagement with dynastic propaganda like the *Baile*. She suggests that for the redactor

> the mythic past provided a defensive strategy in a threatening present. The depiction of the designation of rulers by the sovereignty-goddess linked sacred time with historical time, and accorded the former legitimating status for the latter.[29]

This is certainly true, but Herbert's observation can also be taken further. The legitimation provided by narratives like *Baile in Scáil* is not only conferred by mythic time, but also by fantastical space, in the form of the otherworld.

Baile in Scáil is a striking example of how the removal of a narrative to an otherworld can enable engagement with the political realities of the historical world, although it is somewhat unusual in its overt declaration of its political interests and in its clear elucidation of its symbolism. Later texts implicate the otherworld in treatments of kingship, but rarely explicate the relationship between one and the other so clearly. The otherworld in *Baile in Scáil* is analogous to the hand of providence; Lugh and his retinue are deeply invested in this-world affairs and exist within the text solely to validate political reality. An otherworld encounter of this sort tends to confirm rather than reveal. The sort of magic depicted in accounts of otherworld journeys is unlikely to uncover a lost heir or to challenge the existing order, despite the prevalence of such incidents elsewhere in medieval literature.[30] It might be suggested that this confirmatory function had considerably greater political value in a society like Ireland where potential succession to kingship was open to several individuals, rather than a single designated heir, and where kingly authority was more open to challenge as a result. Although the king could lay claim to being the best or (realistically) the most powerful individual the dynasty had to offer at a particular moment, the natural need for an external authority to validate this power is answered by these texts.

There is rarely any expectation that the otherworld is a realm that might be brought under anyone's control. Attacks on the otherworld tend to be very much guerrilla operations. Heroes like Reinbrun and Orfeo venture into the otherworld to retrieve something that has been taken, in order to restore the natural order of the actual world, not to extend its patrimony. The encounter with the otherworld is the only arena, apart from the

---

[29] Máire Herbert, 'Goddess and King: The Sacred Marriage in Early Ireland', in *Women and Sovereignty*, edited by Louise O. Fradenburg (Edinburgh: Edinburgh University Press, 1992), pp. 264–75 (p. 272).

[30] Cooper, *English Romance in Time*, pp. 324–60.

encounter with the Divine, in which a king's prowess might legitimately be seen as limited or ineffectual; yet, it is precisely this position of powerlessness that allows the otherworld journey to be turned to political advantage. Acknowledging the superior power of a realm that is not-of-this-world does little to undermine the authority of a ruler in the human world. It also helps matters that the authority the otherworld gives to figures like Conn Cétcathach and Cormac Mac Airt is conferred with complete freedom and is untainted by any suggestion of duress or self-interest. The otherworld encounter is a particularly effective means of confirming kingly power since the denizens of that realm can act with complete independence.

The wide pool of candidates from which a royal successor in medieval Ireland could be selected might also make the loss of potential heirs to the otherworld seem less grievous. The permanent departure of eldest sons to the otherworld is not as fatal for the dynasty from which they come as it might otherwise be. For instance, Connla has a younger brother, Art, who, despite having his own otherworldly adventures, would remain in Ireland and continue the line.[31] The departure of a royal to the otherworld could be a cause of dynastic pride: *Echtrae Chonnlai* seems to have been particularly widely disseminated, presumably, in part, as a means of bolstering the authority of the Uí Néill. The singling out of a human ancestor—albeit a collateral one—as worthy of a more-than-human world can certainly be read as a mark of prestige that reflects well on the bloodline as a whole. It is not usually the weak that are chosen, but the best and the bravest, and *Echtrae Chonnlai* lays heavy emphasis on Connla's 'worth'. There is a sense throughout the story that the protagonist's qualities are more otherworldly than worldly; in an inversion of the convention, Connla's physical beauty is made a subject of more comment than that of the otherworld woman and it is explicitly stated that it is his beauty that has won her love. But this is a double-edged sword. Although the story does not dwell on the implications of Connla's departure, his father makes every attempt to prevent and dissuade him from leaving, and the qualities attributed to the young man that render his departure from this world almost inevitable are also those qualities that would be of most benefit within the power structures of the actual world. That Connla is his

---

[31] Perhaps significantly, writers in the post-conquest English tradition are less likely to transport the progeny of a king to the otherworld on a permanent basis. Men like Lanval, who go to live with their fairy mistresses, are knights, not royalty, and their loss is not as potentially damaging to the body politic. Since primogeniture only becomes a fixture in English political life after the Norman Conquest, it might be supposed that any earlier otherworld accounts would mirror the Irish narratives in this regard. However, since no otherworld account of this sort has survived from Anglo-Saxon England, such considerations must remain speculative.

dynasty's 'king in waiting' is also implied at the outset,[32] and, to drive home the point, the otherworld woman declares he has a 'kingly form'.[33] There is a telling episode in the twelfth-century text *Cogadh Gaedhel Re Gaillaibh* (The War of the Irish with the Foreigners, i.e. the Vikings) that suggests that such departures could, at times, be viewed as deeply problematic. The night before the key Battle of Clontarf in 1014, Dunlang arrives late because his fairy lover has been trying to persuade him to stay away. He relates that he chose to forgo her inducements and laments what he has lost. Murchadh reproaches him saying:

> Often... was I offered in hills and in fairy mansions this world and these gifts, but I never abandoned for one night my country nor mine inheritance for them.[34]

The difference in attitude between this account and that of *Echtrae Chonnlai* is, largely, a matter of perspective. In the *Cogadh*, judgement is being offered from within the narrative by a character who has no certainty about the course of future events. The focus of the *Echtrae Chonnlai* author is rather different. Such a work would be of limited value to an extinct dynasty, and the knowledge that the line continued and flourished despite the voluntary disappearance of an heir to the otherworld must surely have cast the loss in a rather more positive light. On the night before a crucial battle, of course, such choices take on a considerably less rosy hue. The prestige of an ancestral figure being chosen by the inhabitants of the otherworld has an obvious value for the authors of dynastic narratives. Although the tone of *Echtrae Chonnlai* is essentially celebratory, the post-hoc perspective of its author allows it to be so.

It is not unusual for such narratives to highlight the more personal ramifications of these departures in the same breath as they emphasize the political ones. Sometimes an undertone of loss gestures towards how closely the journey to the otherworld parallels the encounter with death.[35] In *Echtrae Láegairi maic Crimthainn* (The Adventure of Láegaire

---

[32] See McCone's discussion of the phrase 'for láim a athar', *Echtrae Chonnlai*, edited by McCone, p. 129.

[33] The physical perfection of the ideal king was a standard topos in medieval Irish literature. See further, Jaski, *Early Irish Kingship*, pp. 82–7.

[34] 'Is menic... tarcas damsa i sithaib ocus i sithbrugaib, in betha sin, ocus na comada, ocus nir treigius oen aidchi mo tir, no mo ducus oro'. *Cogadh Gaedhel re Gallaibh: The Wars of the Gaedhil with the Gaill*, edited by James Henthorn Todd, RS 48 (London: Longmans, 1867), p. 172. I have romanized the Gaelic script used in Todd's edition.

[35] It is possible that a narrative of a tragic death may lie behind the otherworld departure of Connla in *Echtrae Chonnlai*. Writing in the seventeenth century, but working from medieval sources, Geoffrey Keating testifies to an alternative tradition wherein Connla was not lost to the otherworld but killed in battle by his uncle. Geoffrey Keating, *Foras Feasa ar*

mac Crimthainn), the earliest parts of which date to the ninth century,[36] Láegaire's father is distraught at his son's decision to remain in the land beneath the waves and he implores him to stay:

'Do not leave me,' said Crimhthann; 'you shall have the kingship of the Three Connaughts, their gold and their silver, their horses and their bridles, and their fair women at your pleasure; and do not leave us.'[37]

The promises of great wealth and temporal power stress just how high the stakes become when a man of royal blood chooses to remain in the otherworld, but the text also emphasizes that the things promised to Láegaire are the worldly equivalents of what he already has, in more perfect form, in the otherworld. In response to his father's plea, he enumerates the supernatural riches and battle-spoils that are his and praises the beauty of his fairy wife before concluding, with a degree of exultation that seems almost callous in the context: 'one night of the fairy nights / I will not exchange for your kingdom'.[38] In this episode, the claims of familial affection are given particular weight: the father's final personal plea 'ocus nachan fácaib' ('and do not leave us') picks up once more the 'n' sounds of the alliterating cluster 'a n-ór ocus a n-arcat a n-eich' ('their gold and their silver, their horses') at the start of his statement. The aural effect is to place particular and poignant stress on this final, most personal, plea. These journeys require the breaking of all this-worldly bonds and, as such, demand that something be relinquished in the same breath in which they promise possession.

APPROPRIATING AVALON

Perhaps the most famous link between an otherworld location and kingship is made in the story of Arthur's journey to Avalon. Much ink has been spilled attempting to unravel the tangled mass of material associated with this island and its cultural origins, but the place of this realm within the

---

Éirinn: the history of Ireland, edited by David Comyn and Patrick S. Dinneen, 4 vols, ITS, 4, 8, 9, 15 (London: David Nutt, 1902–1914), ii (1908), pp. 270–1.

[36] 'The Adventure of Laeghaire mac Crimhthainn', edited by Kenneth Jackson, *Speculum*, 17 (1942), 377–89 (p. 377).

[37] 'Nacham fhácaib', or Crimthand; 'ríge teora Connacht duit, a n-ór 7 a n-argat, a n-eich 7 a sréin, 7 a mná coema do t' reir, 7 nachan fácaib'. 'Laeghaire Mac Crimhthainn', edited by Jackson, 385.

[38] 'oín adaig d'aidchib síde / ní thibér ar do ríge'. 'Laeghaire Mac Crimhthainn', edited by Jackson, 356.

tradition of the otherworld encounter and its role within imaginative literature are less frequently discussed. Despite the profound cultural impact of the idea of Avalon, Patch's book touches on the place only in passing[39] and a full-length scholarly treatment of the literary uses of the realm has yet to be produced.[40] This comparative neglect of what is often thought of as the quintessential medieval otherworld is perhaps partly explained by the fact that depictions of Avalon frequently fail to conform to the conventions of otherworld descriptions. Accounts of Arthur's life rarely take the opportunity to describe Avalon at any length, an unusual and surprising fact, given medieval writers' propensity for producing lengthy accounts of marvellous lands. Indeed, in the British Arthurian tradition the encounter with Avalon is almost always at one remove; Arthur is taken there, but the narrative does not follow him. This otherworld is perpetually hidden beyond the horizon of the text. Of course, the imagination can be piqued as much by removal of detail as by superfluity of it, and I would suggest that the historical impact of the idea of Avalon is partly dependent on this absence of detail and that a wide range of otherworld themes and motifs could be, and were, invoked by writers throughout the Middle Ages to fill this highly suggestive textual lacuna.

This pattern of description, or rather lack of description, is set in the *Historia*, where Geoffrey devotes just a few lines to describing Arthur's departure for Avalon:

> The illustrious king Arthur too was mortally wounded; he was taken away to the island of Avalon to have his wounds tended and, in the year of Our Lord 542, handed over Britain's crown to his relative Constantinus, son of Cador duke of Cornwall.[41]

Although the succession of events which precipitate the fall of Arthur appear to impel this portion of the narrative towards as absolute a conclusion as possible, the introduction of Avalon halts the story in its tracks. Geoffrey transforms what should rightly be the close of the work into a suspension *in medias res*. Wace's version of events is similarly

---

[39] Indeed, two of the seven indexed allusions to it refer to its appearance in non-Arthurian texts such as *Ogier le Danois*; see the index to Patch, *The Other World*, p. 374.

[40] There is a recent chapter-length treatment in Wade, *Fairies*, pp. 39–72.

[41] 'Sed et inclitus ille rex Arturus letaliter uulneratus est; qui illinc ad sananda uulnera sua in insulam Auallonis euectus Constantino cognato suo et filio Cadoris ducis Cornubiae diadema Britanniae concessit anno ab incarnatione Domini .dxlii.'. Geoffrey of Monmouth, *The History of the Kings of Britain*, edited by Michael D. Reeve, translated by Neil Wright, Arthurian Studies, 69 (Woodbridge: Boydell, 2007), pp. 252–3.

cursory, though far more explicit about the implications of Arthur's departure for Avalon:

> He had himself carried to Avalon for the treatment of his wounds. He is still there, awaited by the Britons, as they say and believe, and will return and may live again...Merlin said of Arthur rightly that his death would be doubtful, the prophet spoke truly: ever since, people have always doubted whether he is dead or alive. Truly, 542 years after the Incarnation he did have himself carried to Avalon.[42]

Laȝamon also goes further than Wace in having Arthur promise to return rather than merely implying the possibility of his return: 'And seoðe ich cumen wulle to mine kineriche / And wunien mid Brutten mid muchelere wunne'.[43] The lines go some way towards shifting the generic affiliation of the text, transforming the tragic death of a king into a potentially triumphal variant on the familiar exile-and-return narrative. Of the three accounts, Laȝamon's text also goes furthest in descriptive terms, identifying Arthur's healers as 'aluen' folk and putting special stress on the supernatural associations of the island. Yet, even this fullest of early accounts fails to give any specifics about the nature or location of the realm to which Arthur is heading. Geoffrey's *Historia*, Wace and Laȝamon's *Brut*s, and various later works such as the Alliterative *Morte Arthure*, the Stanzaic *Morte Arthur*, and Malory's version of the tale, are united in the sparingness of their accounts of Avalon. As far as the mainstream Arthurian tradition goes, the island is a largely vacant site and, as with all such sites, becomes both a locus of contention and a prompt to the imagination.

That Geoffrey's reticence about Avalon in the *Historia* was not an imaginative failing or a product of indifference is evidenced by the very full and thoroughly otherworldly account he gives of the island in the *Vita Merlini*:

> The *Island of Apples* gets its name 'The Fortunate Island' from the fact that it produces all manner of plants spontaneously. It needs no farmers to plough the fields. There is no cultivation of the land at all beyond that which is

---

[42] 'En Avalon se fist porter / Pur ses plaies mediciner. / Encore i est, Bretun l'atendent, / Si cum il dient e entendent; / De la vendra, encor puet vivre. / ... Merlin dist d'Arthur, si ot droit, / Que sa mort dutuse serreit. / Li prophetes dist verité; / Tut tens en ad l'um puis duté, / E dutera, ço crei, tut dis, / Se il est morz u il est vis. / Porter se fist en Avalun, / Pur veir, puis l'Incarnatiun / Cinc cenz e quarante dous anz'. *Wace's Roman de Brut, A History of the British: Text and Translation*, edited and translated by J. Weiss (Exeter: University of Exeter Press, 1999), pp. 332–4, ll. 13277–81, 13285–93.

[43] 'And afterwards I will return to my kingdom and dwell with the Britons in great contentment.' Laȝamon, *Brut or Hystoria Brutonum*, edited by W. R. J. Barron and S. C. Weinberg (Harlow: Longman, 1995), ll. 14281–2.

Nature's work. It produces crops in abundance and grapes without help; and apple trees spring up from the short grass in its woods. All plants, not merely grass alone, grow spontaneously; and men live a hundred years or more.[44]

The passage goes on to invest the isle with distinctly supernatural associations, describing the nine sisters who rule it, and the healing and shape-shifting properties of Morgan, the first among them. The marvellous nature of the island is reinforced in a further allusion to Arthur's departure over the sea to the 'palace of the nymphs'.[45] Geoffrey also takes this opportunity to raise the question of Arthur's possible return—a subject never broached in the *Historia*—though he gives no further account of Arthur's existence once he arrives in the otherworld.[46] Of course, given the very limited circulation of the *Vita Merlini*, it almost certainly cannot have provided the imaginative background against which the audience of the *Historia* read the reference to Avalon. It is in no sense the authoritative account of the realm. However, the profound debt of the work to such widely circulated texts as Isidore's *Etymologiae* and the *Navigatio Sancti Brendani Abbatis*[47] is evidence enough that the culture in which Geoffrey was writing was more than adequately supplied with descriptions of marvellous islands. The conventions of otherworld description provided a wide range of prompts to the imagination of those moved to speculate on what the *Historia* left unsaid. A case in point is the *Gesta Regum Britanniae* (written sometime between 1235 and 1254) usually attributed to William of Rennes.[48] The work is a Latin verse adaptation of Geoffrey of Monmouth's *Historia*. It clearly derives from a Breton context and is dedicated to Cadioc, bishop of Vannes. William tracks Geoffrey's account very closely until he comes to Arthur's death, at which point he follows the king to Avalon and gives an account of the island and events that take place there subsequently. He provides the sort of lavish set-piece

---

[44] 'Insula pomorum que Fortunata vocatur / ex re nomen habet quia per se singula profert. / Non opus est illi sulcantibus arva colonis, / omnis abest cultus nisi quem natura ministrat. / Ultro fecundas segetes producit et uvas / nataque poma suis pretonso gramine silvis. / Omnia gignit humus vice graminis ultro redundans, / annis centenis aut ultra vivitur illic'. Geoffrey of Monmouth, *Life of Merlin: Vita Merlini*, edited and translated by Basil Clarke (Cardiff: University of Wales Press, 1973), ll. 908–15.

[45] Geoffrey, *Vita Merlini*, l. 1124.

[46] Geoffrey, *Vita Merlini*, ll. 954–7.

[47] It is stated in the *Vita* that the boat which took Arthur to Avalon was piloted by Barinthus because of his knowledge of the seas (ll. 930–1). This character appears at the opening of the *Navigatio*, where he tells Brendan of his journey westwards to a marvellous, paradisal island.

[48] On the question of the text's authorship and regional origins, see *The Historia Regum Britanniae of Geoffrey of Monmouth V: Gesta Regum Britanniae*, edited and translated by Neil Wright (Cambridge: D. S. Brewer, 1991), pp. xi–xiv.

description conventional to otherworld accounts, yet lacking in most accounts of Avalon. William enthusiastically rehearses the conventions of the fertile, sorrowless island of flowering plains and apple trees with no extremes of heat or cold, where wealth is held in common and where a fairy king reigns over all. The daughter of this king heals Arthur's wounds and becomes his mistress. There is no allusion to Arthur's possible return, but the stress on his immortality fits with the Breton loyalties apparent elsewhere in William's work.[49] It is a remarkable passage and appears to be entirely William's own invention. Siân Echard has commented that 'in attempting to account for this final flourish, I lose any sense of an overall purpose for William's Arthuriad'.[50] The addition certainly jars in this otherwise sober rendition of Geoffrey's narrative, but, in the context of otherworld narratives more generally, it can be read as William making the most conventional sense he can out of Geoffrey's departure from narrative norms, rather than any attempt to make a larger comment about Arthur and his world. William's impulse may be narratological rather than political and it is, perhaps, the most natural response to the *Historia's* tantalizing silence on Avalon to insert a conventional otherworld description complete with a fairy mistress to plug the gap.

No gap-filler comparable to William's survives from Britain, but his sudden flight of fancy reflects the imaginative suggestiveness of Avalon. Geoffrey's introduction of an otherworld site into the narrative has a rather paradoxical effect. His entire text treads a narrow line between history and fiction, and the removal of Arthur to Avalon would seem to be the sort of plot twist that risks fatally undermining his audiences' suspension of disbelief. Yet, in removing Arthur from the actual world, Geoffrey contrives to substantially enhance the historical impact of his text. Arthur's journey exploits the disruptive potential of the otherworld encounter which, like so many manifestations of the ambiguous supernatural in medieval literature, is apt to produce a rather unmanageable proliferation of meanings. Imagining a space removed from the known world, where time potentially moves at a different rate to historical time, and where the usual laws of human mortality may not necessarily apply, erodes certain sources of authority within the actual world. The possibility of Avalon's existence suggests that linear kingly succession in historical time is not as fixed and inevitable as it might appear to be. The concept of

<hr/>

[49] *Gesta Regum Britanniae*, edited and translated by Wright, IX: 314–17, p. 248. For a fuller account of William's work, see Rosemary Morris, 'The *Gesta Regum Britanniae* of William of Rennes: an Arthurian Epic?', *Arthurian Literature*, 6 (1986), 60–123 (on William's Breton identity, see pp. 97–123, in particular).

[50] Siân Echard, *Arthurian Narrative in the Latin Tradition* (Cambridge: Cambridge University Press, 1998), p. 105.

a 'once *and* future king' cuts at the root of assumptions about kingship and allows open-ended accounts of Arthur in the Galfridian tradition to graft themselves onto the historical world in a remarkably persistent fashion.

The most prominent historical engagement with this open ending is the exhumation of the bodies of Arthur and Guinevere at Glastonbury in the reign of Henry II.[51] The discovery of the bodies is as elaborate a piece of archaeological fiction as one could wish to find and did not merely drag Arthur back within the limits of historical time, but also divested Avalon of some of its most problematic otherworldly qualities. The inaccessible *insula pomorum* was rewritten as one of the most visited sites in England, bound by historical time and subject to change and decay. Of course, the disenchantment was not absolute, and writers show considerable sensitivity to the possible otherworldly attributes of Glastonbury. As an ancient religious site located on a fertile sometime island on England's western seaboard, Glastonbury had just enough mystique for the Arthurian narrative to retain its grandeur and sufficient familiarity to eliminate any sense of threat to the established order.[52] Indeed, Gerald of Wales' attempt to demonstrate the etymological appropriateness[53] of the identification of the site with Avalon in his *De Principis Instructione Liber* brings several otherworld associations to the surface:

> Now the place which is now called Glaston, was in ancient times called the isle of Avalon. For it is as it were an isle, covered with marshes, wherefore in the British tongue it was called Inis Avallon, that is 'the apple-bearing isle'.... It was also once called 'Inis gutrin' in the British tongue, that is, the glassy isle, wherefore when the Saxons afterwards came thither they call that place Glastingeburi. For 'Glas' in their language has the same meaning as *uitrum*, while 'buri' means *castrum* or *ciutias*.[54]

---

[51] The most extensive contemporary sources for this exhumation are the two accounts by Gerald of Wales: firstly, in his *De Instructione Principis Liber*, which dates to the 1190s, and secondly, in in his *Speculum Ecclesiae* from around 1217. The discovery is also reported by Ralph of Coggeshall in the *Chronicon Anglicanum*, which he composed between 1187–1234 (*Chronicon Anglicanum*, edited by Stevenson, p. 36). For a comparison and overview of the various accounts of the exhumation, see *Le Haut Livre du Graal: Perlesvaus*, edited by William A. Nitze, 2 vols (Chicago: University of Chicago Press, 1932, 1937), II, 62–72.

[52] James Carley gives an account of the wider historical and mythological associations of Glastonbury in his Introduction to John of Glastonbury, *An Edition, Translation and Study of John of Glastonbury's Cronica sive Antiquitates Glastoniensis Ecclesie*, edited by James P. Carley, translated by David Townsend (Woodbridge: Boydell, 1985), pp. xi–lx.

[53] For a full account of the possible origins of the toponym, see Louis H. Gray, 'The Origin of the Name of Glastonbury', *Speculum*, 10 (1935), 46–53.

[54] 'Quae nunc autem Glastonia dicitur, antiquitus insula Avallonia dicebatur. Est enim quasi insula tota paludibus obsita, unde dicta est Britannice, Inis Avallon, id est, *insula pomifera*. Pomis enim, quae *aval* Britannica lingua dicuntur, locus ille quondam abundabat . . . Dicta quoque quondam Britannice *Inis gutrin* fuerat, hoc est, *insula vitrea*; ex quo vocabulo supervenientes postea Saxones locum illum *Glastingeburi* vocitabant. Glas enim

Both the island of apples and the island of glass have well-established otherworld connotations. Apples are a recurrent motif in Irish depictions of the otherworld, where they are closely associated with the notion of kingship.[55] Items of glass or crystal were a staple component of otherworld descriptions throughout the Middle Ages.[56] An allusion specific to the cultural context in which Gerald was working occurs in the Welsh Arthurian poem *Preideu Annwfyn*. The poem, which almost certainly predates Gerald's account, alludes to a glass fortress (*caer wydyr*) that is located in, or is identical with, the otherworld *Annwfyn*. Furthermore, the *Historia Brittonum*, which was in wide circulation at the time, and with which Gerald was certainly familiar, recounts how Spanish sailors encountered an impenetrable glass tower off the south coast of Ireland.[57] The account in the *De Principis Instructione Liber* showcases Gerald's sensitivity to the power of linguistic history. In it he recruits British culture, so frequently associated with the perpetuation of belief in Arthur's immortality, to argue the case for this death. In a similar vein, Gerald's second account of the exhumation, in his *Speculum Ecclesiae*, notes that it was the tales of the Britons that prompted the excavations at Glastonbury.[58] The irony would surely not have been lost on his audience. Neither the *Speculum* nor the *De Principis Instructione Liber* scrape away the layer of oral historical tradition surrounding Arthur's second coming, but they harness the nebulous yet imaginatively potent 'British fables' to their own ends.[59] Gerald's accounts of the Glastonbury 'discovery' not only contradict the

---

lingua eorum *vitrum* sonat, et bury *castrum*, vel *civitas* appellatur.' *De Principis Instructione Liber*, in *Giraldi Cambrensis Opera*, edited by J. S. Brewer and others, 8 vols, RS, 21 (London: Longmans, 1861–1891), VIII (1891), p. 128. The translation is from Gerald of Wales, *The Autobiography of Gerald of Wales*, translated by H. E. Butler, 2nd edn (Woodbridge: Boydell, 2005), pp. 120–1.

[55] For an account of the otherworld associations of apples in the Irish tradition, see Eleanor Hull, 'The Silver Bough in Irish Legend', *Folklore*, 12 (1901), 431–45.

[56] A later, and perhaps unconscious, echo of the passing of Arthur to a glass dwelling occurs in Lydgate's *Fall of Princes*, which describes how the dying king was transported to 'Arthuris constellacioun / Wher he sit crownid in the heuenly mansioun / Amyd the paleis of stonis cristallyne, / Told among Cristen first of þe worthi nyne'. John Lydgate, *The Fall of Princes*, edited by Henry Bergin, 4 vols, EETS, e.s., 121–4 (1924–1927), III (1923), Book VIII, ll. 3105–8. See further, R. A. Dwyer, 'Arthur's Stellification in the *Fall of Princes*', *Philological Quarterly*, 57 (1978), 155–71.

[57] Nennius, *British History and the Welsh Annals*, edited and translated by John Morris (London: Phillimore, 1980), p. 61.

[58] Gerald of Wales, *Speculum Ecclesiae*, in *Giraldi Cambrensis Opera*, edited by J. S. Brewer and others, 8 vols, RS, 21 (London: Longmans, 1861–1891), IV (1873), II: 9, pp. 48–50.

[59] Further sensitivity to the 'canon' of Arthurian legend is, perhaps, discernable in a late twelfth-century interpolation in William of Malmesbury's *Early History of Glastonbury* that relates that the king died at Glastonbury at the age of a hundred years. This dovetails rather neatly with the account of Avalon given in the *Vita Merlini*, where 'men may live a hundred year or more' (l. 915).

widespread belief in Arthur's return, they seek to supply the sort of highly detailed narrative necessary to supplant such an imaginatively potent and deeply entrenched cultural belief.

If the removal of Arthur to Avalon establishes a timeline that challenges that of historical kings, then it also opens an alternative territory where he may reign parallel to the kings of Britain. Avalon itself may be read as a sort of mirror of Britain. Its western location, fertility, temperate climate, and insularity are all qualities associated with Britain by successive generations of writers.[60] But rather than drawing explicit links to Britain, writers more frequently canvassed the unknown and mysterious regions of the world as possible sites for Arthur's kingdom. In his *Draco Normannicus* (written sometime in the late 1160s), Étienne of Rouen imagines Arthur as ruler of the Antipodes, who engages in an epistolary exchange with Henry II in a vain attempt to convince the latter to withdraw from his campaigns in Brittany. Étienne's loyalties are very much with the Angevins, and the exchange seems designed to mock the idea of the Breton Hope. The *Draco Normannicus* gives explicit voice to the parallel tracks on which Arthur's reign and those of historical kings run. Uniquely, Étienne's text countenances the possibility that Arthur has already returned: 'Not long ago from the Antipodes I have returned... to your world... Indeed, I myself await, posted near the forests of Cornouaille, refreshing my weary legions'.[61] These are, as it transpires, fairy legions, unsurprising in light of the association of Morgan 'Le Fay' with Avalon and the frequency with which the notion of fairyland is entangled with the idea of the Antipodes in writings of this period. In making him king of the underside of the world, Étienne's text expresses the notion that Arthur's kingship runs parallel to Henry's in very spatial terms. As J. S. P. Tatlock observes, the letters of the *Draco* are, at heart, a piece of court entertainment,[62] yet it is clear that the idea of the British king's continued life made the Arthurian world a particularly compelling lens through which to view contemporary historical events.

Another, more proximate, location for Arthur's afterlife is suggested by Gervase of Tilbury in his *Otia Imperialia*. This story collection was written

---

[60] This is discussed further in Chapter 4.

[61] 'Nuper ab antipodum pro te tellure recessi / ... Ipse quidem siluas fessas refouens legiones, / Incolo Cornubie, proxima castra loco.' Étienne de Rouen, *Epistola Arturi regis ad Henricum regem Anglorum*, in *Latin Arthurian Literature*, edited Mildred Leake Day (Cambridge: D. S. Brewer, 2005), pp. 236–57, ll. 272, 292–3. For a discussion of the treatment of Arthur and the contemporary political backdrop that prompts it, see Echard, *Arthurian Narrative*, pp. 85–93.

[62] J. S. P. Tatlock, 'Geoffrey and King Arthur in *Normannicus Draco*', *Modern Philology*, 31 (1933), 1–18. For a more recent account, see Hiatt, *Terra Incognita*, p. 115.

for the half-English Holy Roman Emperor Otto IV in the years around 1210, though, according to Gervase, he had first started planning such a work thirty years earlier. The *Otia*'s three component books give a history and description of the world and an account of numerous marvels. There are thirty known manuscripts of the work now in existence and a high proportion of them are localizable to Italy or Southern France. The spread of apparent dates of the manuscripts indicates that the popularity of the work endured throughout the Middle Ages. I have already mentioned Gervase's story of an English swineherd who travels to the otherworld through a hollow hill. He tells a similar tale about a Sicilian groom, but this time with an Arthurian flourish. Given how frequently hollow mountains serve as entrances to the otherworld, it is not entirely surprising to find Arthur ensconced in Mount Etna in Gervase's *Otia Imperialia*.[63] Just as the swineherd followed a pig into a cave, this groom follows his master's runaway horse into the side of the mountain.

> Finding a very narrow but level path the servant came out onto an immensely wide and beautiful plain, full of delights of every kind; there in a palace constructed with marvellous workmanship, he found Arthur reclining on a couch of royal splendour.[64]

Arthur returns the horse to the groom and describes how he has dwelt in this place for a long time, suffering from wounds he received during the battle of Camlann and which break open again each year. It is not entirely clear whether Mount Etna is to be identified with Avalon. Gervase makes reference to Arthur having left for Avalon at the end of his reign at another point in the *Otia*, but does not connect Sicily and Avalon explicitly.[65]

Like Gerald's account of the Glastonbury find, Gervase seems to root his story firmly in the oral tradition. He tells us that there is a well-established tradition among the populace of Sicily which places Arthur in Mount Etna.[66] However, as with Gerald's account, this appeal to local

---

[63] In the *Otia*, Etna is also identified as an entrance to the infernal regions, though there is no suggestion that Arthur's realm is identical with Hell. There is a survey of the tradition that associates Arthur with Mount Etna in Arturo Graf, *Miti, leggende e superstizioni del Medioevo*, 2 vols (Turin: Ermanno Loescher, 1892–1893; repr. Bologna: A. Forni, 1965) II, 303–25. Antonio Pioletti provides a more recent analysis in 'Artù, Avallon, l'Etna', *Quaderni Medievali*, 28 (1989), 6–35.

[64] 'Artissima semita sed plana inuenta, puer in spatiosissimam planiciem iocundam omnibusque deliciis plenam aduenit, ibique in palatio miro opere constructo reperit Arcturum in strato regii apparatus recubantem.' Gervase, *Otia Imperialia*, II: 12, p. 336.

[65] Gervase, *Otia Imperialia*, II: 17, p. 429.

[66] Gervase, *Otia Imperialia*, II: 12, p. 336. Gervase's *Otia* seems to be the earliest written account of such a tradition, but there are numerous subsequent accounts that associate Sicily with the Arthurian legend. The closest in date is a similar story that appears in Caesarius of Heisterbach's *Dialogus miraculorum*. This and later medieval texts which connect Sicily

folklore does not tell the full story and there is a very literate dimension to Gervase's anecdote about Arthur under Etna. The account seems to have been influenced not only by Geoffrey's *Historia*, but also by the far less widely disseminated *Vita Merlini*; for instance, the 'couch of royal splendour' on which Gervase places Arthur is a clear echo of the 'golden bed' of the *Vita Merlini*.[67] Although the story supports the idea that Arthur survived, Gervase pours scorn on the notion of his return. The achievements of the *Otia*'s Arthur are very much those of the past—Gervase's king is in a sort of limbo, rendered largely impotent by his wounds, and presents very little threat to the status quo.

There were good political reasons for originating, or perpetuating, the notion that Arthur now dwelt within Etna, and Gervase's interest in the story is rather personal. In the late 1180s, he had spent time at the court of King William II of Sicily, whose death without an heir in 1189 precipitated the decline of Norman rule on the island. Gervase may have remained in Sicily until as late as 1194, under the rule of Tancred, who, after some initial teething problems, also allied himself to the kings of England. Gervase's position probably became untenable after the island was taken over by the Hohenstaufen emperor, Henry VI, in 1194. Nonetheless, this was not the end of Gervase's contact with Sicily—the *Otia*'s patron, Otto, attempted to invade the island in 1211 during the period of the work's composition. Locating Arthur in Sicily provides a striking pseudo-historical link between the northern and southern Norman kingdoms.[68] The immediate context of the Mount Etna narrative in the *Otia* emphasizes the connection. After concluding the story of the Sicilian groom, Gervase notes that '[m]oreover, similar things are reported to have happened in the forests of Great Britain or Brittany . . .' and goes on to tell of how foresters often see troops of huntsmen who claim to be Arthur and his knights in these regions.[69] The presence of Arthur embedded, quite literally, in the landscape of the island, gestures to the rightness of the northern interest in Sicily. Like the Glastonbury texts, this story exploits fully the political potential of Arthur as a *rex quondam* while

with Arthurian figures are discussed in Pioletti, 'Artù, Avallon, l'Etna'. In a similar vein, the sixteenth-century writer Étienne Forcadel described an attempt by Arthur to enter Saint Patrick's Purgatory in his 'De Gallorum Imperio et Philosophia'. Thomas Wright, *Saint Patrick's Purgatory: An Essay on the Legends* (London: John Russell Smith, 1844), pp. 62–3.

[67] Geoffrey, *Vita Merlini*, l. 934.

[68] On the wider cultural connections of Sicily in this period, particularly the impact of Anglo-Norman and French romance traditions, see William Burgwinkle, 'Remembering the Future: Cultural Hybridity in Sicily?', *Journal of Romance Studies*, 4 (2004), 79–96. The extent to which Gervase himself operated as a cultural conduit between Britain and Sicily is discussed at pp. 85–6.

[69] 'Sed et in siluis Britannie maioris aut minoris consimilia contigisse referuntur . . .' Gervase, *Otia*, II: 12, p. 336.

ignoring the possibility of his future return. From the perspective of writers like Gervase, this Arthur of the past is a far less problematic, though not much less effective, servant of the present than the messianic returning king of the future.

In the mainstream Arthurian tradition in Britain, Avalon is less a textual presence than an imaginatively charged absence. In opening up an otherworldly space into which the wounded Arthur is carried, Geoffrey radically altered the premise on which a conventional history of kings might be founded. The profound ambiguity of Arthur's passing prompts the creation of a range of new narrative worlds, both textual and oral, beyond the *Historia* and, it seems, underpins some existing ones. The opening of the Arthurian story into a largely undefined otherworld space allowed a diverse range of narratives and their attendant political interests to flood in to fill the gap. These potential worlds are grounded in a range of highly divergent evaluations of the contemporary meaning of Arthur and his rule. In the British tradition, Avalon is contested ground, and the elaborate attempts of the Angevin rulers to promote the Glastonbury find testify to the continuing impact of Arthur's departure to the otherworld on political reality.

ALEXANDER'S JOURNEY TO THE EARTHLY PARADISE

Like the authors of accounts of Arthur's removal to Avalon, writers treating Alexander the Great's journey to the Earthly Paradise take the opportunity afforded by the encounter with the otherworld to interrogate the nature and limitations of human authority. Avalon provides the means by which Arthur's power can survive beyond what should have been his natural death and it challenges authority in the historical world by raising the possibility of his future return. Alexander's encounter with the Earthly Paradise also engages with death, though in this case the otherworld visit exposes the ruler's limitations and presents him with tidings of his own demise. This component of the Alexander legend stands out within the tradition of otherworld narratives insofar as it features a hero who believes that he can impose his will on an otherworld location. Such an attitude is not entirely without precedent. *Preideu Annwfyn*, wherein Arthur and his men appear to be on an expedition to attack an otherworldly location, is open to such an interpretation.[70] In *Echtrae Láegairi maic Crimthainn*,

---

[70] *Preideu Annwfyn*, edited and translated by Haycock.

Láegaire responds to the fairy Fiachna's request for help in winning his wife back from another otherworld being. In the course of battle, the human hero takes the lead in the attack on the fort where the woman is kept.[71] The story closes with the statement that Láegaire now rules the *síd* jointly with Fiachna. Though the encounter is initiated by an otherworld being and the human's rule in the *síd* is the reward freely given by its denizen, Láegaire is an unusually proactive and martial human protagonist. Alexander's case is somewhat different from these since the goal he sets himself is not the conquest of a secular otherworld, but the subjugation of the Earthly Paradise itself.

The imaginative power and rich thematic interest the Earthly Paradise would have held for a medieval Christian audience is obvious. Paradise was widely believed to still exist within the boundaries of the earth and was often depicted as the most easterly land on medieval *mappae mundi*.[72] In being understood as humanity's point of origin and 'true' home, the location held a fascination and an immediate personal relevance that no doubt contributed to the extent and vitality of the literature that treats it in this period. Few medieval depictions of a happy or beautiful otherworld resist the pull of Edenic imagery. Imagery associated with the location is ever-present, even if rarely identified as such, in otherworld descriptions, and awareness of the Edenic narrative provides a resonant cultural backdrop to medieval experience of such depictions. The Earthly Paradise is a figure both of human hope and primordial tragedy, it is the ultimate terrestrial 'land of heart's desire', but it is almost defined by its inaccessibility to mortals. The biblical narrative of the Creation and the Fall established the land as a locus for thematic concerns ranging across beauty, desire, sexuality, abundance, mortality, evil, exile, loss, and sin, and these concerns are unpacked and explored in numerous literary depictions of both Paradise and 'Edenic' otherworlds. The Earthly Paradise is less frequently the catalyst for explorations of various types of authority, but a rare, and particularly interesting, exception is the popular narrative of Alexander the Great's journey there. As George Cary notes, the legend may originate in the Babylonian Talmud before the year 500, but it became widely known in the West through the *Iter Ad Paradisum*, a short Latin work composed in the eleventh or early twelfth century by a Jewish author identified in five of the extant manuscripts as 'Salomon

---

[71] 'Laeghaire mac Crimhthainn', edited by Jackson, 382.

[72] For a recent treatment of medieval attempts to locate paradise on the map, see Scafi, *Mapping Paradise*. The treatment of the Alexander legend on the Hereford map and other medieval maps is discussed in Reed Kline, *Maps of Medieval Thought*, pp. 165–90.

didascalus Judaeorum'.[73] The *Iter* now survives in fourteen manuscripts, but the number of allusions to, and vernacular adaptations of, the narrative suggest a wide cultural influence that is not reflected in the number of extant manuscripts or in the limited scholarship that has been devoted to the work.

In its original Latin version, the narrative recounts how Alexander, in his travels through Asia, sees huge leaves floating down a broad river. He is informed that the leaves come from the 'paradise of pleasure' (*paradisus voluptatis*).[74] With five hundred companions he endures a thirty-four day journey up the turbulent river before arriving at a city bounded by towering, impenetrable, mossy walls. After sailing around the city for three days, the company finally discern a small window in the walls. They knock and an aged man appears at the aperture. Alexander's envoys demand that the city give the king tribute, at which point the old man upbraids them for their brashness and impatience before disappearing. He returns some time later with a gemstone in the shape of a human eye that he describes as a portent. Alexander and his men return down the river and are greeted with great rejoicing by the remainder of his army. At Susa, Alexander consults with learned men on the possible significance of the stone. Many try and fail to interpret its symbolism before its meaning is finally elucidated by an elderly Jew named Papas who places the (seemingly light) stone in a scale and demonstrates that no quantity of gold or gems in the opposite pan will outweigh it. Finally, Papas covers the stone in dust, at which point it is outweighed by a single coin. A mystified Alexander asks the man to explain these events and the nature of the city whence he has just returned. He is told that what appears to be a city is, in fact, the place where souls await the resurrection of the body and that no living person may enter there. The stone, he says, symbolizes Alexander's own eye which, in life, is consumed by desire, curiosity, and ambition, and is unsated by riches but which, when covered with the dust of the grave, will serve no purpose and seek for nothing. Duly rebuked, Alexander

---

[73] George Cary, *The Medieval Alexander*, edited by D. J. A. Ross (Cambridge: Cambridge University Press, 1956), p. 19.

[74] *Iter Alexandri Magni ad Paradisum*, edited by Alfons Hilka, in *La Prise de Defur and Le Voyage d'Alexandre au Paradis Terrestre*, edited by Lawton P.G. Peckham and Milan S. La Du (Princeton: Princeton University Press, 1935), pp. xli–xlviii (p. xlii). Translations are from *Alexandri Magni Iter ad Paradisum*, in *The Romances of Alexander*, translated by Dennis M. Kratz (London: Garland, 1991), pp. 127–34 (p. 127). The term 'paradise of pleasure' (*paradisus voluptatis*) is used of Eden in the Vulgate Genesis 2. 8, 15 and 3. 23, 24. However, it is also possible that the text's Jewish author derived the term directly from the Hebrew Bible's Eden, meaning 'delight'.

thanks the old man and strives to restrain his cupidity and greed. The text ends with a brief account of Alexander's death.[75]

Few other medieval narratives convene such a comprehensive range of themes associated with Paradise in religious and popular thought. Although Alexander directs his quest towards the decidedly hubristic goal of conquering Paradise, or at the very least exacting tribute from it, he simultaneously articulates a type of desire that is less obviously martial: 'I have accomplished nothing in the world and consider the results of all my ambition as nothing unless I earn a share of this joy'.[76] Desire for power is linked to desire for joy, and the conjunction of these themes gives Alexander's ambition an altogether more universal application. Alexander is seduced by the promise of beauty and wonder. The limited potency of human agency conventional to encounters with the other-world is given particular emphasis in this narrative and is first articulated by the old man at the window. As he hands over the stone to Alexander's men, he informs them:

> The inhabitants of this place send a message to the king: 'In whatever way you regard it, as either a gift or tribute owed to you, accept this stone. We are sending it to you in loving consideration as a portent and a warning, for it will be able to put an end to your avaricious desires. Once you have learned its nature and power, from then on you will desist from all ambition. Know also that it will not be advantageous for you or your men to delay here any longer, because if this river is churned up by even a gentle wind you will undoubtedly suffer a shipwreck that will cost you your life. Therefore return to your companions and do not appear ungrateful to the God of Gods for the kindness conferred upon you.[77]

The gesture and accompanying speech accomplish a series of inversions, shifting authority from Alexander to the inhabitants of Paradise at the very point at which he might appear to have asserted his authority over them. The clarity of the power relation that the giving of a tribute would conventionally symbolize is immediately muddied by the man's declaration that

---

[75] *Iter*, edited by Hilka, pp. xli–xlviii; translated by Kratz, pp. 127–34.

[76] 'Nichil profeci in mundo totiusque meę ambitionis questum nichili pendo, nisi huius voluptatis participium promeruero'. *Iter*, edited by Hilka, ll. 20–1; translated by Kratz, p. 127.

[77] 'Mandant huius loci incolę regi: "Quocumque modo sive dono sive tributario debito decreveris, prodigii commonitorium in hoc suscipe, quem tibi karitatis intuitu mittimus lapidem, qui terminum tuis cupiditatibus poterit imponere. Nam cum naturam et virtutem eius didiceris, ab omni ambitione ultra cessabis. Noveris etiam tibi tuisque non expedire hic ulterius immorari, quoniam, si fluvius hic vel modico spiritu procellę afflatur, procul dubio naufragium incurretis cum detrimento vitę vestrę. Quapropter te sociis restitue et deo deorum pro tibi collatis beneficiis ne ingratus esse videaris."' *Iter*, edited by Hilka, ll. 66–75; translated by Kratz, p. 129.

the stone may be regarded as a 'tribute' *or* as a 'gift'. The apparent lack of concern over how the king chooses to regard the stone is of a piece with the largely disdainful manner in which the man treats Alexander's emissaries from the point at which he opens the window. It underscores the sense that not only can the authority of Alexander not penetrate the walls of Paradise, but Alexander is largely an irrelevance to the people within. Previous cities have acknowledged Alexander's power by submitting to, or by vigorously resisting, him, but this city's disengaged response goes some way to depriving him of that power itself. And, although the wonder-stone is repeatedly described as a 'tribute' from Paradise throughout the remainder of the text, the audience is never allowed to lose sight of the fact that it is an odd sort of tribute. The old man's closing words limit the reach of Alexander's authority still further. The 'tribute' which should be the fulfilment of Alexander's desires will, in fact, put an end to them. Equally, this token which should represent the accomplishment of Alexander's loftiest ambition is described as the item which will cause him to abandon such goals. Like the old man, Papas's words further undercut the authority of Alexander and the role played by his own will in the entire episode. Alexander's account of the perils of his journey and its 'successful' conclusion prompt Papas to exclaim that he owes his success entirely to God and that the king's safe passage is a gift of divine generosity granted to no other mortal.[78] The re-inscription of the journey in terms of a divine gift recalls the earlier suggestion that the wonder-stone might be a gift rather than a tribute. The final and most complete inversion comes with the revelation that the stone is a symbol of Alexander's mortality—in reaching the land of the immortals, he is given proof and prophecy of his own death. In the context of a journey which began with Alexander's declaration that he would assert his will over Paradise itself, the contrast is striking. The text enacts a complex negotiation of the extremes of human authority and limitation. When incorporated, as it often was, into full-length versions of the Alexander legend, the *Iter* provides a point of reversal where the limits of human agency and will are thrown into sharp relief by the encounter with a supernatural world.

One of the most striking aspects of medieval accounts of Alexander is the diversity of judgements various medieval authors pronounce on him. For some, he is an exemplum of hubris, overarching ambition, and blasphemy; at the other end of the scale, he can be depicted as an example of wisdom and good kingship, and even a Christ-like figure.[79] The account of his journey to the Earthly Paradise holds a rather ambiguous place in this moral tradition. Although it often appears on its own in

---

[78] *Iter*, edited by Hilka, ll. 117–18; translated by Kratz, p. 131.
[79] Cary, *Medieval Alexander*, p. 156.

manuscripts, the *Iter* seems to have been conceived of as an interpolation into the Alexander legend popular throughout medieval Europe, and there is little evidence that Alexander's detractors were more likely to incorporate it into their accounts than his admirers.[80] It seems likely that the nature of this story contributed to its versatility. The interpretation appears to turn on whether individual adaptors choose to highlight the personal or universal in their treatment of the narrative. Authors antagonistic to Alexander treat the story as the most extreme example of his cupidity and pride. In positive portrayals, Alexander, cut down to size by the encounter with the divine, becomes a mere everyman and is barred from entering Paradise by his humanity rather than any exceptional pride or acquisitiveness on his own part.

Accounts of Alexander's journey to Paradise survive from England and Scotland in the Anglo-Norman *Roman de Toute Chevalerie* and Sir Gilbert Hay's Middle Scots *The Buik of King Alexander the Conquerour*, which appears to date from around 1460.[81] Mary Lascelles has argued convincingly that the story had a popularity in England and Scotland which is not reflected in the comparative rarity of its inclusion in accounts of Alexander.[82] The *Roman de Toute Chevalerie*, composed in the late twelfth century by a writer usually identified as Thomas of Kent, includes a brief account of the wonder-stone episode, which appears in only one of the five surviving manuscripts.[83] The section is almost certainly not part of Thomas's original text and Alexander himself does not travel to the walls of the Earthly Paradise in this version; rather, he is given 'ceo petite piere' (this little stone) as 'treuage' (tribute) from Paradise, without ever visiting

---

[80] Whether incorporated into a larger work or not, the Latin version opens with the word 'Igitur', suggesting authorial consciousness of a broader narrative into which it might have been inserted. For further discussion, see *Le Prise*, edited by Peckham and La Du, p. xxxiii.

[81] The earliest manuscript, British Library MS Add. 40732, dates from the 1530s. Hay's authorship of the poem has been the subject of some dispute: for a good recent account of the evidence, see Joanna Martin, '"Of Wisdome and of Guide Governance": Sir Gilbert Hay and *The Buik of King Alexander the Conquerour*', in *A Companion to Medieval Scottish Poetry*, edited by Pricilla Bawcutt and J. H. Williams (Woodbridge: D. S. Brewer, 2006), pp. 75–88. Emily Wingfield also analyses the background and surviving manuscripts of this text in 'The Composition and Revision of Sir Gilbert Hay's *Buik of King Alexander the Conquerour*', *Nottingham Medieval Studies*, 57 (2013), 247–86.

[82] M. Lascelles, 'Alexander and the Earthly Paradise in Mediaeval English Writings', *Medium Aevum*, 5 (1936), 31–47, 79–104, 173–88.

[83] Thomas of Kent, *The Anglo-Norman Alexander: Le Roman de Toute Chevalerie*, edited by Brian Foster and Ian Short, 2 vols, ANTS, 29, 31 (London: Birbeck College, 1976–1977). For a discussion of the date, see the 'Introduction' to volume 2, pp. 75–6, and for the author, see Brian Foster, 'The *Roman de Toute Chevalerie*: Its Date and Author', *French Studies*, 9 (1955), pp. 154–8. As yet, the text lacks an English translation.

that place.[84] By contrast, Gilbert Hay's work is particularly noteworthy for its extensive engagement with Alexander's journey to Paradise and its apparently innovative treatment of the episode.[85]

Hay's book, which runs to a mammoth 19,368 lines, has received scant critical attention until recent years.[86] Hay himself is, perhaps, best known for his translations of *L'arbre des batailles*, Ramon Lull's *L'ordre de chevalerie*, and the pseudo-Aristotelian *Secretum secretorum*. His treatment of the Earthly Paradise episode in his *Buik* is adapted from the French translation of the *Iter*, *Le Voyage au Paradis Terrestre*, which is often included in the French *Roman d'Alexandre*. The *Voyage* is relatively faithful to the *Iter*, but Hay's adaptation of it contains several elements unique to his poem and which, if they are his own innovations, are evidence of considerable poetic ability.[87] The episode is soaked with a sense of exile and loss. Uniquely, Alexander is permitted to see within the walls of Paradise when the sea on which he is sailing miraculously rises to the height of the boundary walls. The description rehearses several motifs conventional to otherworld accounts. The theme of the distortion of time in the otherworld is played out, though here rationalized as a symptom of the delightfulness of paradise:

Suppois a man þare tuentie ȝere suld be,	
He vauld nocht think it tuentie dayis lang,	
For sic a melody of birdis sang,	[such
With all pleasance þat mannis witt mycht think,	
That thame lest nocht of vther mete and drink,	[desire no other
That quehn that thai thre dayis thare had bene,	[when
Thai tocht thai had bot cummyn ȝistrene.[88]	[arrived yesterday

There is perpetual daylight there, extensive flowering plains, and the scent of spices and balsam. A 'golden crag' stands beside it and even the walls of

---

[84] Thomas of Kent, *Anglo-Norman Alexander*, ll. 5563–4.

[85] Gilbert Hay, *The Buik of King Alexander the Conquerour*, edited by John Cartwright, 2 vols, STS, 4th Ser., 16, 18 (Aberdeen: Aberdeen University Press, 1986–1990). The section recounting the journey to Paradise has also been printed in *Longer Scottish Poems, 1375–1650*, edited by Priscilla Bawcutt and Felicity Riddy, 2 vols (Edinburgh: Scottish Academic Press, 1987) I, pp. 85–6.

[86] For a recent summary of critical work on the text, see Anna Caughey, '"Als for the worthynes of þe romance": Exploitation of Genre in the *Buik of King Alexander the Conqueror*', in *The Exploitations of Medieval Romance*, edited by Laura Ashe, Ivana Djordjević, and Judith Weiss (Cambridge: D. S. Brewer, 2010), pp. 139–58.

[87] For an account of the points of similarity and difference between the *Iter* and the *Voyage*, see *Le Prise*, edited by Peckham and La Du, pp. xxxiii–xl.

[88] Hay, *Buik of King Alexander*, ll. 16283–9.

the land are of shining gold.[89] Apart from being highly dramatic, the moment at which Alexander surveys the interior of the land is also poignant. The rich description of the delights within the land heightens the pain with which Alexander recognizes that his very humanity excludes him from it:

> Than Alexander in sprete sa revist was   [ravished
> He wauld richt fane have bene within the place,
> Bot that wald never be, of na kyn wise.[90]

Hay's version also replaces the old man at the window with an angel who comes to Alexander as he overlooks the walls and hands him an apple. This angelic messenger is a more emphatic gesture towards biblical themes than the wise man, and must surely have recalled the cherubim described as guarding the eastern wall of Eden after the expulsion of Adam and Eve.[91] The substitution of the apple for the wonder-stone is not Hay's innovation (it first appears in one of his sources, the Old French adaptation of the *Iter*, *Le Voyage au Paradis Terrestre*), but Hay's persistent allusions to the Genesis narrative create a context that brings out the item's lapsarian symbolism most fully.[92]

Alexander's journey to the walls of Eden reads like the climax of Hay's version of the legend. This Scottish text displays a particularly persistent concern with the journey to Paradise, and few accounts so successfully avoid betraying the episode's origins as an interpolation into the legend. The Earthly Paradise is a constant presence throughout the text, even before Alexander declares his intention to visit it. As Alexander progresses through Asia, he encounters cities situated on one of the rivers that flow out of paradise: 'The citie was wele fundit at devise [skillfully] / Apoun ane flude [river] þat come fra Paradise'.[93] Alexander's famous flight with the griffins is also reimagined by Hay as the means by which he plots his passage to Eden.

---

[89] Although the description is relatively conventional, the combination of details recalls no text so firmly as John Mandeville's description of Paradise: John Mandeville, *The Book of John Mandeville*, edited by Tamarah Kohanski and C. David Benson (Kalamazoo, MI: Medieval Institute Publications, 2007), ll. 2705–35. Lascelles has suggested that elements of Mandeville's account of the Earthly Paradise are derived from a recension of the *Iter*. However, Hay's text may reflect the Mandeville account feeding back into the Alexander tradition.

[90] Hay, *Buik of King Alexander*, ll. 16281–3.

[91] 'And he cast out Adam; and placed before the paradise of pleasure Cherubims, and a flaming sword, turning every way, to keep the way of the tree of life'. Genesis 3.24.

[92] The *Buik*'s editor, John Cartwright, has argued that, in Hay's account of the journey to Paradise, 'the storyteller and the homilist are mutually supportive, and help Hay to make more interesting sense of the whole Alexander story than any other writer in Western Europe managed to do'. John Cartwright, 'Sir Gilbert Hay's "Alexander": A Study in Transformations', *Medium Aevum*, 60 (1991), 61–71 (p. 61).

[93] Hay, *Buik of King Alexander*, ll. 11296–7.

Hay describes Alexander's gaze moving across the earth, from Macedonia through Asia toward Paradise. The motion mirrors the line of his conquests and sets up Paradise as their furthest extreme, mapping time onto space. Indeed, throughout the episode's account of the lands of the world, Paradise is the point to which the description repeatedly returns. To drive the connection home, Alexander's journey on the rising waters to survey Paradise functions like a mirror of the flight with the griffins in Hay's text, firmly linking the two episodes within the narrative. There is a recurrent sense in Hay's work that all roads are leading towards this climactic encounter with the otherworld. The Earthly Paradise is also the point at which much of the thematic material of the work converges.

In general, Hay portrays Alexander in a positive light and, predictably, produces an account of the journey to Paradise where the emphasis is less on the king's hubris than on the limitations inherent in his humanity. The description of the episode is couched in language that highlights Alexander's smallness in contrast to the realm he has encountered. The walls are 'richt hie', so much so that no man might see the top of them, and the water that flows from Paradise is 'mekill, and of grete quantetie' and 'like to þe se'.[94] The linguistic choices Hay makes also bring out Alexander's human limitation and his comparative insignificance in the face of the supernatural. Paradise itself is described in terms of superlatives. Faced with its huge walls, Alexander

. . . wist wele in his power na was	[knew
To gett nane ansure of þat haly place,	[answer
Na fynd the way to past vp to that hicht,	
Bot gif it war throw grace of God almycht.	[except by God's grace
Than slepit he, [as] all man-kynd man do.[95]	

The sheer height of the walls and the impenetrability of the citadel renders Alexander 'mare abaissit na before'.[96] Alexander's reactions to this state of affairs are depicted almost exclusively in terms that stress his helplessness and his limitation. He can conceive of no means to reach the top of the wall. The repeated use of the word 'nocht' (thrice in the course of lines 16229–32) underscores this sudden impotence. Hay also chooses this moment to inform us that Alexander is not dressed in his kingly attire, but in the clothes of a messenger. Lascelles has argued that the insertion of this detail reflects 'the disjointed manner of an unskilful narrator';[97] the

---

[94] Hay, *Buik of King Alexander*, ll. 16214, 16218, 16219.
[95] Hay, *Buik of King Alexander*, ll. 16236–40.
[96] Hay, *Buik of King Alexander*, l. 16227.
[97] Lascelles, 'Alexander and the Earthly Paradise', 89.

lines certainly contribute little to narrative momentum but, in a passage that constantly seeks to stress Alexander's humanity, they have much to contribute on a thematic level. Following close on the heels of this assertion of Alexander's impotence, the sleep which overtakes him serves as a reminder of his humanity and the limitations of his will—a point confirmed by the assertion that the conqueror must sleep as 'all man-kynd man do'.[98]

Indeed, the text dwells on how far Alexander's will is overcome by the encounter and how far the experience of wonder deprives him of control of his senses. The overwhelming impact of the Earthly Paradise, conveyed through Hay's rich and emphatic language, renders Alexander helpless—even his delight underlines his limitation. Hay described how the environs of paradise are so beautiful to Alexander and his two companions: 'That fra þare-selff þai war sa revist quyte / That of nane erdly thing þai tuke sa grete delite'.[99] This involuntary 'taking over' of Alexander and his men by the delights of the location underscores the idea that Paradise is a place where human will gives way to the self-abandonment inherent in wonder.

The Alexander who encounters Paradise in Hay's work is an altogether more devout and humble figure than the Alexander of the *Iter*. In surveying the globe during his flight, Alexander's ambition to ask for tribute from Paradise is founded on, and rendered less problematic by, the fact that the gods have given him permission to do so. Alexander sets out for Paradise 'with grete devotioun', a term which casts him more as a pilgrim than a conqueror.[100] Faced with the impenetrable walls of Paradise, Hay's Alexander recognizes that he may only gain entry by the 'grace of God almycht' and resorts to prayer.[101] Furthermore, the waters bear him up to the top of the wall while he is on his knees in prayer—a somewhat unconventional position from which to ask tribute. The tribute-giving, when it comes, is described with great economy, in contrast to the extended description of Eden that has preceded it. As in all versions of the story, the episode is structured around oppositions, life and death, will and abandonment, desire and denial. The angel comes to the wall, greets Alexander, and hands him the apple, before departing. As in all other versions of the text, the token Alexander receives from Paradise is symbolic of his death. Unlike other versions of the text, Alexander does not have to call upon any authority to interpret the gift: the interpretation is made readily by the angel, who, when giving it to him, enjoins him to 'think that þou has schorte

[98] Hay, *Buik of King Alexander*, l. 16240.
[99] Hay, *Buik of King Alexander*, ll. 16209–10.
[100] Hay, *Buik of King Alexander*, l. 16112.
[101] Hay, *Buik of King Alexander*, l. 16239.

tyme for to liff'.[102] The fulfilment of desire is also the encounter with death and the multiple reversals articulated in this exchange are reflected in the imagery and rhetoric that follow. The description of the receding waters and the description of Alexander's departure take place over a mere four lines and both are couched in terms which stress diminution, passing, and descent: the water 'wanyt' and the ship 'devalit doun' before Alexander and his two companions 'passit doun' the river whence they came.[103] And, indeed, although the poem has a further 3,000 lines to run, and Alexander undertakes one more campaign, it really is all downhill from there. Given Hay's pointed evocations of the Genesis narrative, it is difficult to read this rhetorical emphasis on descent as anything other than a nod in the direction of the original Fall.

Although the encounter fixes the *ne plus ultra* to Alexander's conquests, the remoteness of Paradise's location and its supernatural properties allow that limit to be read as a badge of achievement. In Hay's narrative and other adaptations, the vastness of Alexander's empire is extolled by describing it as stretching from the Pillars of Hercules, or the western sea, to Paradise. On his deathbed, Hay's Alexander describes his conquests as ranging from 'Paradice to þe Pilleris of Hercules'.[104] Both before and after his journey to it, Paradise features in Hay's text as both the limit and summit of Alexander's achievement. The extent of his conquests is repeatedly conceptualized with reference to Paradise at their eastern extreme.[105] The dual reading of Paradise as both a summit and a limit reinforces the sense that the encounter with it has introduced a second scale of measurement into the account of Alexander's achievements. The wall between Paradise and the rest of the world is also the point at which human standards of authority meet divine ones. The encounter with the otherworld precipitates a shift in the audience's horizon of expectations, and casts the text's treatment of authority in an entirely different light.

In the accounts of Alexander's journey to the Earthly Paradise, the encounter with the otherworld is both a validation of Alexander's authority and a constraint on it: it confirms him as the greatest of mortal kings, but circumscribes his power firmly within the human sphere. It develops the theme of the limits of human agency repeatedly treated in otherworld descriptions and, in applying it to the greatest of human empire-builders, gives it added depth and power. The token Alexander receives from

---

[102] Hay, *Buik of King Alexander*, l. 16299.
[103] Hay, *Buik of King Alexander*, ll. 16304–6.
[104] Hay, *Buik of King Alexander*, l. 18303.
[105] See, for instance, the formulations of the scope of Alexander's conquests in Hay, *Buik of King Alexander*, ll. 2676, 4668–89, 14794–5, 18319–22.

Paradise, whether it takes the form of the wonder-stone or of the apple, is a particularly effective elaboration on the conventional motif of the precious object retrieved from the otherworld. The story allows considerable scope for thematic adaptation, enrichment, and alteration. For instance, the *Iter* reads as a (largely unambiguous) warning against ambition, pride, and greed. Three centuries later, Gilbert Hay's emphasis falls on human loss, exile, and the hunger for beatitude, but in both cases the basic elements of the plot remain the same. The encounter with the Earthly Paradise is the point at which the main themes in the Alexander legend converge: ambition and wonder, desire and death, authority and limitation. In all accounts, Alexander's encounter with the Earthly Paradise is the point at which authority shifts most fully away from the conqueror.

The encounter with a supernatural realm radically alters the sense of relative proportion which has held true in the narrative up to this point. The Alexander legends frequently set up the Macedonian conqueror as the scale against which all achievement and authority is measured. The encounter with the Earthly Paradise provides the first moment in the narrative when the figure of Alexander is cut down to size. On a human scale, he retains his authority and his claim to be called 'the Great', but the encounter with the otherworld introduces a scale that is altogether larger and against which Alexander is thoroughly dwarfed.

The fact that the theme of authority is so prevalent in otherworld narratives from very different cultures and periods reflects the extent to which these encounters lend themselves to such reflections. The presence of two different and, in many ways, unequal worlds within a narrative will repeatedly convene issues, and provoke treatments, of both authority and power. The operations of authority within and beyond the text treated in this chapter are usually 'triangulated': actual-world figures within the narrative and, at times, figures in the historical world outside it, may have their authority validated and their power amplified by the encounter with the otherworld. A cluster of medieval Irish narratives launch a king, or a potential heir to a kingdom, with strong links to historical dynasties, on an otherworld journey and the imaginative appeal of these otherworld narratives could sweeten the taste of dynastic propaganda. Similarly, the Avalon of the Arthurian tradition had a particularly profound impact on political reality in the historical world. At its most heightened, the authority of the otherworld is brought into direct conflict with the most powerful human ruler of all—Alexander the Great. Not only was the fantastical nature of these realms no impediment to their use for political and didactic purposes, it seems to have facilitated such explorations and deployments by a range of authors who recognized the imaginative potency of these otherworlds and who tended to take them very seriously indeed.

4

Archipelagic Otherworlds

Although they are among the most fantastical of medieval literary fictions, otherworld accounts could be enlisted by their authors and audiences to a variety of entirely serious ends. What this final chapter considers is a particularly heightened instance of this seriousness: the use of otherworldly imagery to describe lands that are not only indisputably 'actual' to the writer, but also geographically proximate and easily reachable. In some cases, the very country in which the text originates is reimagined in these terms. We have already touched on some cases like this. For instance, Mount Etna's geographical circumstances mesh rather neatly with the well-established components of medieval otherworld narratives. The island was very fertile, and trade with North Africa, in particular, had made the island rich in jewels and expensive cloths. In the central Middle Ages, Sicily was notable for its gold coinage, and the German chroniclers who wrote of Henry VI's takeover of the island at the end of the twelfth century were astonished at the island's wealth.[1] Islands and hollow hills are by far the most frequent locations for otherworld realms in medieval writing and the combination of both in one location must have been particularly resonant.

There are two strands of recent scholarship that provide a natural way into the question of 'actual' otherworlds. The notion that the geographical distinctiveness of the island of Britain was reimagined as a specific source of 'national' pride by medieval writers (usually English ones) has received scholarly attention in the last decade. In her 2006 book, *Angels on the Edge of the World*, Kathy Lavezzo has suggested that closely related discourses of peripherality, westernness, and insularity were developed by various English writers into a symbolic geography that underpinned English identity.[2] Catherine A. M. Clarke and Fabienne Michelet have also focused on the

---

[1] Graham A. Loud, 'Coinage, Wealth and Plunder in the Age of Robert Guiscard', *English Historical Review*, 114 (1999), 815–43 (pp. 817–18).

[2] Kathy Lavezzo, *Angels on the Edge of the World: Geography, Literature, and English Community, 1000–1534* (Ithaca, NY: Cornell University Press, 2006).

symbolic dimension of insular geography.[3] However, the extent to which rhetoric and imagery associated with otherworld accounts are used by such authors is yet to be addressed. In highlighting this discourse, this chapter also proposes an alternative framework through which to view insular literature in a comparative context. A concurrent movement in recent scholarship, spearheaded by scholars such as Jeffrey Jerome Cohen, has been to reorientate medieval English studies towards a more authentically archipelagic perspective.[4] Alfred Siewers has recently connected this to the idea of the otherworld, suggesting that the 'doubled landscape' of the otherworld finds a 'geographical doppelgänger' in the archipelago.[5] He uses the idea of an archipelago, a multiplicitous, fragmented space characterized by 'difference with identity', as a framework for thinking about the otherworlds of early Irish literature.[6] Siewers considers that literary depictions of otherworlds, accessible through hills, water, and fog barriers across medieval Ireland 'extended the geography of the Irish sea province into an archipelago of varied temporalities on land as well as across the sea.'[7] Perhaps this model can also work in the opposite direction? Depictions of the otherworld may have provided a model for thinking about insular geography, not only in Ireland, but also throughout the island group we term the British Isles. This study has argued that comparative approaches to literature based on assumptions about shared 'Celtic' sources are problematic and unproductive. What follows proposes an alternative framework within which to compare writings in the various insular languages. This framework is geographical, rather than chronological, and is grounded in the imaginative impact of shared archipelagic geography on insular literatures, which, I believe, provides a fruitful and under-explored avenue through which to address the history of ideas in these multicultural, multilingual islands.

The evidence suggests that medieval writers saw a clear analogue to the particular qualities of the British Isles in otherworld accounts and drew on imagery and ideas associated with such accounts in describing these territories. However, there is likely to be a degree of imaginative give and take in such portrayals: it is arguable that part of the interest insular

---

[3] Catherine A. M. Clarke, *Literary Landscapes and the Idea of England, 700–1400* (Cambridge: D. S. Brewer, 2006), in particular, p. 67 *et passim*; Fabienne Michelet, *Creation, Migration, and Conquest: Imaginary Geography and Sense of Space in Old English Literature* (Oxford: Oxford University Press, 2006).

[4] Cohen, ed., *Cultural Diversity*. The notion of the archipelago provides the framework for Sebastian I. Sobecki, ed., *The Sea and Englishness in the Middle Ages: Maritime Narratives, Identity and Culture* (Cambridge: D.S. Brewer, 2011).

[5] Siewers, *Strange Beauty*, p. 8.   [6] Siewers, *Strange Beauty*, p. 18.

[7] Siewers, *Strange Beauty*, p. 20.

writers evince in otherworld accounts in the first place is a result of the distinctive nature of archipelagic geography, a distinctiveness that would have appeared considerably more pronounced in the Middle Ages than today. The 'otherness' of Britain, Ireland, and the surrounding islands was inherent in their geography long before it was elaborated upon in literature and history. From almost any medieval European perspective, the islands of the Atlantic were something of an anomaly. The known world was largely reducible to the single landmass of Asia, Africa, and Europe. The only known location comparably dense with islands was the Mediterranean, but its islands lay in an enclosed area of sea, whose limits were clearly discernable. Britain and Ireland lay in the unmapped world ocean, beyond the *orbis* of land that enclosed the Mediterranean. If such geography provided the cue for, and enhanced the relevance of, otherworld accounts in medieval literary texts, it is not a large leap to assume that the imagery of such descriptions might have been (re)applied to the various regions of the insular world by writers working in a more historical mode. As such, it is not always possible to distinguish between responses that take their immediate cue from the geographical context and those with more literary sources, and, indeed, the two are by no means mutually exclusive; one may reinforce the other.

THE NORTH ATLANTIC *ORBIS ALTER*

The 'otherness' of Britain, Ireland, and the surrounding islands was inherent in their geography and, as such, available to be exploited by a host of writers in the premodern world. Their singular position is particularly obvious from a cursory examination of almost any medieval world map. In these works, Britain and Ireland tend to be placed at the edge of the world image, often somewhat distorted in shape, as if mapmakers had trouble accommodating them in a framework designed to hold the neat, circular form of the three continents. A particularly striking example of this perception is a twelfth-century world map in Oxford, St John's College MS 17, f. 6r (Figure 4.2). This manuscript is a miscellany of computistical texts written at Thornley Abbey in Cambridgeshire and features an elaborated T-O map that lays out the regions of the world within a circular frame that lies within another larger circle denoting the world ocean. On the map, the island of Britain is represented pressing up against the outer rim of the world ocean on the left side of the map, while Ireland and Thule (usually interpreted as Iceland) are represented beyond the boundary of the map altogether, the only lands thus positioned. Of course, writers had responded to this geographic situation long before the

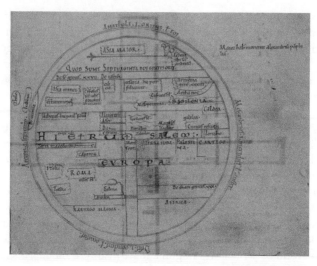

Fig. 4.2. World Map from Oxford, St John's College MS 17, f. 6r. (Reproduced by permission of the President and Fellows of St John's College, Oxford.)

Middle Ages, and the influence of classical descriptions of the archipelago can be discerned in medieval writing on the subject. The idea that the lands which Latin writers referred to as the 'islands of the ocean' (*oceani insulae*) were in some way exceptional is a recurrent feature of classical accounts of the region. From the perspective of this study, one Latin formula for describing Britain and Ireland is of particular interest: *alter orbis*. This term, or the variant *orbis alius*, is reasonably well established in the scattered geographical accounts of Britain and Ireland, particularly Britain, from Antiquity. It should be noted that the term was not only applied to the Atlantic islands: Pliny uses it with reference to Scandinavia and Ceylon, while Pomponius Mela describes Ceylon/Taprobane and the Antipodes in the same terms.[8] However, such a term seems to have been used most frequently and most emphatically in relation to Britain and Ireland, and to have been taken up with some enthusiasm by medieval authors.

As early as the first century AD, Virgil described Britons as 'wholly sundered from the world', and, in his enduringly popular late fourth-century commentary on Virgil, Servius noted of this phrase that Britain is 'called an other world by the poets'.[9] In the early third century, Origen

---

[8] Patrick Sims-Williams, *The Irish Influence on Medieval Welsh Literature* (Oxford: Oxford University Press, 2011), p. 54.

[9] 'et penitus toto divisos orbe Britannos'. Virgil, *Eclogues*, edited and translated by Len Krisak and Gregson David (Philadelphia: University of Pennsylvania Press, 2010), I: 66,

writes of Britain in similar terms: '[t]he power of the Lord and Saviour is with those who are in Britain separated from our world'.[10] Virgil's line also finds a later echo in Claudian, who describes Britain as 'cut off from our world',[11] and in the late fourth century, Paula and Eustochium noted in a letter about travel to the Holy Land that '[t]he Briton, separated from our world, no sooner makes progress in religion than he leaves the setting sun and seeks the place known to him only in from hearsay and from the account in Scriptures'.[12] In the same century, Solinus noted that 'the coasts of France would be called the end of the world if Britain did not deserve the name of almost another world'.[13] Isidore of Seville describes Britain as 'cut off from the whole globe by the intervening sea'.[14] There is a good deal of evidence that writers working in Britain itself took their cue from these classical accounts. Solinus's statement proved particularly influential throughout the Middle Ages and beyond: it was repeated and elaborated by Trevisa (via Higden), John Harrison in his *Description of Britain*, Camden in his *Britannia*, and Fabyan in his *Chronicle*.[15] Higden also

---

p. 8; 'a poetis alter orbis terrarum dicitur'. Servius, *Servii Grammatici qui feruntur in Vergilii carmina commentarii*, edited by Georg Thilo and Hermann Hagen, 3 vols (Leipzig: Teubner, 1881–1902.), III (1902), *in Eclogues*, I: 66, p. 15. On the influence of Servius in the Middle Ages, see Christopher Baswell, *Virgil in Medieval England: Figuring the* Aeneid *from the Twelfth Century to Chaucer* (Cambridge: Cambridge University Press, 1995), pp. 47–53.

[10] 'Virtus Domini Salvatoris et cum his est, qui ab orbe nostro in Britannia dividuntur', Origen, *Die Homilien zu Lukas in der Übersetzung des Hieronymus und die griechischen Reste der Homilien und des Lukas-Kommentars*, edited by Max Rauer, in *Origenes: Werke*, 12 vols, Die Griechischen Christlichen Schriftsteller, 35 (Berlin: Akademie-Verlag, 1899–1955), IX (1931), homily VI, pp. 32–40, (p. 39); Translation from Origen, *Homilies on Luke*, translated by Joseph T. Leinhard (Washington, DC: Catholic University of America Press, 1996), p. 27.

[11] 'nostro diducta Britannia mundo', Claudian, 'Panegyricus, Dictus Manlio Theodoro Consuli', in *Claudian*, translated by Maurice Platnauer (London: William Heinemann, 1922), pp. 338–63, (p. 342).

[12] 'Divisus ab orbe nostro, Britannus, si in religione processerit, occiduo sole dimisso, quaerit locum fama sibi tantum et scripturarum relatione cognitum.' Paula and Eustochium, 'Epistola ad Marcellam', in *Itinera Heirosolymitana et Descriptiones Terrae Sanctae*, edited by Titus Tobler and Augustus Molinier (Geneva: J.-G. Fick, 1879–1885), I, pp. 43–7 (p. 44). Translation from Paula and Eustochium, 'On Visiting Jerusalem', in *Lives of Roman Christian Women*, edited by Caroline White (Penguin: London, 2010), pp. 165–75 (p. 174).

[13] 'Finis erat orbis ora Gallici litoris, nisi Brittania insula non qualibet amplitudine nomen paene orbis alterius mereretur', Solinus, *Collectanea Rerum Memorabilium*, edited by T. Mommsen (Berlin: Weidmann, 1895), pp. 99–100.

[14] 'Brittania Oceani insula interfuso mari toto orbe divisa', Isidore of Seville, *Isidori Hispalensis Episcopi Etymologiarum Sive Originum*, edited by W. M. Lindsay, 2 vols (Oxford: Clarendon Press, 1911), II, XIV: 6. 2. Translation from Isidore of Seville, *The Etymologies of Isidore of Seville*, translated by Stephen A. Barney and others (Cambridge: Cambridge University Press, 2006), p. 294.

[15] Josephine Waters Bennett, 'Britain Among the Fortunate Isles', *Studies in Philology*, 53 (1956), 114–40.

uses similar terms but adduces sources closer to home, quoting Alfred, 'English Britain is called another world, which formerly Charlemagne called his own chamber because of the abundance of good things there'.[16] In Eadmer's *Vita Anselmi* (*c*.1124), the author cites Pope Urban II's description of Anselm's position as primate of Canterbury as the apostle and patriarch of that 'other world' (*alter orbis*).[17] A short time later, the quotation is taken up and repeated by William of Malmesbury in *De Gestis Pontificum Anglorum*, where he has Urban describe Anselm as being like the pope of 'an other world' (*alter orbis*).[18] Bede never uses this precise term, but lays great emphasis on Britain's alterity and isolation. In his Preface to the *Cantica Canticorum*, Bede describes himself and his readers as 'born and reared far from the world, that is, on an island of the Ocean sea'.[19] The term *alter orbis* is, however, used by William of Malmesbury in his account of Bede.[20]

As we have seen, translating the phrase *orbis alter* as an 'otherworld' is problematic, since it brings a series of associations into play which simply did not exist in the Middle Ages. However, even though it does not have the same semantic range as the modern term, the phrase does lay stress on the island group's alterity and also its singularity, ideas that are key to the depiction of otherworlds in literary texts. There is a recurrent sense in these accounts that an exceptional location gives rise to exceptional qualities; for instance, in Higden's quotation from Alfred, the British *alter orbis* is a place of peculiar beauty and abundance. This stress on the special qualities of these isolated islands also links these accounts to otherworld descriptions. Classical writers frequently comment on the islands' strangely temperate climate, which, as Josephine Waters Bennett notes, must have seemed to them 'contrary to nature or supernatural'.[21] The islands are endowed with exceptional qualities in Plutarch, Procopius of Caesarea, and Pomponius Mela. Plutarch quotes Demetrius, who was

---

[16] 'Anglia Britannica alter orbis appellatur; quam olim Carolus Magnus prae omnium bonorum copia cameram suam vocavit'. Ranulf Higden, *Polychronicon Ranulphi Higden Monachi Cestrensis*, edited by Churchill Babington and J. R. Lumby, 9 vols, RS, 41 (London: Longmans, 1865–1886), II (1869), 4–6.

[17] Eadmer, *The Life of St Anselm, Archbishop of Canterbury*, edited and translated by R. W. Southern (Oxford: Clarendon Press, 1972), II: 29, p. 105.

[18] '"Includamus", inquit, "hunc in orbe nostro, quasi alterius orbis papam"'. William of Malmesbury, *De Gestis Pontificum Anglorum*, edited by N. E. S. A. Hamilton, RS, 52 (London: Longmans, 1870), I: 53, p. 100.

[19] 'longius extra orbem, hoc est in insula maris Oceani nati et nutriti'. Bede, *In Cantica Canticorum*, edited by D. Hurst, Corpus Christianorum, Series Latina, 119 (Turnhout: Brepols, 1983), Preface.

[20] 'Nam et Britannia, quae a quibusdam alter orbis appellatur, quod oceano interfusa non multis cosmographis comperta est, habet in remotissima sui plaga locum natiuitatis et educationis eius, Scottiae propinquum'. William of Malmesbury, *Gesta Regum Anglorum*, edited and translated by R. A. B. Mynors, R. M. Thomson, and M. Winterbottom, 2 vols (Oxford: Clarendon Press, 1998), I, I: 53. 1, p. 82.

[21] Bennett, 'Fortunate Isles', p. 119.

in Britain in about AD 82, to the effect that the British believed in an island paradise to the west.[22] Procopius of Caesarea recounts a third-century legend that the souls of the dead are taken to Britain from Continental Europe,[23] suggesting an early identification of the island with liminality and, perhaps, the association of the west—the region of the setting sun— with death. The near contemporary Pomponius Mela recounts a Gaulish belief in the Island of Sena, believed to be opposite Brittany and where nine priestesses perform wonders and cure the incurable—an idea that is very close to Geoffrey of Monmouth's *insula pomorum*.[24] The second-hand nature of this information makes it difficult to be assertive about the extent to which it reflects authentic local or 'Celtic' beliefs. Otherworld islands inhabited by nine women crop up in Irish and Welsh, yet, as Patrick Sims-Williams has recently noted, the notion may also be discerned in Norse writings and, of course, the nine muses have an island home in various classical accounts.[25] It appears that these texts may be more revelatory of Mediterranean ideas of the west and of the islands in the Atlantic than they are about the inhabitants and living environment of the archipelago. To suggest that such ideas reflect Celtic beliefs that were known by classical authors and then somehow survived and were echoed in medieval insular literature is considerably less plausible than suggesting a line of influence from classical authors to medieval writers.

Three central and related ideas can be isolated from these accounts which are linked to the special, even supernatural, properties of Britain and Ireland: insularity, peripherality, and westernness. A sense that islands and peripheries are a natural site for the production of marvels is discernable in many medieval texts, particularly the numerous accounts of natural wonders. Barry Cunliffe suggests that islands 'had a special quality', and that: 'Perhaps it was the idea of boundedness . . . that was the attraction. That islands were liminal places, neither entirely of the land nor of the sea, would have endowed them with unusual power in the minds of those who lived at the interface between land and ocean.'[26] Cunliffe's comments, of course, say more about how islands must have appeared to their inhabitants than to people arriving from elsewhere. For the traveller

---

[22] Plutarch, 'De Defectu Oraculorum', in *Moralia*, edited by Frank Cole Babbitt (Whitefish, MT: Kessinger Publishing, 2005), pp. 350–501.

[23] Procopius of Caesarea, *History of the Wars*, edited and translated by H. B. Dewing, 7 vols (London: W. Heinemann, 1914–1940), v (1928), pp. 266–70.

[24] Pomponius Mela, *Description of the World*, translated by Frank E. Romer (Ann Arbor, MI: University of Michigan Press, 1998), III: 6, p. 115.

[25] Sims-Williams, *Irish Influence*, pp. 63–4.

[26] Cunliffe, *Facing the Ocean*, p. 31. See also, Nathalie Bouloux, 'Les îles dans les descriptions géographiques et les cartes du Moyen Âge', *Médiévales*, 47 (2004), 47–62.

arriving at the island, its 'special quality' would surely have been further enhanced by the necessity of crossing an expanse of water in order to reach it—a natural barrier which by the Middle Ages had become a conventional entry point to otherworld realms. Gerald of Wales' account of the marvels of Ireland, for instance, focuses on numerous inland islands.[27] Ireland itself emerges from his text as a place where everything is heightened, where extremes of beauty and barbarity are cemented by geographical isolation and insularity.

Bounded, enclosed spaces had a powerful claim on the medieval imagination. Their connotation of purity was not lost on national mythographers, nor was the sense of resistance to outside interference. Britain's boundedness was conceived in fortress-like terms long before Shakespeare's 'fortress built by Nature for herself'. Gildas speaks of Britain as 'fortified on all sides by a vast and more or less uncrossable ring of sea',[28] while Geoffrey of Monmouth, for instance, sees Britain as an *insula optima* surrounded by a fierce, monster-infested sea.[29] Medieval cartographers tend to give special treatment to islands, frequently infilling them in a bold colour (or a range of colours) while leaving the expanse of the continents in largely neutral tones. The Catalan Atlas, compiled in 1375–8, is a prominent example of this tendency, providing elaborate decorations, gilding, and colours for its islands.[30] The structure of Isidore's *Etymologiae* both reflected and perpetuated perceptions of the anomalous nature of islands generally. The islands of the ocean are grouped into a section of their own in Book XIV, Chapter 6, titled 'De insulis'. Europe, Asia, and Africa have already been treated in separate sections. Indeed, Isidore's work provides accounts of Britain and Ireland that lay the foundation for much later writing on the subject. Ireland is described as next to Britain and 'more fertile in its site . . . [t]here no snakes are found, birds are scarce, and there are no bees, so that if someone were to sprinkle dust or pebbles brought from there among beehives in some other place, the swarms would desert the honeycombs'.[31] Such properties of Irish soil might be considered merely exceptional, rather than

---

[27] Gerald, *Topographia*, II: 4, 5, 6, 12, pp. 80–4, 94–5.

[28] 'quae arcuatis oceani sinibus ambiuntur, tenens, cuius diffusiore et, ut ita dicam, intransmeabli undique circulo absque meridianae freto plagae'. Gildas, *De Excidio Britonum: The Ruin of Britain and Other Sources*, edited and translated by Michael Winterbottom (London: Phillimore, 1978), pp. 89–90.

[29] Sebastian I. Sobecki, *The Sea and Medieval English Literature* (Cambridge: D. S. Brewer, 2008).

[30] *Mappamundi: Der Katalanische Weltatlas vom Jahre 1375*, edited by George Grosjean (Dietikon: Urs Graf Verlag, 1977).

[31] 'Scotia idem et Hibernia proxima Brittaniae insula, spatio terrarum angustior; sed situ fecundior . . . Illic nulla anguis, avis rara, apis nulla, adeo ut advectos inde pulveres seu

supernatural; however, the notion takes on a rather more marvellous hue in Bede's elaboration of Isidore's account:

> No reptiles are found there; for, though often carried thither out of Britain, as soon as the ship comes near the shore, and the scent of the air reaches them, they die ... almost all things in the island are good against poison. In short, we have known that when some persons have been bitten by serpents, the scrapings of leaves of books that were brought out of Ireland, being put into water, and given them to drink, have immediately expelled the spreading poison, and assuaged the swelling.[32]

Gerald of Wales makes the supernatural properties of islands more explicit: 'some countries, islands especially, and parts remote from the centre of the earth, are remarkable for prodigies which are peculiarly their own'.[33] The purity of islands—a symptom of their separation from the rest of the world—could also be developed into an association of such spaces with health and, indeed, with the sort of healing properties often associated with paradise-like otherworld realms.

Peripherality as a mark of exceptionality is a key theme in Gerald of Wales' accounts of Ireland. The Ireland of the *Topographia Hibernica* is depicted thus:

> Thus separated from the rest of the world, and in some sort to be distinguished as another world [*alter orbis*], not only by its situation, but by objects out of the ordinary course of nature contained in it, Ireland seems to be nature's especial repository, where she stores up her most remarkable and precious treasures.[34]

Ireland's status as an *alter orbis* is linked to its preponderance of natural wonders. The island is imagined as a landscape of desire. For the most

---

lapillos si quis alibi sparserit inter alvaria, examina favos deserant'. Isidore, *Etymologies*, XIV: 6. 6; translated by Barney et al., p. 294.

[32] 'nullum ibi reptile uideri soleat, nullus uiuere serpens ualeat. Nam saepe illo de Brittania adlati serpentes, mox ut proximante terris nauigio, odore aeris illius adtacti fuerint, intereunt; quin potius omnia pene quae de eadem insula sunt, contra uenenum ualent. Denique uidimus, quibusdam a serpente percussis, rasa folia codicum qui de Hibernia fuerant, et ipsam rasuram aquae inmissam ac potui datam, talibus protinus totam uim ueneni grassantis, totum inflati corporis absumsisse ac sedasse tumorem.' Bede, *Ecclesiastical History of the English People*, edited by Bertram Colgrave and R. A. B. Mynors (Oxford: Oxford University Press, 1969), I: 1, pp. 18–20.

[33] 'Quaelibet nimirum regiones, insulae praesertim et partes a centro remotissimae, propriis quibusdam prodigiis pollent.' Gerald, *Topographia*, II: Praef., p. 75; translated by Forester, p. 58.

[34] 'Quae videlicet Hibernia, quanto a cetero et communi orbe terrarum semota, et quasi alter orbis esse dignoscitur, tanto rebus quibusdam solito naturae cursui incognitis, quasi peculiaris ejusdem naturae thesaurus, ubi insignia et pretiosiora sui secreta reposuerit, esse videtur.' Gerald, *Topographia*, I: 2, p. 23; translated by Forester, p. 18.

part, the strangeness of its natural marvels is seen as something that attracts rather than repulses. In his *Preface* addressed to Henry II, Gerald describes his *Topographia*, a description of the land itself, as a gift that outdoes gold or hunting birds, suggesting that the marvels of Ireland are a worthy object of desire.[35]

The persistent thematic linking of geographical peripheries with death and the limits of human time in literary texts is also discernable in historical accounts. The idea is articulated at an early stage by Saint Patrick in his *Confessio* (*c.*450), which describes the saint's perception that he was being taken to the very ends of the earth when he was taken as a slave to Ireland. As Thomas O'Loughlin has noted, Patrick links this geographical extreme to the position which he believes his mission occupies in salvation history.[36] In the course of his *Confessio*, he repeatedly refers to his being brought to Ireland *ad ultimum terrae* and appears to link the fact that he has arrived to work at the ends of the earth to the closeness of the end of time.[37] Chapters 34 to 40 of the *Confessio* contain Patrick's most extensive elaboration of this connection. Patrick states his gratitude to God for being chosen to proclaim the gospel 'in the last days', recalling Christ's promise that the gospel would be proclaimed 'to all the nations before the end of the world' and stating that 'we are witnesses that the gospel has been preached to the point beyond which there is no one'.[38] He describes the Irish as coming to the faith only in his day and living at the ends of the earth. Patrick draws on a wide range of biblical passages in support of his mission, many of which emphasize the conjunction of the ends of the earth and the end of time: 'I have put you as a light among the nations, to be a means of salvation to the ends of the earth' (Acts 13. 47); 'They shall come from east and west and shall sit down at table with Abraham and Isaac and Jacob' (Matt. 8. 11); 'This gospel of the kingdom shall be preached throughout the whole world as a testimony to all nations; and then the end shall come' (Matt. 24. 14). Patrick appears to believe that, having brought the gospel to the ends of the earth, there is now no

---

[35] Gerald, *Topographia*, I: Praefatio Secunda, p. 21; translated by Forester, p. 10.

[36] Thomas O'Loughlin, 'Patrick on the Margins of Space and Time', in *Eklogai: Studies in Honour of Thomas Finan and Gerard Watson,* edited by Kieran McGroarty (Maynooth: Cardinal Press, 2001), pp. 44–58.

[37] Patrick, *Confessio*, in *St. Patrick: His Writings and Muirchu's Life*, edited and translated by A. B. E. Hood (London: Phillimore, 1978), pp. 23–34, Chapters 1, 11, 34, 38.

[38] 'ut ego inscius et in novissimis diebus hoc opus tam pium et tam mirificum auderem adgredere, ita ut imitarem quippiam illos quos ante Dominus iam olim praedixerat praenuntiaturos evangelium suum in testimonium omnibus gentibus ante finem mundi—quod ita ergo vidimus itaque suppletum est: ecce testes sumus quia evangelium praedicatum est usque ubi nemo ultra est'. Patrick, *Confessio*, p. 29.

obstacle to the Second Coming: Ireland stands at the extremity of the world and, in a certain sense, at the end of history. The islands of the ocean, it would appear, exist in a space between life and death, time and eternity. Patrick is by no means the only writer who makes this connection. A few decades earlier, Saint Augustine, in his letter to Hesychius, also connected the end of time to the fact of the gospel reaching the ends of the earth, specifically the 'islands in the ocean'.[39] A similar way of thinking is also apparent in a later period, in Bede's work.[40]

The association of this geographical periphery with the end of time is made still more natural by the association of the west with the setting sun. Writing like Patrick's emphasizes the eschatological significance of this location, but the idea of the west as an end point was also explored by writers working towards more secular and political ends. Patrick's thinking finds an echo in the widespread notion of the *translatio imperii*, a concept best summed up by Hugh of St Victor:

> In the succession of historical events the order of space and the order of time seem to be in almost complete correspondence. Therefore divine providence's arrangement seems to have been that what was brought about at the beginning of time would also have been brought about in the east . . . and then as time proceeded towards its end, the centre of events would have shifted to the west.[41]

Such a spatio-temporal perspective tends to place the islands of the ocean in a privileged position and to underscore not just the symbolic significance of peripheries, but of the western periphery in particular. In many ways, westernness, the *translatio imperii*, the marvellous, peripherality, and insularity form a complex of related ideas whose associations are rarely explicitly articulated, but which lie behind and inform a wide range of writings, and which have a particularly profound resonance for writers working in the peripheral *alter orbis* of Britain and Ireland.

---

[39] Augustine, *S. Aureli Augustini Hipponiensis episcopi Epistulae, pars iv, ep. CLXXXV–CCLXX*, edited by A. Goldbacher, Corpus Scriptorum Ecclesiasticorum Latinorum, 57 (Vienna: Tempsky, 1895), letter 199, pp. 243–92.

[40] A. H. Merrills, *History and Geography in Late Antiquity*, (Cambridge: Cambridge University Press, 2005), pp. 235–9.

[41] 'Ordo autem loci et ordo temporis fere per omnia secundum rerum gestarum seriem concurrere videntur. Et ita per divinam providentiam videtur esse dispositum, ut que in principio temporum gerebantur, in oriente . . . gererentur, ac deinde ad finem profluente tempore usque ad occidentum rerum summa descenderet.' Hugh of St Victor, *De archa Noe morali*, edited by Patrice Secard and D. Poirel, Corpus Christianorum, Continuatio Mediaevalis, 176 (Turnhout: Brepols, 2001), IV: 9. 22–7, p. 111.

THESE OTHER EDENS

Among the most topographically accurate of medieval maps are the series of portolan charts produced primarily in the western Mediterranean from the thirteenth century onwards. Discussion of these charts has tended to highlight their topographical accuracy and to discern in them the beginnings of modern cartography.[42] They appear to be highly practical documents that are little concerned with the symbolic and ideological discourses that occupied the makers of the *mappae mundi*. However, a striking exception to this general sobriety comes in the depiction of the west coast of Ireland in a series of charts in use in the fourteenth and fifteenth centuries. Deviating significantly from geographical reality, these maps depict a huge bay half way down that coastline, within which are depicted numerous tiny islands. The legend that accompanies this feature usually runs, 'The Happy Lake [*lacus fortunatus*], on which there are 367 islands which are called holy and blessed'.[43] The map-makers would appear to be compensating for their general ignorance of that section of coastline by recourse to garbled stories and, perhaps, pure fantasy. There does not seem to be any written account from which the idea of a 'Happy Lake' at this location could have immediately derived, though the complex of ideas about Ireland's supernatural characteristics in circulation in medieval Europe is likely to have been a contributory factor.

One of the conduits for the dissemination and exploitation of such associations is the, rather less utilitarian, *mappae mundi* tradition.[44] The fact that, by most accounts, Britain was a leader in the production of such maps seems difficult to account for at first glance.[45] These maps typically situate Britain at the westward limits of the known world, isolated from the Pangea-like single landmass of Europe, Asia, and Africa. The typical orientation of *mappae mundi* in this period (east is at the top) only serves to further marginalize Britain; the island appears peripheral to the casual observer, inserted at the bottom of the page, a footnote to the central

---

[42] For an overview, see Tony Campbell, 'Portolan Charts from the Late Thirteenth Century to 1500', in *The History of Cartography*, edited by J. B. Harley and David Woodward, 6 vols (Chicago: University of Chicago Press, 1987–1994), I (1992), 371–463.

[43] 'Lacus fortunatus ubi sunt insule que dicuntur sancte beate ccclxvii' (my transcription). There has been no systematic study of the occurrences of this depiction, but it appears (with minor variations, usually in the number of islands mentioned) on most late medieval charts that depict the British Isles, including those of Franceso Beccari (1403) and Grazioso Benincasa (1467). The latter is reproduced in Delumeau, *History of Paradise*, p. 103.

[44] See Peter Barber, 'The Evesham World Map: A Late Medieval English View of God and the World', *Imago Mundi*, 47 (1995), 13–33.

[45] Lavezzo, *Angels*, p. 7.

geographical narrative. The term 'narrative' is particularly apposite here, since in many ways medieval maps are more like literary texts than clear accounts of topography. They are as much accounts of history and ideology as they are of geography; indeed, they synthesize time and space in ways that are highly sophisticated.

Recent research on how these maps express ideas of national identity has focused on how they convey the idea of the *translatio imperii*.[46] Many of these maps appear in the pages of manuscript volumes and accompany texts. This context encourages a reading of the maps like a text, from top to bottom, which, in most cases, means reading from east to west. The extent to which such a reading can be laden with symbolic potential is evident from examination of the famous Ebstorf Map.[47] This map was in a collection in Germany until it was lost in an Allied bombing raid in 1943. Although it was probably produced locally, it may be located within the English cartographical tradition since there is some evidence that it was designed to illustrate the works of the English-born Gervase of Tilbury and may have been produced by him, or on his instruction, during his time in Germany.[48] To read the map from top to bottom as one would a text is to discover that westward movement is synonymous with the advance of history. At the very top of the map, human history begins with Adam and Eve depicted in Eden in the east; a little further to the west are various Old Testament sites including the Tower of Babel; Jerusalem follows, accompanied by an image of the resurrection, then Rome and then Paris. For English writers, these ideas had a very logical conclusion and they seized upon them as signs of the predestined greatness of their country. In this context, the absence of Ireland from some *mappae mundi* can be interpreted as not only a function of necessary abbreviation, but of a deeply rooted ideology. Here, western peripherality is something to be prized at the expense of geographical accuracy.

That said, the degree to which these maps can be read as diagrams of the *translatio imperii* can easily be overemphasized. As Stephen McKenzie

---

[46] Summarized in Stephen McKenzie's critique of this position, 'The Westward Progression of History on Medieval *Mappaemundi*: An Investigation of the Evidence', in *The Hereford World Map: Medieval World Maps and their Context*, edited by P. D. A. Harvey (London: British Library, 2006), pp. 335–44.

[47] The map is reproduced with extensive commentary in Hartmut Kugler, in collaboration with Sonja Glauch, Antje Willing, and Thomas Zapf, eds., *Die Ebstorfer Weltkarte: Kommentierte Neuausgabe in zwei Bänden* (Berlin: Akademie Verlag, 2007).

[48] Gervase's possible connection to the map is discussed in Hartmut Kugler, 'Die Ebstorfer Weltkarte ohne Gervasius von Tilbury', in *Kloster und Bildung im Mittelalter*, edited by Nathalie Kruppa and Jürgen Wilke (Göttingen: Vandenhoeck & Ruprecht, 2006), pp. 497–512, and in Armin Wolf, 'The Ebstorf Mappamundi and Gervase of Tilbury: The Controversy Revisited', *Imago Mundi*, 64 (2012), 1–27.

notes, a relatively small number of maps respond readily to this reading.[49] In most instances, no clear east–west axis of progressive historical events can be discerned. However, less emphatic visual qualities of these images also lend themselves to consideration of the island of Britain's special status. A particularly notable further elaboration of this symbolic geography saw Britain as the mirror of Eden. The two, more or less, faced each other on the map. Eden was traditionally considered to have been walled off at the Fall; it was fortress-like, enclosed, remote, and inaccessible; some medieval maps depict it as an island surrounded by the ocean.[50] The imaginative leap required to see Britain's isolation and enclosed insular nature in similar terms was very small indeed.

Although English depictions of the island of Britain as an 'other Eden' have attracted considerable interest, particularly in recent years, a similar trend in Irish literature has gone almost entirely uncommented upon.[51] In many ways, Ireland was a more natural location for the making of such national myths. Its isolation and westernness were more pronounced than that of Britain, and its freedom from venomous reptiles, particularly snakes, had already elicited comment from classical authors. Early descriptions dwell on the purity of its soil and its holiness, and, as late as the thirteenth century, the Norse *Speculum Regale* states of Ireland, 'so holy is this land beyond all others that no venomous animal can exist there, neither snake nor toad', before linking this holiness to the preponderance of natural marvels found there.[52] Ireland's holiness and exceptionality were, as we have seen, stated most emphatically by Bede in his *Ecclesiastical History*, a work that had considerable influence in England throughout the Middle Ages.[53] Numerous romances bear out the notion of the idyllic nature of the west; as Cooper notes, 'writers were more likely to use the west as the setting for utopias rather than quest—a land of promise, like Brendan's, rather than threat.'[54] At various points in his *Topographia Hibernica*, Gerald of Wales lays great stress on both the purity and supernatural characteristics of the Occident. He writes:

---

[49] McKenzie, 'Westward Progression', pp. 335–44.

[50] See, for instance, the Sawley World Map (Cambridge, Corpus Christi College MS 66, p. 2), reproduced in Lavezzo, *Angels*, p. 47.

[51] On Irish accounts of the wonders of the country, see Elizabeth Boyle, 'On the Wonders of Ireland: Translation and Adaptation', in *Authorities and Adaptations: The Reworking and Transmission of Textual Sources in Medieval Ireland*, edited by Elizabeth Boyle and Deborah Hayden (Dublin: Dublin Institute for Advanced Studies, 2014), pp. 233–61.

[52] *The King's Mirror (Speculum regale—Konungs skuggsjá)*, translated by L. M. Larson, Scandinavian Monographs, 3 (New York: Twayne, 1917), p. 105.

[53] Bede, *Ecclesiastical History*, pp. 334–45, 474–7. Discussed in Lavezzo, *Angels*, pp. 54–7.

[54] Cooper, *English Romance in Time*, p. 75.

The air is so healthy that no clouds bring infection, and there are no pestilent vapours or tainted breezes. The islanders have little need of physicians for you will find few sick persons, except those who are at the point of death.[55]

This celebration of the temperate western periphery is set alongside an account of the contrasting 'toxic airs' and 'poisons' that abound in the Far East. However, although the Irish western extreme of the world is unlike the East in its purity, it mirrors the Orient in its abundance of marvels:

> For as the countries of the East are remarkable and pre-eminent for some prodigies peculiar to themselves and originating there, so also the Western parts are dignified by the miracles of nature performed within their limits. For sometimes, like one wearied with serious affairs and realities, she withdraws and retires for a little space, and, as it were, sportively employs herself with extraordinary freaks in secret parts reverently and mysteriously veiled.[56]

The conjunction of purity, isolation, and supernatural properties makes comparisons with Paradise almost inevitable.

A striking medieval comparison of Ireland and Eden appears in the *Míniugud* recension of *Lebor Gabála Érenn*. The Irish foundation legend *Lebor Gabála Érenn*, often translated as the 'Book of Invasions' or the 'Book of the Taking of Ireland', is a vast collection of material brought together, perhaps in the tenth century, to form a single narrative which exists in numerous recensions. The *Míniugud* recension opens with a striking passage that dwells on Irish exceptionality and the paradisal connotations of extreme westernness. The form in which it appears in the *Book of Lecan* is worth quoting at length:

> The island of Ireland is situated in the west; as the Paradise of Adam is situated on the southern coast of the east, so Ireland is in the northern portion, toward the west. Those lands are as similar by nature, as they are similar by their positions on the earth: for as Paradise hath no noxious beast,

---

[55] 'Aeris quoque clementia tanta est, ut nec nebula inficiens, nec spiritus hic pestilens, nec aura corrumpens. Medicorum opera parum indiget insula. Morbidos enim homines, praeter moribundos, paucos invenies.' Gerald, *Topographia*, I: 33, p. 67; translated by Forester, p. 51.

[56] 'Sicut enim orientales plagae propriis quibusdam et sibi innatis praeeminent et praecellunt ostentis, sic et occidentales circumferentiae suis naturae miraculis illustrantur. Quoties quippe, tanquam seriis et veris fatigata negotiis, paululum secedit et excedit, remotis in partibus, quasi verecundis et occultis natura ludit excessibus.' Gerald, *Topographia*, I: Praefatio Secundo, pp. 20–1; translated by Forester, p. 9. In 1375–8, Gerald's celebration of the marvels of Ireland finds its way (probably through intermediate sources) into the celebrated Catalan Atlas, which summarizes material from the *Topographia* in recounting how in Ireland there are 'moltes illes meravellosas'. *Der Katalanische Weltatlas*, edited by Grosjean.

so the learned testify that Ireland hath no serpent, lion, toad, injurious rat, dragon, scorpion, nor any hurtful beast, save only the wolf. And so Ireland is called 'the island of the west': 'Hiberoc' in Greek is called 'occasum' in Latin; 'nia' or 'nyon' in Greek is called 'insula' in Latin.[57]

The claim is justified in a mixture of historical, scientific, geographical, and etymological terms. The celebrated absence of venomous animals from the island is invoked as evidence for kinship with Eden, and the passage suggests that it is only logical that two lands of comparable global marginality should mirror each other in their natural phenomena. The description appears to move rather abruptly from eulogizing description to etymology lesson in the final line; however, more may underlie this than mere authorial clumsiness. This etymology stresses two qualities intrinsic to the notions of exceptionality under discussion here: insularity and westernness. Coming directly after the comparison with Paradise, it is impossible not to read this as indicative of an immensely privileged geographical position. Interpolated matter that accompanies this text quotes Isidore to the effect that Ireland is more fertile than Britain. The quotation from Isidore also underscores the symbolic cachet of western-ness and perhaps even a degree of competitiveness between writers of different nationalities in attempting to situate their own country most firmly within this context. The later version of the *Miniugud* description in Rawlinson B. 512, alluded to above, also supplies Ireland's location in relation to Paradise with a temporal context, noting: 'Just as Adam's Paradise is located at the sunrise, so Ireland is at the Sunset'.[58] The association of the East with the sunrise and so with the beginning of time, and the west with the setting sun and so with its end, is mapped onto the relationship of Eden and Ireland, the former standing at the dawn of history and the latter at its culmination.

---

[57] 'Hybernia insola possita est in occidente; sicut Ade Paradisus in australi plaga orientis poissitus est, ita Hibernia in septimprionali parte, apud occasum sita est. Sic similes sunt natura humi, sicut similes sunt ambo locis in orbe: quoniam sicut absque bestia Paradisus est, ita periti Hiberniam non habere serpentem uel leonum uel ranam uel murem nocentem uel draconem uel scorpium uel unum noxium animal nisi lupum tantum testantur. Hibernia ergo dicitur "insola occasus". "Hyberoc" Grece, "occasum" dicitur Latine; "nia" autem uel "nyon" Grece, "insula" Latine dicitur.' *Lebor Gabála Erenn: The Book of Invasions*, edited and translated by R. A. S. Macalister, 6 vols, ITS, 34, 35, 39, 41, 44 (Dublin: Educational Company of Ireland, 1938–1956), I (1938), p. 164–5.

[58] 'Amal ata Paradas Adaim icon turcbail is amlaid ata Heriu ocun fuiniud.' Quoted from Rawlinson B 512 in *The Tripartite Life of Patrick: With Other Documents Relating to that Saint*, edited and translated by Whitley Stokes, 2 vols, RS, 89 (London: H.M. Stationery Office, 1888), I, p. xxix.

The *translatio imperii* provides a neglected context for *Lebor Gabála*'s vast geographic scope and its sweeping movement from east to west through history and pseudo-history. The text is deeply concerned with establishing Irish exceptionality, and suggests that the island was considered a plausible refuge for those who wished to escape the coming of the biblical Flood. *Lebor Gabála*'s treatment of the antediluvian inhabitants of Ireland provides further evidence of Irish attempts to underline the exceptionality of their island by tapping into the association of insularity with purity. Most recensions agree that the granddaughter of Noah, Cessair, sought out Ireland, which was then uninhabited, when her sinfulness prevented her from taking a place on the Ark. In one account Noah advises her to go 'to the western border of the world, perhaps the Flood will not reach it'.[59] In another recension, Cessair takes counsel from her druids and flees to Ireland since:

> she thought it probable that a place where men had never come till then, where no evil nor sin had been committed, and which was free from the reptiles and monsters of the world, that such a place should be exempt from a Flood. And her wizards, indeed, told her that Ireland was in that case, and that on that account she should come to Ireland.[60]

Although the exceptional purity of Ireland, insofar as it is associated with a lack of human inhabitants, was obviously a thing of the past at the time of *Lebor Gabála*'s compilation, the account also connects this purity to its lack of snakes and monstrous creatures, a quality that still held true. In both versions of the episode, Ireland is treated as sufficiently exceptional, whether on account of its remoteness or on account of its purity, for authority figures like Noah, Cessair, or the druids to consider it likely to avoid the coming Flood. In the event it does not; all but one of Cessair's company are wiped out, the survivor living on by dint of sealing himself in an underground cave until the waters recede. *Lebor Gabála* never makes it explicit whether Ireland's submergence is a function of the sinful Cessair's arrival or whether it would have occurred in any case.

Lebor Gabála's description of Ireland finds an echo in a passage in a Latin *Life of Saint Brigid*, usually attributed to Donatus of Fiesole (d.876). Donatus's lines in praise of his homeland are worth quoting in full:

---

[59] 'co himeall īarthorach in domain, beas gu ria in dīli'. *Lebor Gabála*, edited by Macalister, II (1939), pp. 202–3.

[60] 'ba dōig lese dū na rāncatar dōini rīam cossin, ⁊ nach dērnad olc na himurbus, ⁊ ro sāerad ar bíastaib ⁊ mīchuirthib in domuin, combad sāer in dū sin ar dīlind. Ocus ro indisetar dana a druidhi di Hēriu fon innas sain, ⁊ ara tíset co Hērinn'. *Lebor Gabála*, edited by Macalister, II (1939), pp. 184–7.

> The noblest share of earth is the far western world
> Whose name is written Scottia in the ancient books;
> Rich in goods, in silver, jewels, cloth, and gold,
> Benign to the body, in air and mellow soil.
> With honey and with milk flow Ireland's lovely plains,
> With silk and arms, abundant fruit, with art and men.
> No fury of bears is there, and the Irish land
> Never has nurtured the savage seed of lions;
> There no poison harms, no serpent glides in the grass,
> No frog harshly sings his loud complaint in the lake.
> Worthy are the Irish to dwell in this their land,
> A race of men renowned in war, in peace, in faith.[61]

The description is introduced by stressing Ireland's isolation and western location. The statement that 'with honey and with milk flow Ireland's lovely plains' suggests a comparison with the Promised Land, but the stress on the island's abundance of gems and gold recalls biblical accounts of Paradise. The comparison with Eden is less explicit here than in the *Lebor Gabála*, but phrases like 'the sod is sacred' and the stress on its freedom from serpents and dangerous animals invite the connection. As the text's editor, D. N. Kissane, has observed, these lines owe something to Virgil's praise of Italy in his *Georgics* and there are also apparent echoes of Bede's account of Ireland.[62] The precise relationship of these verses to the similar praise of Ireland in the *Lebor Gabála* is unclear, and their similarities have hitherto gone unnoticed. However, there is no evidence that the text circulated outside of Italy in the Middle Ages. All five of the surviving manuscripts are Italian in origin, so the primary interest of Donatus's work would appear to lie in how far it might reflect contemporary ideas about Ireland rather than in the extent to which it influences them.[63]

---

[61] 'Finibus occiduis describitur optima tellus, / Nomine et antiquis Scottia scripta libris. / Diues opum, argenti, gemmarum, uestis et auri: / Commoda corporibus, aere, putre solo. / Melle fluit pulchris et lacte Scotia campis, / Uestibus atque armis, frugibus, arte, uiris. / Ursorum rabies nulla est ibi, seua leonum / Semina nec umquam Scotica terra tulit. / Nulla uenena nocent nec serpens serpit in erba / Nec conquesta canit garrula rana lacu. / In qua Scottorum gentes habitare merentur, / Inclita gens hominum milite, pace, fide.' 'Uita Metrica Sanctae Brigidae: A Critical Edition', edited by D. N. Kissane, *Proceedings of the Royal Irish Academy*, 77 (1977), 57–87, ll. 125–36. Extract translated in Máire and Liam de Paor, *Early Christian Ireland* (London: Thames and Hudson, 1958), p. 130.

[62] For a full account of the Virgilian allusions in this description, see Kissane's notes to these lines.

[63] For an account of the surviving manuscripts, see 'Uita Metrica', edited by Kissane, 73–5.

ISLANDS OF MAGIC

The perception that the islands of the ocean might constitute an other-world was not limited in its application to the two islands of Britain and Ireland. A neglected Irish poem in praise of Raghnall (or Rǫgnvaldr), King of the Isle of Man, composed sometime between 1187 and 1208, provides one of the most explicit instances of an historical realm being reimagined in terms usually reserved for literary otherworlds.[64] The first eight of its forty-nine quatrains are devoted to praise of the Isle of Man itself:

> A fruitful place is the fairy mound of Eamhain, beautiful the land in which it is found, a fair rath [fort] surpassing every dwelling in which are many bright apple branches.
>
> Eamhain Ablach the freshest, it will take on a summer hue which is the brightest, few forts or hills more fair, in its fresh verdant mantle.[65]

The poem's editor, Brian Ó Cuív, has posited a straightforward iden-tification between the Isle of Man and the *síth Emna* of the poem; however, it seems more likely that a specific location on Man is being referred to here, in all probability Raghnall's own dwelling or, possibly, an inauguration site.[66] Regardless of the precise location on the Isle of Man involved, the term *Emhain Albach* has very definite otherworldly connotations. It is literally 'Emhain of the Apples', suggesting a direct connection with Avalon.[67] *Eamhain* is an ambiguous

---

[64] Edited with a translation and notes by Brian Ó Cuív in 'A Poem in Praise of Raghnall, King of Man', *Éigse*, 8 (1956–1957), 283–301. The late twelfth- or early thirteenth-century dating is Ó Cuív's (p. 283), but the earliest copy of the poem appears in the fifteenth-century Book of Fermoy. For a fuller account of Raghnall's career, see R. Andrew McDonald, *Manx Kingship in its Irish Sea Setting, 1187–1229: King Rǫgnvaldr and the Crovan Dynasty* (Dublin: Four Courts Press, 2007).

[65] 'Baile suthach síth Emhna, / cruthach in chrích a ttarla, / raíth chaem os cinn cech dingna / 'nab imdha craeb fhinn abhla. / Emhain Abhlach is úire, / samdath gebhaidh is gluaire, / terc dún ná cnoc is chaeime / 'na brot naeighi n-úr n-uaine.' 'Raghnall', edited by Ó Cuív, p. 288, st. 1–2.

[66] There are several possibilities, including the inauguration site on Castleward Mound and, more famously, Tynwald Hill, but no clear identification with either of these locations can be made from the internal evidence of the poem itself.

[67] The Welsh *Ynys Afallach* has often been cited as the direct source for Avalon, but the ending *-ach* suggests this term is a borrowing from the Irish. See further, the entry for 'Ellan Vannin (Isle of Man)' in *Celtic Culture: A Historical Encyclopedia*, edited by John T. Koch, 5 vols (Santa Barbara: ABC-CLIO, 2006), ii, 673–89 (p. 677). Ceridwen Lloyd-Morgan argues that the use of the term *Ynys Afallach* to mean Avalon is actually a post-Galfridian development in Welsh. See Ceridwen Lloyd-Morgan, 'From *Ynys Wydrin* to *Glasynbri*: Glastonbury in Welsh Vernacular Tradition', in *Glastonbury Abbey and the Arthurian Tradition*, edited by James P. Carley, Arthurian Studies, 45 (Cambridge: D. S. Brewer, 2001), pp. 161–77.

word.[68] It has been variously identified as describing a place connected with water or a stream and as a 'holy mound' or otherworld hall.[69] The association of apple branches with the otherworld and with kingship is readily made in other Irish texts, notably *Immram Brain*, where the fairy woman's branch is described as coming from Eamhain.[70] It seems quite likely that the praise poem is explicitly evoking the earlier *immram* in which, after all, the deity most frequently associated with the Isle of Man, Manannán mac Lir, makes a notable appearance.[71] By the eighth and ninth stanzas of the work, the poem's addressee, Raghnall, has become completely identified with the image of the apple branch: 'Thou, the son of noble Sadhbh, thou art the most beautiful apple-branch'.[72] Every facet of this 'Eamhain' is idyllic, it is consistently described in terms that emphasize its fertility and freshness, but the description goes further than merely stressing the location's beauty. The description of Eamhain as a 'fairy mound' (*síth*) in the very first line enjoins the audience to imagine this place as not merely naturally, but supernaturally, attractive. Further supernatural associations are developed in the course of the poem. The poet speculates that Raghnall is not merely the son of a human man, but begotten by a 'god from the brink of the Boyne' and in whose hair 'the wind of Paradise has played'.[73] The idea of Eamhain as a *síd* is repeated explicitly in stanzas 4 and 6. Stanzas 15 and 16 develop the otherworld imagery further:

> Many are the doorways of thy land, brighter are they than blue skins, among them, o branch of the haven of Eamhain, are the cave of Fern and the fair cave of Cnoghdha.
>
> If I were to follow the fair cave of Corann I would go without a great ship into this Manainn which I praise so that I should be beside thy land in the north.[74]

---

[68] See further, the discussion of this term in Chapter 1.

[69] Kay Muhr, 'Manx Place-Names: An Ulster View', in *Mannin Revisited: Twelve Essays on Manx Culture and Environment*, edited by Peter Davey and David Finlayson (Edinburgh: Scottish Society for Northern Studies, 2002), pp. 37–52 (p. 41).

[70] 'Cróeb dind abaill a hEmain', *Immram Brain*, edited by Mac Mathúna, p. 33.

[71] For a comprehensive survey of Manannán's role in the Irish tradition, see Charles W. MacQuarrie, *The Biography of the Irish God of the Sea from* The Voyage of Bran *(700AD) to* Finnegans Wake *(1939): The Waves of Manannán* (Lampeter: The Edwin Mellen Press, 2004).

[72] 'Tussa, mac Sadbha saeire, / tusa in tslat abhla as áille', 'Raghnall', edited by Ó Cuív, st. 9.

[73] 'dia do bhrú na Bóinne'; 'do ermais gaeth phuirt Pharrdhais', 'Raghnall', edited by Ó Cuív, st. 9, 42.

[74] 'Doirsi t'fherainn as imdha, / soillsiináit sreabhainn ghorma, / is díb, a chraebh chuain Emna, / uaim Ferna, uaim chaem Cnoghdha. / Do-raghainn-si can raluing / isin Manaind-si molaim, / cu mbeind tuaidh re taeibh t'fheraind / dá leanainn uaim caeim Coraind'. 'Raghnall', edited by Ó Cuív, st. 15–16.

The notion that the Isle might be accessed through caves on the Irish mainland would seem, in the context, to be evoking otherworld locations accessed through caverns. The three caves that are named, Ferns, Cnoghdha (almost certainly the tumulus at Knowth in the Boyne Valley), and Corann, are well known in literary accounts. The caves at Knowth and at Ferns are listed among the 'three dark places in Ireland' in the *Triads of Ireland*.[75] Knowth, in particular, is associated with both the otherworld and with the kingship of Ireland; the poet Tadhg Dall Ó hUiginn refers to a patron as 'a charmed diadem from the fairy mound of Knowth'.[76] The cave of Corann, in modern-day Sligo, also has supernatural associations in literature. For instance, it makes an appearance as an abode of supernatural beings in the *Duanaire Finn*.[77] The poem's depiction of the island would be straightforwardly idyllic in any other account, but the insistence on the location's supernatural status gives several details a distinctly otherworldly colouring. For instance, the fruitfulness, beauty, sweet smells, and greenness of the place are all redolent of the conventions of otherworld description. The use of superlatives in the account, such as the statements that the rath at Eamhain surpasses every other dwelling and that Eamhain is the best hillock on earth, is a further poetic device associated with supernatural realms.[78] The peculiar warmth of the climate, which allows tilling to take place after autumn has passed,[79] reads, in this context, like the suspension of the usual laws of seasonal change associated with otherworld locations.

The background to the poem's composition is obscure. Raghnall was of Viking stock but had marriage connections with Gaelic families in Scotland, Wales, and probably Ireland. He made repeated truces with King John and was a brother-in-law of the Anglo-Norman ruler of Ulster John de Courcy. The poem is almost certainly Irish rather than Manx or Scottish in origin as the poet situates himself firmly in Ireland. The two dominant themes in this praise poem are kingship and the supernatural, and, given the associations otherworld literatures tend to develop between the two, this connection is unlikely to be merely accidental. Although Raghnall's achievements were confined to the consolidation of his position

---

[75] *The Triads of Ireland*, edited by Kuno Meyer (Dublin: Hodges Figgis, 1906), p. 4.

[76] 'a mhionn séanta a Síodh Chnodhbha'; see further, F. J. Byrne, 'Historical Note on Cnogba (Knowth)', *Proceedings of the Royal Irish Academy*, 66 (1967–1968), 383–400, (pp. 382–4).

[77] *Duanaire Finn: The Book of the Lays of Fionn*, edited and translated by Eoin MacNeill and Gerard Murphy, 3 vols, ITS, 7, 28, 43 (London: Simpkin and Marshall, 1908–1953), II (1933), p. 8.

[78] 'Raghnall', edited by Ó Cuív, st. 1, 14.

[79] 'Raghnall', edited by Ó Cuív, st. 5.

on Man and in various other Irish Sea islands, it seems likely that his ambition was considerably greater.[80] Writing in the first decades after the Anglo-Norman invasion of Ireland in 1169, the poet appears to be suggesting that Raghnall may re-establish the link between Dublin and Man.[81] The texts seems highly allusive, drawing on a range of images and concepts from (predominantly earlier) Irish writing. The piece moves from an exposition of the otherworldly qualities of Eamhain in the first nine stanzas to an account of Raghnall's suitability for kingship. As we have seen, linking the otherworld and kingship is entirely conventional, and this poet's shift from supernatural to political considerations is entirely apt when viewed within the literary context. The praise poem casts Raghnall in the role of an Irish king and bolsters that depiction with a wide range of symbolism associated with Gaelic kingship. Although Raghnall is of Viking stock, and his immediate descent from Godred Crovan is alluded to on numerous occasions in the course of the poem, he is described as ultimately being of the thoroughly Gaelic and kingly line of Conn Cédcathach and his grandson Cormac Mac Airt. Indeed, given the confirmatory role otherworld encounters play in narratives about the lives of these two kings, naming them might also further reinforce the theme of the supernatural validation of Raghnall's kingship. Developing the treatment of kingship, the poem, in what must be considered a hyberbolic, but entirely conventional, mode, calls Raghnall 'the king of the world'[82] and suggests that *Emhain Ablach* itself is equivalent to Tara, the site most firmly associated with the sacral kingship of Ireland: 'Eamhain of the fragrant apple-trees is the Tara of Man without deceit'.[83] The poet describes Raghnall as Eamhain's 'lover'[84] and claims that Raghnall's kingship will be confirmed by the *Lia Fáil* (Stone of Destiny)—an oracular stone at Tara, which was believed to cry out under the feet of the rightful king.[85]

The work accomplishes a series of syntheses between Viking lord and Irish king, and between Ireland and the Isle of Man. The many caves on the Irish mainland, which provide entry points to travel to the Island without a ship,[86] not only function as a means of heightening the island's

---

[80] McDonald, *King Rǫgnvaldr*, p. 101 *et passim*.

[81] 'Raghnall', edited by Ó Cuív, st. 19.

[82] 'rí in domnán'. 'Raghnall', edited by Ó Cuív, st. 20.

[83] 'Emain na n-aball cumra / Teamair Mhanann cin mhebhla'. 'Raghnall', edited by Ó Cuív, st. 8.

[84] 'Raghnall', edited by Ó Cuív, st. 14.

[85] 'Raghnall', edited by Ó Cuív, st. 10. Whether the stone was still at Tara by the twelfth century is a matter of some dispute, but its presence or absence at that location does not necessarily undermine its efficacy as a poetic means of confirming Raghnall's authority.

[86] 'can raluing'. 'Raghnall', edited by Ó Cuív, st. 16.

otherworld associations, but may be read as an affirmation of the perceived links between the kingdom of Ireland and that of Man. Thus, while the poet's otherworldly imagery rarefies and distances the Isle of Man, that same imagery is also used to bring it closer to Ireland. The poem exoticizes Man while simultaneously suggesting a natural affinity between the island and Ireland that underscores Raghnall's status and ambition. The poem reimagines the landscape of Ireland and the Isle of Man in supernatural terms that also have an immediate political force. The magical and the desirable are interwoven in this poem, and the rich resources of Irish-language otherworld imagery are exploited to recast the island in terms that are complex and mysterious but, above all else, alluring.

The association of Man and the otherworld seems to arise quite naturally from its geography. The island's appearance and location mark it as a liminal and mysterious zone. It is usually described as precisely midway between Britain and Ireland. Depictions of the Isle of Man in Irish literature appear to be characterized by 'a combination of exotic and mysterious marginality and centrality'.[87] The stress laid on its beauty in the praise poem to Raghnall is not mere poetic fancy; most medieval sources describe the island as both fertile and attractive. A further other-world connection may have come from the fact that the Isle of Man, then as now, was subject to heavy fog. A barrier of mist appears to have been a fairly conventional entry point to the otherworld in literature; for instance, in *Baile an Scáil*, the protagonist finds himself in the fairy otherworld when a thick fog descends on him, and in the *Navigatio Sancti Brendani*, the Earthly Paradise is approachable only through a *caligo grandis*.[88] The island was also the subject of a long-standing territorial conflict. This was not merely a function of its celebrated fertility but, as Gerald of Wales notes in his *Topographia*, stemmed from the strategic importance of its location between Britain and Ireland.[89] The island changed hands throughout the Middle Ages, and Norse influence was particularly strong. It was under the rule of the Scandinavian kings of Dublin and the earls of Orkney before passing into the hands of the Norse Godred Crovan as part of the kingdom of Man and the Isles in the late eleventh century. Throughout this time it maintained close links with Gaelic Ireland and

---

[87] *Celtic Culture*, edited by Koch, entry for 'Ellan Vannin'. Charles W. MacQuarrie gives the fullest analysis of the supernatural associations of the Isle of Man in medieval Irish literature in 'The Isle of Man in Medieval Gaelic Literature', in *A New History of the Isle of Man: Volume 3, The Medieval Period, 1000–1405*, edited by Seán Duffy (Liverpool: Liverpool University Press, forthcoming). I am very grateful to Professor MacQuarrie for sending me a pre-publication copy of this paper.

[88] Sobecki, *Sea*, p. 88.

[89] See, for instance, Gerald, *Topographia*, II: 15, p. 97.

Scotland. Various Irish regional kings sought control of it. In the eleventh century alone, kings of Leinster, Ulster, and Munster attempted to bring it under their sway.[90] The island fell under Norwegian and then sporadic Scottish and English influence, before passing definitively into English hands in the fourteenth century.

The praise poem to Raghnall is not the only instance of the Isle of Man being reimagined as an otherworld realm by an Irish writer with political ends in mind. Other texts provide evidence (albeit fragmentary) that the Isle of Man had some associations with the kingship of Ireland. The Lia Fáil was, according to *Baile an Scáil*, brought to Ireland from *Inis Fáil* (the Island of Destiny):

> 'Fál... indeed', said the poet, 'is the name of the stone and the island of Fál is its place of origin and it was placed in Tara in the Land of Fáil. It [will] remain forever in the Land of Tailtiu'.[91]

Inis Fáil is more usually a poetic term for Ireland, but the context of the passage from the *Baile* suggests an island other than Ireland is at issue. As John Carey has argued, it is possible to trace an Irish literary tradition in which Inis Fáil and the Isle of Man are equated.[92] The Middle Irish tradition generally identifies the Lia Fáil as having its origins with the fairies, the Tuatha Dé Danann, but does not suggest a specific geographical location from which it is taken into Ireland. However, the short Middle Irish text *Forfess Fer Falgae* equates the *firu Faal* (the men of Fál) and the men of Man in its account of a raid on what seems to be an otherworldly fort by legendary heroes.[93] In an echo of other Irish otherworld accounts, like *Immram Brain*, the narrative catalyst is the arrival of a magical bird from the island who bears a beautiful branch to the stronghold of the Ulster heroes. The otherworldly qualities of the island are further suggested by the identification of Gét, the king of Man, as one of the supernatural race of the Fomoiri. Carey speculates that the *Lia Fáil* may have been regarded as booty from such a raid.[94] A textual analogue which might provide some support for this idea is *Aided Chon Roí*, which sees Irish warriors besiege the palace of the king of the Fír Fálgae (not identified as

---

[90] Seán Duffy, 'Emerging from the Mist: Ireland and Man in the Eleventh Century', in *Mannin Revisited*, edited by Davey and Finlayson, pp. 53–6, (p. 54).

[91] John Carey, 'Tara and the Supernatural', in *The Kingship and Landscape of Tara*, edited by Edel Bhreathnach (Dublin: Four Courts Press, 2005), pp. 32–48.

[92] "Fál... ém,' ol an fili 'a hainm na cloche ⁊ Inis Fáil asa torlad ⁊ is i Temraig tíre Fáil fo-ruirmed. Tír Tailten hi tairiss hí co bráth'. *Baile*, edited and translated by Murray, pp. 33, 50. See also, Carey, 'Tara', p. 32 *et passim*.

[93] 'Forfess Fer Fálgae (Aus Egerton 1782 fol. 19a)', edited by Kuno Meyer, *Zeitschrift für Celtische Philologie*, 8 (1912), 564–5 (p. 564).

[94] Carey, 'Tara', p. 38.

Man in this instance) in order to bring his treasures back to Ireland. As we have seen, the removal of an item of supernatural power from the otherworld to this one is a recurrent motif in literary accounts. The item is most often a means of authenticating the otherworld journey, but it can also elucidate problems such as the course of the future. Such items often have an element of prestige, and a stone of supernatural power imported into Ireland from the Manx otherworld could be seen as bringing with it a sort of political legitimization that mirrors the confirmatory function otherworld beings often perform in narratives of kingship and political rule.[95]

Irish literature was not alone among insular literatures in reimagining the territories of its neighbours in terms of the otherworldly. The Welsh *Preideu Annwfyn* (The Spoils of Annwfyn) recounts an attack by Arthur on the otherworld land of Annwfyn which results in the seizure and importation of a magical cauldron to Wales. 'Annwfyn' is a difficult location to pin down. In *Preideu Annwfyn*, it appears to be underwater.[96] Reconstructing a coherent narrative from this enigmatic poem is similarly difficult, but this much is generally agreed upon: Arthur and three shiploads of men sail to Annwfyn and, en route, or on arrival, they encounter resistance at a glass fort, they capture a cauldron and the Brindled Ox, and return home with only seven survivors. Both *Branwen ferch Llŷr* (Branwen Daughter of Lyr) and *Culhwch ac Olwen* (Culhwch and Olwen) describe similar overseas expeditions, led by Bran in the former text and by Arthur in the latter. In *Branwen*, the objective is the rescue of Branwen, and the Britons are hampered by the Irish use of a magical cauldron of rebirth, which one of Bran's retinue finally destroys.[97] In *Culhwch*, the cauldron is the sole object of Arthur's quest and is successfully seized and taken back to Britain.[98] In both texts a fight in a

---

[95] The fact that the term Inis Fáil is more widely used as a toponym for Ireland itself raises the possibility that the Isle of Man might also be used as a figure for Ireland in these texts. In her recent treatment of English national identity, Catherine A. M. Clarke has suggested that certain inland islands in Britain were used as metonyms for the island as a whole (Clarke, *Literary Landscapes*, p. 67 *et passim*). It may be possible to discern a similar connection between Man and Ireland in Irish literature. The only other island known as Inis Fáil is Beggery in Wexford Harbour. Perhaps significantly, the name 'Beggery' derives from the Irish *Becc Ériu*, which means 'Little Ireland' (Carey, 'Tara', p. 38n).

[96] *Preideu Annwfyn*, edited by Haycock, p. 440.

[97] *Branwen Uerch Lyr, the Second of the Four Branches of the Mabinogi*, edited by Derek S. Thomson (Dublin: Dublin Institute of Advanced Studies, 1961). Translated as *The Second Branch*, in *The Mabinogion*, translated by Sioned Davies (Oxford: Oxford University Press, 2007), pp. 22–34.

[98] *Culhwch ac Olwen: Testun Syr Idris Foster*, edited by Rachel Bromwich and D. Simon Evans (Cardiff: University of Wales Press, 1988). For a translation, see *How Culhwch Won Olwen*, in *The Mabinogion*, translated by Sioned Davies (Oxford: Oxford University Press, 2007), pp. 179–213.

hall results in the death of the Britons' enemies and in the return of seven survivors to Wales. Significantly, in both these later versions of what appears to be the same story, Annwfyn is replaced by Ireland.[99] The textual evolution of this group of related tales is obscure. Sims-Williams concludes: 'While it is likely enough that the four versions of the story influenced each other, it is more convincing to think of them as reworkings of a common story-pattern for different purposes than as text to be related by a stemma.'[100] Whatever the root of the differing uses of Annwfyn and Ireland in these texts, they appear to suggest a close association between Ireland and the otherworld in this strand of the Welsh tradition. The cauldron of *Culhwch ac Olwen* is the property of an Irishman, Diwrnach, who is identified as a giant elsewhere in the corpus.[101]

The presence of a cauldron of rebirth in Ireland in *Pedeir Keinc y Mabinogi* (The Four Branches of the Mabinogi) may be a further allusion to the traditional association of Ireland with healing. This association is developed in Geoffrey of Monmouth's *Historia*. The removal of the Giant's Ring (Stonehenge) from Ireland to Britain can also be located within this tradition of the importation of a marvellous authority-conferring object from a supernatural, or, at least, an exoticized, realm. Geoffrey recounts a journey from Britain to Ireland in search of a supernatural object (or, in this case, series of objects) and the defeat of those Irish who resist. Merlin describes the stones' provenance and properties thus:

> The stones are magic and can effect various cures. They were brought long ago from the farthest shores of Africa by giants, who erected them in Ireland while they lived there. Their purpose was to set up baths among them whenever they were ill. They used to wash the stones and pour the water into the baths to cure illnesses.[102]

[99] Prionsias MacCana, *Branwen Daughter of Llŷr: A Study of the Irish Affinities and of the Composition of the Second Branch of the Mabinogi* (Cardiff: University of Wales Press, 1958), p. 147.

[100] Patrick Sims-Williams, 'The Early Welsh Arthurian Poems', in *The Arthur of the Welsh: The Arthurian Legend in Medieval Welsh Literature*, edited by R. Bromwich and others (Cardiff: University of Wales Press, 1991), pp. 33–71 (p. 56).

[101] He is described as such in the account of the Thirteen Treasures of the Island of Britain: *Trioedd Ynys Prydein: The Triads of the Island of Britain*, edited and translated by Rachel Bromwich (Cardiff: University of Wales Press, 1961; rev. 2006), pp. 259–60.

[102] 'Mistici sunt lapides et ad diuersa medicamenta salubres. Gigantes olim asportauerunt eos ex ultimis finibus Affricae et posuerunt in Hibernia dum eam inhabitarent. Erat autem causa ut balnea infra ipsos conficerent cum infirmitate grauarentur. Lauabant namque lapides et infra balnea diffundebant, unde aegroti curabantur.' Geoffrey, *History of the Kings*, pp. 172–3.

Although the giants have long since departed the scene, Geoffrey's text appears to suggest a supernatural association for Ireland. The healing properties of the stones recall the health-giving properties widely associated with Ireland's air, plants, and soil in Isidore, and developed by Bede and various later writers.[103] Indeed, Geoffrey himself makes reference to the concept in the *Vita Merlini*: 'If some earth or a stone is taken from there [Ireland] and added to the soil of any other place it drives away snakes and bees.'[104] As noted above, the westward position of Ireland may have partly inspired such associations, or, at the very least, rendered them more plausible. In a more literary mode, a similar association of healing with the west may lie behind the recuperation of Tristan in Ireland in *Tristan and Isolde* and, indeed, the removal of the wounded Arthur westwards to the island of Avalon. Obviously, a magical stone circle does not an otherworld make, but it would appear that the supernatural properties of the Giant's Ring are closely tied to its Irish origins and invoke a well-established discourse that linked the island with healing. The fact that the stones are won from the ruler of another territory further underscores their status as authority-conferring objects, irrespective of their supernatural origins. Introduced as objects for healing, the stones are intimately linked to leadership and kingship in the remainder of the work. Their installation at Salisbury coincides with a festival where lands are divided up and where Aurelius's status as king is celebrated. Later, several kings, including Aurelius himself, are buried inside the ring. Although the shift in emphasis from the supernatural healing properties of the stones to their association with kingship in the *Historia* may seem abrupt, when viewed in the context of traditional beliefs about kingship and healing powers, the thematic shift is more apparent than real.

MONSTROUS PERIPHERIES

One recurrent theme in these accounts is the frequency with which the supernatural is associated with territories that are politically contested. Such territories are, perhaps, liable to be more demanding of analysis than their stable counterparts and, as such, the subject of a greater number of explorations of every kind. The aptness of the otherworld account as a frame through which to view such regions derives largely from the fact that it provides such a highly malleable and imaginatively potent model for

---

[103] William of Malmesbury, *Gesta Regum Anglorum*, p. 11.
[104] 'Unde fit ut tellus illinc avecta lapisve /, si superaddatur, serpentes tollat apesque'. Geoffrey, *Life of Merlin*, ll. 891–2.

imagining space, and, crucially, lends itself particularly well to the exploration of political authority. Reimagining actual-world territories in terms usually reserved for Paradise would seem a relatively straightforward and natural use of otherworld motifs. However, since such realms may only mirror, but not be identified with, Paradise, accounts of them are always qualified and liable to fall back on more ambiguous forms of supernatural associations than the straightforwardly Edenic. The potentially disruptive effect of this ambiguity is something writers take pains to guard against; the author of Raghnall's praise poem, for instance, dwells only on the less threatening qualities of the *sídhe* in his accounts of an otherworldly Isle of Man. However, in some instances, the ambiguity of otherworld spaces was exploited by writers who recognized the ease with which the wondrous and novel qualities of the supernatural could also be read as threatening. If the resources of otherworld paradisal imagery could be employed in the service of national self-mythologizing, then the imagery associated with monstrous otherworlds could also be used to denigrate national enemies. Indeed, sometimes both savage and idyllic otherworlds could be evoked with reference to the same territory. For instance, long before the medieval period, writers developed an association between the Irish periphery and monstrosity. Diodorus Siculus, Strabo, and Jerome all claim that the Irish practice cannibalism, while Pomponius Mela and Solinus assert that they are a particularly savage people.[105]

Solinus's description is rather more complex than that of the others; on the one hand, he stresses the savagery of the people, but, on the other, he testifies to the natural fruitfulness and attractiveness of Ireland itself. Something similar happens in Gerald of Wales' *Topographia Hibernica,* where the author holds beauty and barbarity, desire and revulsion in a delicate balance. Here the landscape of Ireland is figured as both idyllic and fantastical, and its marvellous nature is also spoken of in terms that fuel desire. Yet, while the land itself is desirable and beautiful, the people who inhabit it are uncivilized. In many respects, Gerald has his cake and eats it too. The same peripherality that renders the island so abounding in natural marvels renders its people barbarous:

> But habits are formed by mutual intercourse; and as this people inhabit a country so remote from the rest of the world, and lying at its furthest extremity, forming as it were another world, and are thus secluded from civilized nations, they learn nothing, and practise nothing but the barbarism

---

[105] These accounts are summarized and analysed in James F. Kenney, *The Sources for the Early History of Ireland: Ecclesiastical* (New York: Columbia University Press, 1929), pp. 127–34.

in which they are born and bred, and which sticks to them like a second nature.[106]

While writers like Bede and Donatus stress how the beauty of Ireland is mirrored in the holiness of its people, much of the *Topographia* is concerned with driving a wedge between the inhabitants of the island and the land itself. Gerald gives numerous accounts of Irish sexual immorality, including an account of an Irish lord copulating with a mare as part of his coronation ceremony, suggesting to his audience that bestiality was sanctioned at the very highest level of society, as part of the king-making process itself.[107] The natural wonders of Ireland are given a hideous mirror in human disfigurement. Gerald notes:

> Moreover, I have never seen in any other nation so many individuals who were born blind, so many lame, maimed, or having some natural defect.... No wonder if among an adulterous and incestuous people, in which both births and marriages are illegitimate, a nation out of the pale of the laws, nature itself should be foully corrupted by perverse habits.[108]

The rhetorical emphasis on 'nature' echoes that which Gerald employs to account for Irish marvels, and the contrast that results is striking. Set within a land Gerald describes as naturally fertile and productive,[109] the lapsarian connotations are unavoidable—this is the flip side of dwelling in 'another Eden'.

A similar impulse may be discerned in the Middle English poem *Of Arthour and of Merlin* (henceforth *Arthour*), which relates an invasion of England by an army of gigantic Irish pagans.[110] The textual history of *Arthour* is complex. It is evidently translated from a version of the French *Estoire de Merlin*, though it is unclear whether the alterations between the

---

[106] 'Sed cum a convictu mores formentur, quoniam a communi terrarum orbe in his extremitatibus, tanquam in orbe quodam altero, sunt tam remoti, et a modestis et morigeratis populis tam segregati, solam nimirum barbariem in qua et nati sunt et nutriti sapiunt et assuescunt, et tanquam alteram naturam amplectuntur'. Gerald, *Topographia*, III: 10, p. 153; translated by Forester, pp. 125–6.

[107] Gerald, *Topographia*, III: 25, p. 169; translated by Forester, p. 138.

[108] 'Ad haec autem tot caecos natos, tot claudos, tot corpore vitiatos, et naturae beneficio destitutos, in alia non vidimus natione... Nec mirandum si de gente adultera, gente incesta, gente illegitime nata et copulata, gente exlege, arte invida et invisa ipsam turpiter adulterante naturam, tales interdum contra naturae legem natura producat.' Gerald, *Topographia*, III: 35, p. 181; translated by Forester, p. 147.

[109] Gerald, *Topographia*, I: 5, p. 26; translated by Forester, p. 20.

[110] *Of Arthour and of Merlin*, edited by O. D. Macrae-Gibson, 2 vols, EETS, o.s., 268, 279 (London: Oxford University Press, 1973–1979). See further my article, 'West Is East: The Irish Saracens in *Of Arthour and of Merlin*', *Nottingham Medieval Studies*, 55 (2011), 217–32.

English and surviving French texts are primarily the translator's own design or are carried over from a variant version of the *Estoire*, now lost to us. *Arthour* is much occupied with detailed descriptions of battles against Arthur's enemies during an attempted invasion of England. The most significant of these invading groups are the Saxons, the Danes, and the Irish. Both *Arthour* and the *Estoire* describe the invaders as giants, although the English poem does so more persistently and gives fuller descriptions of their great size. *Arthour* tends to underscore the invaders' barbarity while, by contrast, the *Estoire* not infrequently stresses their nobility and knightly qualities.[111] For instance, the French text has the following to say about the reaction of the men fighting for the Irish king Rion when Arthur's troops charge against them: 'they were so worthy and knightly that they were not disheartened for all that. Rather, they kept fighting wondrously hard against King Arthur's men'.[112] Furthermore, the Rion of the *Estoire* is described in distinctly flattering terms: 'Rion who was a most worthy and bold and good knight above all others in his land'.[113] There are no parallels to this praise in *Arthour*.

The most significant departure in the English text's account of the Irish is its clear and consistent portrayal of them as non-Christians. There is no suggestion in the French text that the Irish are heathen or even unduly wicked, yet the Irish of the Middle English poem are consistently depicted as gigantic, 'heþen', and pagan. When the poet introduces four of the invading kings from 'Yrlond', he immediately notes that they are 'heþen kings'.[114] In the corresponding section, the French *Estoire* merely introduces these four as kings 'de la terre as irois' (of the land of the Irish) without any further statement about their Christianity, or lack of it.[115] Their actions in *Arthour* are also far more ruthless than those depicted in the source text. Where the French text describes how they pillaged the countryside for food supplies, the English gives details of the murder of innocent men, women, and children:

---

[111] *Lestoire de Merlin*, in *The Vulgate Version of the Arthurian Romances*, edited by H. Oskar Sommer, 7 vols (Washington, DC: Carnegie Institution, 1908–1913), II (1908), 293, 396–8.

[112] 'il furent si preus & si cheualereus que onques por ce ne se descomforterent anchois tindrent le caple grant & meruilleus encontre la gent le roy artu'. *Lestoire de Merlin*, edited by Sommer, p. 415. Translated by Rupert T. Pickens as *The Story of Merlin*, in *Lancelot-Grail: The Old French Arthurian Vulgate in Translation*, edited by Norris J. Lacy, 5 vols (New York: Garland, 1993), I, 415.

[113] 'rions qui moult estoit preus & hardis & boins cheualiers deseur tous cels de sa terre'. *Lestoire de Merlin*, edited by Sommer, I, 418; *Story of Merlin*, translated by Pickens, p. 398.

[114] *Arthour*, I, ll. 4842–63. All quotations from *Arthour* are taken from Macrae-Gibson's edition of the version in the Auchinleck manuscript.

[115] *Lestoire de Merlin*, edited by Sommer, p. 135.

And [they] were so wroþ þat king Arthour
Hadde ywarnist toun and tour
Þat þe cuntre aboute Lounde
Slowen and brent to þe grounde
Men seiȝe þe fer fer away   [fire
Þennes ouer a iurnay,   [day
Man and wiif and children bo
No hadde þai no pite to slo   [slay
Þe folk schirsten so heiȝe and loude
Þat it schilled into þe cloude.[116]

Alongside the references to them as 'hethen', the word 'sarraȝin' is also used of these invaders; for instance, the term is employed when the Irish invaders are confronted by one of Arthur's knights:

What Sarraȝin so he mett
Wel soriliche he hem grett
Þat wom euer þat he hitt
Þe heued to þe chinne he slitt...[117]   [head

The point is driven home by further details not found in the *Estoire* which tend to associate these invaders with the Islamic world. King Rion's standard is borne by four elephants[118] and *Arthour*'s Irish invaders have a tendency to swear by 'Mahoun'.[119]

On one level, these deviations from the French text may be motivated merely by a desire to make all the enemies of Arthur more malign and his achievement in repelling them more glorious as a result. From this perspective, the Irish would fit rather unremarkably into an overall scheme of adaptation that also paints the Danes and Saxons in darker hues than in the French text. However, considered from a broader cultural perspective, the text's description of the Irish, in particular, stands out rather noticeably. There are numerous examples in medieval romance of peoples from outside the Islamic world being depicted as pagan 'Saracens'. The Vikings, for instance, are not infrequently depicted as gigantic pagans, and the word 'Saracen' is used of them in several romances, most notably in *King Horn*. The *Middle English Dictionary*'s entry for 'Sarasin' gives 'one of the pagan invaders of England, especially a Dane or Saxon' as one of the possible meanings for the term. *Arthour*'s Danish and Saxon invaders fit this definition neatly, but the conferral of such characteristics on the Irish (unacknowledged in the *MED*) would appear to be unique. Not only is

[116] *Arthour*, edited by Macrae-Gibson, ll. 4865–74.
[117] *Arthour*, edited by Macrae-Gibson, ll. 4809–12.
[118] *Arthour*, edited by Macrae-Gibson, ll. 9304–5.
[119] *Arthour*, edited by Macrae-Gibson, ll. 4870–3.

Arthour the only English text in which an historically Christian people are
glossed as 'Saracens', but it is the only instance of a people dwelling west
of England being described in such terms. A final layer of potential
significance for *Arthour*'s treatment of the Irish comes from the fact
that they are the only one of these three enemy peoples whose relationship with England was still a live issue at the time of the poem's putative
date of composition around 1300. As such, it seems unlikely that a
translator would have produced such a strikingly peculiar portrait of the
Irish carelessly or unthinkingly.

In depicting the Irish as gigantic pagans and associating them with the
Islamic world, the *Arthour* poet was not working in an imaginative or
ideological vacuum. This portrayal seems to owe a lot to a set of ideas
about the otherness of the Irish that were circulating in medieval England.[120] Depicting the Irish as heathen may reflect the extensive Viking
settlements on Ireland's eastern seaboard. The Vikings were stereotypic-
ally pagan and could be described as giants or as Saracens in romance.[121] If
Arthour's account of an Irish invasion of England alludes to any historical
events, Viking raids from Ireland are a good fit.[122] The Irish seem to have
been presented as heathen enemies comparable with and often allied with
Saracens from an early point in the *chanson de geste* tradition.[123] For
instance, the Irish are styled as pagan enemies of the French and are
more or less indistinguishable from the Saracens in *Gormont et Isembart*
(early twelfth century) and in several other *chansons de geste*.[124] The
Arthour poet may be drawing on this wider French tradition. Alternatively,
the French *Estoire* itself may even have provided the cue for this, since it
links the Irish armies with the Danes, describing King Mahaglant as 'the
wealthy king of Ireland who was first cousin to the king of Denmark' and

---

[120] This is the position taken by Siobhain Bly Calkin, who observes that the author of
Arthour 'conflates the Saxon invasions of the fifth and sixth centuries with the Viking raids
and settlements of the ninth and tenth centuries'. *Saracens and the Making of English
Identity: The Auchinleck Manuscript* (New York: Routledge, 2005), p. 181.

[121] The propensity of romance authors to depict the Norse as gigantic pagans is
discussed by Diane Speed in 'The Saracens of *King Horn*', *Speculum*, 65 (1990), 564–95.
The Anglo-Norman *Romance of Horn* gives its Danish Saracens African origins. See also,
Ivana Djordjević, 'Saracens and Other Saxons: Using, Misusing, and Confusing Names in
Gui de Warewic and *Guy of Warwick*', in *The Exploitations of Medieval Romance*, edited by
Laura Ashe, Ivana Djordjević, and Judith Weiss (Cambridge: D. S. Brewer, 2010),
pp. 28–42, (p. 34).

[122] Raids by Pictish and Irish pirates are attested in early sources, but are too far removed
in the distant past to have had any impact on the composition and reception of *Arthour*; see
T. M. Charles-Edwards, *Early Christian Ireland* (Cambridge: Cambridge University Press,
2000), pp. 158–63.

[123] P. Rickard, *Britain in Medieval French Literature, 1100–1500* (Cambridge: Cambridge
University Press, 1956), pp. 58–70.

[124] Rickard, *Britain in Medieval French Literature*, pp. 60–1, 68–9.

King Bramangue as lord of part of Denmark and Ireland.[125] The Hiberno-Norse are also deeply integrated into the English romance tradition. The conflict with Colbrond in *Gui* is likely to be a displaced version of Æthelstan's victory over Olaf, the Norse King of Dublin, at Brunanburh in 937 (though Olaf's Irish connections are never mentioned in the romance).[126] This same Olaf is almost certainly the prototype for Havelok the Dane, since his distinctive Gaelic sobriquet *Cuarán* appears in the Anglo-Norman *Lai d'Haveloc*.[127]

Depicting the Irish as gigantic heathens also provides a rationale, indeed an imperative, for conquest. To an audience familiar with the British foundation myth, the presence of giants in a territory could have had a very clear symbolic resonance.[128] Considering the territorial claims of England on Ireland, it is possible to read the association of the island with giants in *Arthour* as part of an *apologia* for conquest. To suggest Ireland is inhabited by giants implies that it is still awaiting its definitive settlement, much like Britain before Brutus's arrival. It is, in a sense, ripe for conquest: the colonization process is figured as a necessary and inevitable part of history that is justified by the example of earlier ages. The proposed date of *Arthour* places it about 130 years after the Anglo-Norman incursion into Ireland, but the process of conquest was slow and in 1300 it was still very much a work in progress. As both Rhiannon Purdie and Siobhain Bly Calkin demonstrate, the Arthur of this text is as much English as he is British, an identification that maps the legendary past more explicitly onto the medieval present.[129]

Gerald of Wales also associates Ireland with a lack of Christianity. In the *Topographia Hibernica*, he insists that many people in the island are not baptized and have no knowledge of Christianity. As evidence, he recounts an anecdote about wildmen dwelling in the most western parts of Ireland who had not heard of Christ. Gerald does not associate these pockets of pagan belief with the presence of Norsemen in Ireland; rather, he finds the story credible because of Ireland's geographical marginality.[130] Throughout his text, Gerald rationalizes his depiction of the Irish as barbarous by reference to the island's peripheral location, its status as an *alter orbis*. The

---

[125] *Story of Merlin*, translated by Pickens, p. 262.
[126] Djordjević, 'Saracens and Other Saxons', p. 33. See further, Robert Allen Rouse, *The Idea of Anglo-Saxon England in Middle English Romance* (Cambridge: D. S. Brewer, 2005), pp. 56–9.
[127] *Le Lai d'Haveloc and Gaimar's Haveloc Episode*, edited by Alexander Bell (Manchester: University of Manchester Press, 1925), l. 258.
[128] Geoffrey, *History of the Kings*, pp. 26–9.
[129] Rhiannon Purdie, *Anglicising Romance: Tail-Rhyme and Genre in Medieval English Literature* (Woodbridge: D. S. Brewer, 2008), p. 97; Calkin, *Saracens and English Identity*, pp. 174–205.
[130] Gerald, *Topographia*, III: 26, pp. 170–1; translated by Forester, pp. 139–40.

idea that Christianity had not yet penetrated the western fringes of the country follows quite naturally and believably from this emphasis.

Ireland's location at the westernmost limit of the world provides a stimulus to Gerald's fertile imagination throughout the *Topographia*. Although Gerald's intense involvement with the Third Crusade has long been acknowledged as a formative element in his life and work, an often neglected facet of his Irish writings is how frequently he brings rhetoric associated with the Crusades to bear on his descriptions of Ireland. His writing repeatedly links the Irish West with the eastern parts of the world: both are peripheral regions abounding in marvels and rendered barbaric by their isolation. Indeed, the literary model for much of *Topographia* is the genre of the 'wonders of the east' and Gerald is not shy about pointing it out:

> As then the prodigies of the Eastern regions have already been brought to the light of public attention through the labours of industrious authors, so those of the West, which have hitherto been almost hidden and unknown, may at length, in these latter days, find an editor through my labours.[131]

As Michelle P. Brown has noted in discussing the illustrations of Irish 'wonders' that accompany the *Topographia* in four extant manuscripts, the idea of the wonders of the east had been used quite widely to further interest in that region as a means of encouraging crusades. She characterizes Gerald's appropriation of the genre in his Irish work as a means of 'capturing publicity for agenda and author alike' by adopting and extending 'a genre which had already helped to direct the attention of European society eastwards'.[132] Gerald had devoted a lot of energy to encouraging Henry II to take a more proactive approach to the Crusades in the East. Throughout Gerald's Irish works, the Angevin interest in the country is depicted not only as a force for civilization, but for true Christianization.

---

[131] 'Ut sicut orientalium regionum prodigia, diligenti auctorum opera, in publicae notitiae lucem dudum prodiere, sic et occidentalia, hactenus quidem abdita fere et incognita, nostro tandem labore his vel occiduis temporibus inveniant editorem.' Gerald, *Topographia*, II: Praef., p. 74; translated by Forester, p. 57.

[132] Michelle P. Brown, 'Marvels of the West: Giraldus Cambrensis and the Role of the Author in the Development of Marginal Illustration', in *Decoration and Illustration in Medieval English Manuscripts*, edited by A. S. G. Edwards, English Manuscript Studies, 10 (London: British Library, 2002), pp. 34–59 (pp. 55–6). See also, Asa Simon Mittman, 'The Other Close at Hand: Gerald of Wales and the Marvels of the West', in *The Monstrous Middle Ages*, edited by Bettina Bildhauer and Robert Mills (Toronto: University of Toronto Press, 2003), pp. 97–112. On the wonders of the east in general, see Rudolf Wittkower, 'Marvels of the East: A Study in the History of Monsters', *Journal of the Warburg and Courtauld Institutes*, 5 (1942), 159–97, and Campbell, *Witness and the Other World*, pp. 47–86. Reed Kline discusses cartographical treatments of the wonders of the east in *Maps of Medieval Thought*, pp. 141–64.

The comparisons Gerald draws between the Occident and the Orient pertain to more than just the marvels of nature and, although he never directly describes the Irish as entirely pagan or explicitly likens them to Saracens, the notion that they might be the western mirrors of these eastern heathens is clearly implied. The step from there to the concept of the 'Irish Saracen' is not a large one.

There is no evidence that Gerald's work directly influenced the *Arthour* author (though such a situation is by no means impossible); however, the tendency of both to imagine the Irish in terms usually reserved for non-Christians in the East or elsewhere appears to reflect similar preoccupations and similar motivations. Since Said, we have grown accustomed to thinking about European depictions of the East as a manifestation of Orientalism[133] and, although postcolonial thinking has been a key ingredient in much recent scholarship on Ireland, the presence of what might be interpreted as an analogous 'Occidentalism' in European treatments of Ireland in the Middle Ages merits further comment. Such an impulse is clearly visible in the *Topographia*'s developed discourse of western peripherality and marvels, and it may provide a rationale for the intriguing series of translations and adaptations that the author of *Arthour* appears to have made. Of course, as many critics of Said have argued, 'Orientalism' is not a monolithic and simple discourse, and medieval 'Occidentalism' appears to have been no different.[134] The wondrous and exceptional nature of the extreme West was also, as discussed above, exploited by Irish writers working in a more celebratory vein. Yet, taken on its own terms, the Middle English translator's choice to depict the Irish as Saracens appears to be an act of linguistic translation that broadens into a politically charged cultural translation where East becomes West and Christians become pagan. The text reflects the narrow line otherworld descriptions often tread between the beautiful and the sinister, and how easily the marvels and wonders that characterize such realms can be interpreted as emblematic of a region's strangeness and, by extension, its threat.

The motif of the monstrous pagan enemy is by no means limited to English texts. Widespread beliefs that remote lands could be the birthing place of natural marvels and deformity were taken to a fantastical extreme in Irish depictions of the Viking territories.[135] Numerous names exist for

[133] Edward Said, *Orientalism: Western Conceptions of the Orient* (London: Penguin, 1978; repr. 1995).

[134] For a recent summary of such criticism, see Daniel Martin Varisco, *Reading Orientalism: Said and the Unsaid* (Seattle, WA: University of Washington Press, 2007), pp. 11–27.

[135] Irish literary treatments of the Viking lands have been given consideration by Prionsias MacCana, 'The Influence of the Vikings on Gaelic Literature', in *Proceedings of the International Congress of Celtic Studies, Dublin, 6–10 July 1959*, edited by Brian Ó Cuív

these lands in Gaelic historical writing and many chroniclers display an extensive knowledge of the various cultural and political situations of these lands. In literary texts, narrowly defined, however, there is no such nuance and these realms are gathered together under the single heading of 'Lochlann'—a term also employed, with considerably greater specificity, in historical writing.[136] Lochlann, in literature, is a sketchily drawn hilly, barren country situated variously in the extreme north or the north-east. It has been suggested that the term originally encompassed part of Scotland and the Northern and Western Isles. Later texts suggest an identification with Norway, and the word is used with reference to this country in Modern Irish. Máire Ní Mhaonaigh has suggested that the very inclusiveness of the term and the 'ensuing elusiveness of Lochlann in the literary landscape... facilitated its gradual acquisition of supernatural associations'.[137]

The inhabitants of Lochlann are sometimes associated with the super-natural Tuatha Dé Danann (People of the Goddess Danu) since they traditionally spent time in the icy north, studying magic. However, the Lochlannaigh were more frequently identified with the Fomoiri, a gigantic and barbarous people of Irish legend.[138] The earliest notable employment of the term in this connection is in the *Síaburcharpat Conculaind* (The Phantom-Chariot of Cúchulainn), where the hero travels north to *aile-thuath* (the 'other land', possibly Scotland), then to Lochlann, and then to the hellish Tír Scaith (the land of shadows). Lochlann is depicted as a remote land where Cúchulainn battles with and defeats a giant, thirty cubits high, and his 350-strong retinue before imposing a tribute.[139] The structure of the text places Lochlann, geographically and ontologically, somewhere between this world and Hell.[140] Prionsias MacCana points to an incident in *Acallam na Senórach* (Colloquy of the Ancients) where Caoilte, the Tuatha Dé Danann, and the fairies of Assaroe beat off an attack by Lochlannaigh, suggesting that it is a 'very obvious com-pound of the semi-realistic Viking attack with the traditional conflict

---

(Dublin: Dublin Institute for Advanced Studies, 1962), pp. 78–118; Máire Ní Mhaonaigh, 'Literary Lochlann', in *Cànan & Cultar/Language and Culture*, edited by Wilson McLeod, James E. Fraser, and Anja Gunderloch, Rannsachadh na Gàidhlig, 3 (Edinburgh: Dunedin Academic Press, 2006), pp. 25–37; Reidar Th. Christiansen, *The Vikings and the Viking Wars in Irish and Gaelic Tradition* (Oslo: Jacob Dybwad, 1931).

[136] For a discussion of the names given to the Vikings in Gaelic historiography and literature, see MacCana, 'Influence of the Vikings', p. 84.

[137] Ní Mhaonaigh, 'Literary Lochlann', p. 34.

[138] MacCana, 'Influence of the Vikings', p. 94.

[139] MacCana, 'Influence of the Vikings', p. 81.

[140] Ní Mhaonaigh, 'Literary Lochlann', p. 30.

between the peoples of the otherworld'.[141] Although the uses of Lochlann in such texts are various, a primary purpose appears to have been political. The decisive victory over the Norsemen in the early eleventh century was mapped back into Ireland's legendary history. As Ní Mhaonaigh notes, by making the enemy both gigantic and monstrous, the glory of the victory was cemented and amplified.[142] This reimagining of the Vikings in otherwordly terms is at its most pronounced and explicit in Irish literature, but it appears not to be unique. Such an association is discernable in the depiction of the Isle of Man in the later romance, *The Turke and Sir Gawain*. *The Turke and Sir Gawain* suggests that otherworldly depictions of Man were not solely the preserve of Gaelic poets, although the emphasis falls on the barbarous rather than on the idyllic in what survives of this romance.

The language of *The Turke and Sir Gawain* suggests that it dates from around 1500 and originates in the north or north midlands of England.[143] The poem occurs in that portion of the Percy Folio where the top halves of the pages were used as fire kindling, so it is now impossible to build a full picture of the manner in which the Isle of Man and its inhabitants were depicted.[144] What remains of the description of Man is the final lines of the account of Gawain and the Turk arriving on the island:

> [The Turk] lett him see a castle faire;
> Such a one he never saw yare,   [before
> Noewher in noe country.
> The Turke said to Sir Gawaine
> "Yonder dwells the King of Man,
> A heathen soldan is hee.   [sultan
> "With him he hath a hideous rout
> Of giants strong and stout
> And uglie to looke upon.
> Whosoever had sought farr and neere
> As wide as the world were,
> Such a companye he cold find none."[145]

The land is cast in terms of extremes of beauty and barbarity. The emphasis on absolutes in the description is characteristic of otherworld accounts: its castle is more fair than any Gawain has ever seen and its

[141] MacCana, 'Influence of the Vikings', p. 86.

[142] Ní Mhaonaigh, 'Literary Lochlann', p. 36.

[143] *The Turke and Sir Gawain*, in *Sir Gawain: Eleven Romances and Tales*, edited by Thomas Hahn (Kalamazoo, MI: Medieval Institute Publications, 1995), pp. 340–58.

[144] In his edition, Thomas Hahn offers 'prose summaries, inevitably somewhat speculative of the sections that are lost' (*Turke*, edited by Hahn, p. 337).

[145] *Turke*, edited by Hahn, ll. 128–36.

inhabitants are more 'hideous' than any that could be found in the whole world. These polarities in the *Turke*'s depiction of Man figure the island's conquest as a proposition that is both attractive and morally necessary: the land itself is a worthy prize, while its incumbent rulers are, patently, not worthy of it. The description of the King of Man as a 'heathen soldan' may be merely a generic description of a cruel and unsympathetic antagonist, but it is not impossible that Man's strong Norse connections are being evoked. Although Scandinavian dominance of the island ended in 1265, William le Scrope, the last ruler of Man to claim descent from the Norse-Gaelic house of Godred Crovan, only relinquished his hold on the island in 1399. The late date of this poem does not preclude such an interpretation, since depictions of Danes as enemies and as invaders in popular culture survive into the Elizabethan era, as the continuing popularity of *Guy of Warwick* testifies. As in *Of Arthour and of Merlin*, the presence of giants in a territory may also be associated with the imperative to conquest.

Depicting Man as a supernatural realm may readily be interpreted as a reflection of English political interests, but this particular text is a product of a set of historical circumstances that appear to be considerably more local and more specific. The action of the romance culminates with the offer of the kingship of Man to Gawain when he has returned to Arthur's court:

> Sir Gromer kneeld upon his knee,
> Saith 'Sir King, and your wil be,
> Crowne Gawaine King of Man.'
> Sir Gawaine kneeld downe by,
> And said "Lord, nay, not I;
> Give it him, for he it wan.   [won
>
> For I never purposed to be noe King,
> Never in all my livinge,
> Whilest I am a living man."
> He said, 'Sir Gromer, take it thee,
> For Gawaine will never King bee
> For no craft that I can.'[146]   [argument I may make

The use of the title 'King of Man' merits further exploration because its peculiarity in an English context cannot be overstressed. From 1405 onwards, the ruler of the Isle of Man was the only individual in medieval England, other than the monarch, entitled to call himself a 'king'. Although the powers it conferred were limited by the small size of the island, the

---

[146] *Turke*, edited by Hahn, ll. 320–31.

symbolic capital to be derived from the title 'king' by the influential Stanley family on whom it was conferred was immense.[147] A sense of this can be gleaned from the fact that a Stanley King of Man appears as an independent signatory in an Anglo-French treaty signed in 1414.[148] The title was used by the Stanleys until the second decade of the sixteenth century, when the incumbent ruler, Thomas Stanley, appears to have decided that flaunting the title of king was politically risky. Man was, perhaps, one of the most remote and least materially significant of the territories in the Stanleys' spheres of influence but, if the evidence of family histories and legends are anything to go by, the one of which they were the most proud.[149] The Kingship of Man was conferred upon Sir John for his service in thwarting the rebellion of the Percy earls of Northumberland, the previous rulers of the island, but who were officially styled lords of Man rather than kings. Although the unique, imperfect copy of *Turke* in the Percy Folio dates from the seventeenth century, the 1405 accession to the kingship of Man by Sir John Stanley provides a compelling backdrop for the action of the narrative.[150]

The first Stanley to bear the title 'King of Man', Sir John Stanley, is a man who manages to be simultaneously everywhere and nowhere in discussions of medieval English literature. He crops up most frequently in analysis of the possible patronage of *Sir Gawain and the Green Knight*. While acknowledging that the dating of the text makes such a connection very unlikely, Helen Cooper has pointed out how closely the life of John Stanley conforms to that which might have been expected for the patron of such a text.[151] John, the second son of the bailiff of the Forest of Wirrall, won fame for himself by his deeds in the wars in France and made his fortune by marrying Isabella Lathom, heiress to Lathom and Knowsley

[147] *The Turke and Sir Gawain* is treated within the wider context of late medieval verse in praise of the Stanley family in Aisling Byrne and Victoria Flood, 'The Romance of the Stanleys: Regional and National Imaginings in the Percy Folio', *Viator*, 46 (2015), 327–52.

[148] Michael J. Bennett, *Community, Class and Careerism: Cheshire and Lancashire Society in the Age of Sir Gawain and the Green Knight* (Cambridge: Cambridge University Press, 1983), p. 217.

[149] For instance, the final word on John Stanley in the so-called *Stanley Poem* is devoted to his attainment of the Kingship of Man, which functions as a sort of climax to this lengthy panegyric. *The Stanley Poem*, in *The Palatine Anthology: A Collection of Ancient Poems and Ballads Relating to Lancashire and Cheshire*, edited by J. O. Halliwell (London: [private circulation], 1850), pp. 208–71, (p. 223).

[150] Echoes of Sir John's biography have been discerned in *Turke* by David A. Lawton in 'History and Legend: The Exile and the Turk', in *Postcolonial Moves*, edited by P. C. Ingham and M. R. Warren (New York: Palgrave, 2003), pp. 173–94 (p. 188). See also, Byrne and Flood, 'The Romance of the Stanleys', 347–50.

[151] Helen Cooper, 'Introduction', in *Sir Gawain and the Green Knight*, translated by Keith Harrison (Oxford: Oxford University Press, 1998), pp. ix–xxxiii.

in south-west Lancashire. He was almost single-handedly responsible for elevating his family, who later became earls of Derby, to an immensely influential position. His eventful career saw him uphold royal authority in Cheshire, Wales, and Ireland. At various points he was made a knight of the garter, steward of the household of the Prince of Wales, controller of the wardrobe, and constable of Windsor castle. He died in Ireland in 1414 while serving a term as Lord Lieutenant and was buried in County Louth. Stanley's rise is, as Cooper has pointed out, the stuff of romance and, indeed, there is evidence that Stanley's descendants thought so too. The so-called *Stanley Poem*, which appears to date from the mid-sixteenth century, paints its account of Sir John's life in a decidedly romance-like hue. Of particular significance for this discussion is the episode where Stanley begs leave of the king to go abroad to seek out adventures and travels extensively throughout Christendom, winning great renown by his feats of arms. Finally, he comes to the Turkish court, where he stays half a year, wins the love of the Grand Turk's daughter, and makes her pregnant. She urges him to flee before her father finds out, expresses a desire to be his wife, and promises to wait for him for seven years. No further mention is made of the Turk and his daughter in the poem, which goes on to recount how Stanley returned to England and married Isabella, but the episode at the Turk's court does indicate that a connection between such a figure and Sir John Stanley was a component in family legends about his life.

A key piece of contextual evidence linking *The Turke and Sir Gawain* to the Stanleys is the manuscript in which it has survived. The dialect in which many of the Percy Folio's texts are written seems firmly that of the north-west and the manuscript contains a high proportion of explicitly Stanleyite verse. Lawton has described the Percy Folio as 'the main repository of the verse of Stanley eulogy' and Gillian Rogers believes that its compiler must have had access to the Stanley library.[152] There are no less than five historical ballads scattered throughout the volume that celebrates the Stanleys (*Scotish Feilde, Flodden Feilde, Bosworth Feilde, Ladye Bessiye,* and *The Rose of Englande*). This is a strikingly high number, given that we only know of one other Stanleyite ballad of this sort from the period.[153] Other texts in the Folio also make reference to the earls of Derby (the Stanleys' title after Bosworth) and the ballad *The Greene*

[152] David A. Lawton, '*Scottish Field*: Alliterative Verse and the Stanley Encomium in the Percy Folio', *Leeds Studies in English*, n.s., 10 (1978), 42–57; Maldwyn Mills and Gillian Rogers, 'The Manuscripts of Popular Romance', in *A Companion to Medieval Popular Romance*, edited by Raluca L. Radulescu and Cory James Rushton (Woodbridge: D. S. Brewer, 2009), pp. 49–66.

[153] This is the ballad which Lawton calls 'Flodden Field II' preserved in British Library, Harley MS 3526 (fols. 100v–133r). Lawton, '*Scottish Field*', p. 50.

Knight mentions the castle of Hooton, where the Stanleys were formerly based.[154]

The external evidence of the geographical origins and the Stanley connections of the Percy Folio, along with the poem's internal evidence of the figure of the Turk associated with Sir John in family legend, and the stress on the unique title 'King of Man' all suggest a Stanley connection of this romance. The *Turke and Sir Gawain* may be a tribute to the Stanleys, in particular Sir John Stanley, but it does not read as a straightforward allegory, with Gawain standing in for Sir John as one might expect. Gawain, as he is imagined in the Middle English Gawain romances including this one, certainly seems an appropriate analogue for John Stanley, who spent much of his life defending England from threats on its borders, but the analogy in this text is not exact. The parallels between Stanley family history (real or imagined) and this romance hold true only at the level of the individual motifs and the geographical interests of the poem, not at the level of its overarching narrative. Gawain, unlike the historical John Stanley, refuses the kingship of Man when it is offered. Furthermore, the Turk occupies a rather different (and more benign) role in this romance than the Grand Turk of the *Stanley Poem*, though the ability of the exotic character to confer authority on the English hero is common to both. The presence of the Turk in the *Stanley Poem* deepens the romance resonances of the work and widens the geographic scope of Stanley's exploits, while the Turk of the Percy Folio romance prompts and enables Gawain's feats of chivalry. However, the disenchantment of the Turk and the revelation that he is, in fact, a knight on whom a spell has been cast, is not a facet of the text that responds to an allegorical interpretation grounded in the Stanleys' family history. With this in mind, it is more logical to think of elements like the Turk and the concern with Man and its kingship as Stanleyite markers in the narrative: badges that announce the text's affiliation to a particular family at a particular place and time rather than indicators of the complete dependence of the romance plot on historical events.

The depiction of the Isle of Man in terms that evoke otherworld accounts is a key component in the romance's territorial politics. The poem appears to suggest that the Turk's release from enchantment, his return to his identity as Sir Gromer, and incorporation into the Round Table is paralleled

---

[154] *The Greene Knight*, in *Sir Gawain*, edited by Hahn, pp. 309–36, l. 493. See also, E. Wilson, '*Sir Gawain and the Green Knight* and the Stanley family of Stanley, Storeton, and Hooton', *Review of English Studies*, n.s., 30 (1979), 308–16.

in the normalizing of the Isle of Man and its incorporation into Arthur's kingdom. The text's most recent editor, Thomas Hahn, argues that:

> Sir Gromer's installation as the new and proper King of the Isle of Man not only converts the alien figure—the 'Turk'—to familiar Christian knighthood, but presumably it demystifies the Isle of Man, changing it from a magic kingdom into a recognizable and accessible feature of the Arthurian (and contemporary) landscape.[155]

This process is perhaps characteristic of the so-called 'Gawain-romances' as a group. It would appear that the outlying territory that the poem had portrayed as a land of savagery and magic is normalized by its absorption into a single British identity. The process provides an interesting contrast to the much earlier Irish praise poem for Raghnall, where it appears that depicting the Isle of Man as an otherworld is a process that cements and authorizes the position of the incumbent Manx ruler rather than one which undermines him. The Isle of Man in the Irish praise poem is enchanted and idyllic rather than enchanted and barbarous. However, the fact that the island's castle in *Turke* is depicted as beautiful may point to a dichotomy between the inhabitants and the land itself, of the type developed in relation to Ireland and the Irish in Gerald's *Topographia*. Man, after all, is a desirable territory, as Sir Gromer's attempts to convince Gawain to accept it as a reward for his courage demonstrate. Indeed, if such a dichotomy is intended, the installation of Sir Gromer as king need not entirely change the island from 'a magic kingdom' as Hahn suggests, but merely replace the monstrous ruler with a human one and return the island to an otherworldly idyll. In both the earlier praise poem and in the *Turke*, depicting the Isle of Man in otherworldly terms allows for a politically charged engagement with the territory, but the malleability of the idea of the otherworld and its ability to accommodate multiple meanings allows it to be exploited to very different purposes in each of these works.

The ends to which writers depict 'real-world' territories in terms of the otherworld are diverse and sometimes nebulous, but certain persistent themes do emerge; foremost among them is territorial politics, broadly conceived. The idea of the 'otherworld' encompassing paradisial, monstrous, and fabulous landscapes has obvious political power. A concept that is so frequently concerned with space, alterity, and desire lends itself to treatments of political authority. The well-developed motif of the otherworld provides a wide range of conventional images and recurrent themes for adaptation. Such alternative worlds may provide a useful counterpoint when superposed on the quotidian world. Reimagining another territory in

---

[155] *Sir Gawain*, edited by Hahn, p. 338.

terms of the otherworld can both distance it and draw it closer, it can render such a land more desirable and so worthy of acquisition or more barbaric and so ripe for conquest. Reimagining one's own land as an otherworld allows a fresh perspective on the familiar. When the rhetoric of the idyllic, or indeed Edenic, otherworld is employed, it can be a means of revitalization and consolation, a means of cementing and developing communal identity. Rather than seeing the narrative otherworld as merely a reflection of known or postulated historical beliefs, this chapter has argued for the force and influence of literary otherworld accounts by illustrating how frequently and effectively imagery associated with them was utilized in treatments of the history and geography of locations within the British Isles.

Despite the linguistic and cultural multiplicity throughout the islands, it appears that writers drew on shared discourses of westernness, insularity, peripherality, and concomitant exceptionality in their analysis of their own relation to the isolated corner of the world in which they were living. The themes of earlier Continental writers were taken up and reshaped to local and national ends. The idea of the *translatio imperii* places the west in a position of privilege in both space and time. Writers in both England and Ireland draw on the same rhetoric of westernness and exceptionality in imagining their island as a western mirror of Eden. Such congruencies may, in part, be due to common native cultural foundations, but they are more obviously a result of shared geography and classical influences. These ideas were wielded with considerable skill and nuance to serve the (usually political) ends of the author. The application of otherworld concepts and imagery to real and proximate locations testifies to the serious and central role performed by the theme of the otherworld in medieval British and Irish culture. It would seem that the notion of the otherworld had a very particular resonance for writers in the North Atlantic archipelago, an area often described by classical writers as an *alter orbis*. The natural features of the island landscapes provided a highly suggestive starting point for these fantasies of national identity. National landscape shapes national literature, and, as the multifarious Greek islands gave episodic shape to the *Odyssey*, the unbounded reaches of the North Atlantic informed fantasies of insular travel and discovery such as the Irish *immrama*. Allied to this were complex attitudes and prejudices on the part of peoples in different parts of the archipelago towards the perceived 'otherness' of one another—attitudes and prejudices that were based on ignorance as well as being shaped and fuelled by political developments. Against this backdrop, the fact that writers working in an archipelago that was so often identified as an 'other world' should show a considerable fascination with notions of the otherworld is entirely unsurprising.

Conclusion

Points of Departure

I began this book by examining some of the words medieval writers use when describing what we now term 'otherworlds'. The sorts of terms they chose suggested that medieval accounts of fantastical realms might not always have been conceived of as quite so utterly 'other' as the modern term 'otherworld' suggests.

This rather counter-intuitive closeness between the otherworld and the human world manifests itself in various ways in the texts I have explored. Although the otherworld is often characterized by its unreal appearance and unnatural properties, pseudo-mimetic description means the otherworld account has all the appearance of reality, in form, if not in content. In a similar way, the pronounced intertextuality of otherworld accounts makes these descriptions mutually confirming and creates the illusion of truth.

Otherworld accounts have a clear, though not absolute, overlap with worlds that medieval Christians would have considered very real—the spaces of the afterlife. In fact, the vista seen by Thomas of Erceldoune places fairyland closer to our own world geographically than the four afterlife realms. The politics of the real world are drawn into otherworld narratives with striking frequency. The Dál Cuinn narratives use the idea of the otherworld to confirm and defend the authority of a dynastic line. Similarly, Arthur's continued life in Avalon has ramifications that move beyond the secondary and tertiary worlds of narrative and into history itself. Avalon's impact is such that some medieval authors try to place Arthur's afterlife in a more manageable location, like Glastonbury or Sicily. In these instances, putting the otherworld on the map actually mitigates, rather than enhances, its impact on the historical world.

The most striking real-world engagement of all, perhaps, is the absorption of the historical world into the otherworld. This sometimes takes shape in metaphorical mode, such as when the anonymous author of the praise poem to Raghnall figures the Isle of Man as a fairy kingdom, or it may take more literal form, as when Gerald of Wales reimagines Ireland (for better or for worse) as an isle of marvels and dubs it an *alter orbis*.

So how might we conceptualize the alterity of medieval otherworlds? The framework presented in this book suggests that the otherworld should not be seen as one exotic space among many, but as a new horizon of expectations *within* the text. It is, in a sense, a means of stepping outside the narrative text while remaining in it, a process that does not sound quite so odd when we consider that literature itself provides just such a conduit in its relationship with the actual world. In the same way that fiction provides a means to step out from reality in order to return to it with a fuller understanding, the otherworld sets up a third perspective from which to view both the secondary fictional and the primary historical worlds. The utility of the otherworld from a literary and historical perspective inheres in this relationship: the myriad ways in which the primary and secondary worlds may be viewed afresh through the encounter with the tertiary world.

There are some important facets of otherworld spaces that mark them out from other challenging and symbolically loaded spaces in medieval writing, such as the forest or the enclosed garden. Encounters with otherworld spaces eschew linear narrative trajectories, meaning medieval otherworlds are not usually experienced as one among many staging posts in a journey. In narrative texts, they are usually either the final destination or the pivot in a process of exile and return; they are points of rupture, rather than part of an evolving topography. The protagonist travels to the otherworld, to be sure, but the land itself is usually rather two-dimensional. Onward journeying deep into this realm is rare, and no further horizon beckons to the hero as it so often does in modern fantasy writing. To take a famous example, Narnia offers multiple very different sites of elaborate adventure that are not available in the text's secondary world of mid-twentieth-century England. Lewis's characters travel widely on a range of quests and explore a variety of marvellous places and beings. By contrast, hit-and-run operations, like those of Orfeo or Reinbrun, are the usual form taken by adventures in the medieval otherworld.

The last decades have seen the marvellous and the fantastical become increasingly serious subjects of study. This trend continues to find strong expression in medieval studies, in no small part due to the fact that medieval culture itself is often distinguished by its willingness to take the marvellous seriously. This seriousness is evident in the medieval treatments of otherworlds explored in these pages and their deep engagement with themes of considerable importance in the historical world. In many ways, otherworlds are the most emphatically fantastical of medieval supernatural concepts. Yet, as we have seen, their capacity for engagement with the historical world is undiminished by this characteristic; if any-thing, it is enhanced by it. The key to both this paradox and to the interchange between fantasy and history that this book has explored is the concept of the otherworld as a new horizon of expectation within the text. It comes as less of a surprise to see the impact of these fantastical realms extend into the historical world, if we view these supernatural realms as new points of fictional departure, analogous with, and bearing the same world-transforming potential as, literature itself.

Bibliography

PRIMARY SOURCES

The Adulterous Falmouth Squire, in *Political, Religious, and Love Poems*, edited by F. J. Furnivall, EETS, o.s., 15 (1866), pp. 93–102.

'The Adventure of Laeghaire mac Crimhthainn', edited by Kenneth Jackson, *Speculum*, 17 (1942), 377–89.

Aislinge Meic Con Glinne, edited by Kenneth Hurlstone Jackson (Dublin: Dublin Institute for Advanced Studies, 1990).

Aislinge Meic Conglinne, The Vision of MacConglinne, a Middle-Irish Wonder Tale, edited and translated by Kuno Meyer (London: David Nutt, 1892).

Alexandri Magni Iter ad Paradisum, in *The Romances of Alexander*, translated by Dennis M. Kratz (London: Garland, 1991), pp. 127–34.

Amadas and Ydoine, translated by Ross G. Arthur (New York: Garland, 1993).

Amadas et Ydoine, edited by John R. Reinhard (Paris: Honoré Champion, 1926).

Annala Uladh: The Annals of Ulster, edited and translated by W. M. Hennessy and B. MacCarthy, 4 vols (Dublin: Thom, 1887–1901).

Apocalypse of St Paul: The Apocryphal New Testament, translated by M. R. James (Oxford: Clarendon Press, 1924).

Of Arthour and of Merlin, edited by O. D. Macrae-Gibson, 2 vols, EETS, o.s., 268, 279 (1973–1979).

Augustine, *S. Aureli Augustini Hipponiensis episcopi Epistulae, pars iv, ep. CLXXXV–CCLXX*, edited by A. Goldbacher, Corpus Scriptorum Ecclesiasticorum Latinorum, 57 (Vienna: Tempsky, 1895).

Augustine of Hippo, *Concerning the City of God Against the Pagans*, translated by Henry Bettenson (Harmondsworth: Penguin, 1972).

Baile in Scáil: The Phantom's Frenzy, edited and translated by Kevin Murray, ITS, 58 (Dublin: Brunswick Press, 2004).

Bede, *Ecclesiastical History of the English People*, edited by B. Colgrave and R. A. B. Mynors (Oxford: Oxford University Press, 1969).

Bede, *In Cantica Canticorum*, edited by D. Hurst, Corpus Christianorum, Series Latina, 119 (Turnhout: Brepols, 1983).

Benedeit, *The Anglo-Norman Voyage of St Brendan*, edited by Brian Merrilees and Ian Short (Manchester: Manchester University Press, 1979).

[Bible], *The Holy Bible Translated from the Latin Vulgate* (Baltimore, MD: John Murphy, 1914).

Biblia Sacra Vulgatae Editionis Sixti V Pontificis Maximi Jussu Recognita et Clementis VIII Auctoritate Edita (London: David Nutt, 1868).

Branwen Uerch Lyr, the Second of the Four Branches of the Mabinogi, edited by Derek S. Thomson (Dublin: Dublin Institute of Advanced Studies, 1961).

[Catalan Atlas], *Mappamundi: Der Katalanische Weltatlas vom Jahre 1375*, edited by George Grosjean (Dietikon: Urs Graf Verlag, 1977).

In Cath Catharda, The Civil War of the Romans: An Irish Version of Lucan's Pharsalia, edited and translated by Whitley Stokes, in *Irische Texte mit Wörterbuch*, edited by Whitley Stokes and Ernst Windisch, 4 vols in 6 (Leipzig: S. Hirzel, 1880–1909), IV.2 (1909).

Chaucer, Geoffrey, 'Sir Thopas', in *The Riverside Chaucer*, edited by Larry D. Benson, 3rd edn (Oxford: Oxford University Press, 1987), pp. 212–16.

Chaucer, Geoffrey, 'The Wife of Bath's Tale', in *The Riverside Chaucer*, edited by Larry D. Benson, 3rd edn (Oxford: Oxford University Press, 1987), pp. 116–22.

Chestre, Thomas, *Sir Launfal*, in *The Middle English Breton Lays*, edited by Anne Laskaya and Eve Salisbury (Kalamazoo, MI: Medieval Institute Publications, 1995), pp. 201–62.

Claudian, 'Panegyricus, Dictus Manlio Theodoro Consuli', in *Claudian*, translated by Maurice Platnauer (London: William Heinemann, 1922).

Cogadh Gaedhel re Gallaibh: The Wars of the Gaedhil with the Gaill, edited and translated by James Henthorn Todd, RS, 48 (London: Longmans, 1867).

Culhwch ac Olwen: Testun Syr Idris Foster, edited by Rachel Bromwich and D. Simon Evans (Cardiff: University of Wales Press, 1988).

How Culhwch Won Olwen, in *The Mabinogion*, translated by Sioned Davies (Oxford: Oxford University Press, 2007), pp. 179–213.

David, 'Hic poeta qui Brendani vitam vult describere', in *The English Origins of Old French Literature*, edited and translated by David Howlett (Dublin: Four Courts Press, 1996), pp. 112–15.

Dicuil, *Liber de Mensura Orbis Terrae*, edited by J. J. Tierney (Dublin: Dublin Institute for Advanced Studies, 1967).

Duanaire Finn: The Book of the Lays of Fionn, edited and translated by Eoin MacNeill and Gerard Murphy, 3 vols, ITS, 7, 28, 43 (London: Simpkin and Marshall, 1908–1953).

Eadmer, *The Life of St Anselm, Archbishop of Canterbury*, edited and translated by R. W. Southern (Oxford: Clarendon Press, 1972).

[Ebstorf Map] Kugler, Hartmut, in collaboration with Sonja Glauch, Antje Willing, and Thomas Zapf, eds., *Die Ebstorfer Weltkarte: Kommentierte Neuausgabe in zwei Bänden* (Berlin: Akademie Verlag, 2007).

'Echtra Airt meic Cuinn: The Adventures of Art Son of Conn', edited and translated by R. I. Best, *Ériu*, 3 (1907), 149–73.

'Echtra Cormaic Maic Airt: The Adventure of Cormac Mac Airt', edited and translated by Vernam Hull, *Papers of the Modern Language Association*, 64 (1949), 871–83.

Echtrae Chonnlai, in *Echtrae Chonnlai and the Beginnings of Vernacular Writing in Ireland*, edited and translated by Kim McCone (Maynooth: Maynooth Monographs, 2000), pp. 121–3.

Étienne de Rouen, *Epistola Arturi regis ad Henricum regem Anglorum*, in *Latin Arthurian Literature*, edited and translated by Mildred Leake Day (Cambridge: D. S. Brewer, 2005).

Étude sur le Purgatoire de Saint Patrice accompagnée du texte latin d'Utrecht et du texte anglo-normand de Cambridge, edited by C. M. Van der Zanden (Amsterdam: H. J. Paris, 1927).

'Forfess Fer Fálgae (Aus Egerton 1782 fo. 19a)', edited by Kuno Meyer, *Zeitschrift für celtische Philologie*, 8 (1912), 564–5.

Geoffrey of Monmouth, *Life of Merlin: Vita Merlini*, edited and translated by Basil Clarke (Cardiff: University of Wales Press, 1973).

Geoffrey of Monmouth, *The History of the Kings of Britain*, edited by Michael D. Reeve, translated by Neil Wright, Arthurian Studies, 69 (Woodbridge: Boydell, 2007).

Gerald of Wales, *Topographia Hibernica*, in *Giraldi Cambrensis Opera*, edited by J. F. Dimock and others, 8 vols, RS, 21 (London: Longmans, 1861–1891), v (1867).

Gerald of Wales, *Itinerarium Kambriae*, in *Giraldi Cambrensis Opera*, edited by J. F. Dimock and others, 8 vols, RS, 21 (London: Longmans, 1861–1891), vi (1868).

Gerald of Wales, *Speculum Ecclesiae*, in *Giraldi Cambrensis Opera*, edited by J. F. Dimock and others, 8 vols, RS, 21 (London: Longmans, 1861–1891), iv (1873).

Gerald of Wales, *De Principis Instructione Liber*, in *Giraldi Cambrensis Opera*, edited by J. F. Dimock and others, 8 vols, RS, 21 (London: Longmans, 1861–1891), viii (1891).

Gerald of Wales, *The Autobiography of Gerald of Wales*, translated by H. E. Butler, 2nd edn (Woodbridge: Boydell, 2005).

Gervase of Tilbury, *Otia Imperialia: Recreation for an Emperor*, edited by S. E. Banks and J. W. Binns (Oxford: Oxford University Press, 2002).

Gildas, *De Excidio Britonum: The Ruin of Britain and Other Sources*, edited and translated by Michael Winterbottom (London: Phillimore, 1978).

Graelent, in *Eleven Old French Narrative Lays*, edited Glyn S. Burgess and Leslie C. Brook (Cambridge: D. S. Brewer, 2007), pp. 349–412.

The Greene Knight, in *Sir Gawain: Eleven Romances and Tales*, edited by Thomas Hahn (Kalamazoo, MI: Medieval Institute Publications, 1995), pp. 309–36.

Le Haut Livre du Graal: Perlesvaus, edited by William A. Nitze, 2 vols (Chicago: University of Chicago Press, 1932, 1937).

Hay, Gilbert, *The Buik of King Alexander the Conquerour*, edited by John Cartwright, 2 vols, STS 4th Ser., 16, 18 (Aberdeen: Aberdeen University Press, 1986–1990).

Hay, Gilbert, *Buik of King Alexander the Conquerour*, in *Longer Scottish Poems, 1375–1650*, edited by Priscilla Bawcutt and Felicity Riddy (Edinburgh: Scottish Academic Press, 1987).

[Hereford World Map], reproduced in P. D. A. Harvey, *Mappa Mundi: The Hereford World Map* (London: British Library, 2006).

Higden, Ranulf, *Polychronicon Ranulphi Higden Monachi Cestrensis*, edited by Churchill Babington and J. R. Lumby, 9 vols, RS, 41 (London: Longman, 1865–1886).

Hugh of St Victor, *De Archa Noe Morali*, edited by Patrice Secard and D. Poirel, Corpus Christianorum, Continuatio Mediaevalis, 176 (Turnhout: Brepols, 2001).

Immram Brain: Bran's Journey to the Land of Women, edited and translated by Séamus Mac Mathúna (Tübingen: Niemeyer, 1985).

Instructio Pie Vivendi Et Superna Meditandi, edited and translated by John McKechnie, 2 vols, ITS, 29, 29a (Dublin: Educational Company of Ireland, 1934–1946).

'The Irish Lives of Guy of Warwick and Bevis of Hampton', edited by F. N. Robinson, *Zeitschrift für celtische Philologie*, 6 (1908), 9–180, 273–338, 9–23, 105–80, 298–320.

Isidore of Seville, *Isidori Hispalensis Episcopi Etymologiarum Sive Originum*, edited by W. M. Lindsay, 2 vols (Oxford: Clarendon Press, 1911).

Isidore of Seville, *The Etymologies of Isidore of Seville*, edited by Stephen A. Barney et al. (Cambridge: Cambridge University Press, 2006).

The Isle of Ladies or the Ile of Pleasaunce, edited by Anthony Jenkins, Garland Medieval Texts, 2 (New York and London: Garland Publishing, 1980).

Iter Alexandri Magni ad Paradisum, edited by Alfons Hilka, in *La Prise de Defur and Le Voyage d'Alexandre au Paradis Terrestre*, edited by Lawton P. G. Peckham and Milan S. La Du (Princeton: Princeton University Press, 1935), pp. xli–xlviii.

John of Glastonbury, *An Edition, Translation and Study of John of Glastonbury's Cronica sive Antiquitates Glastoniensis Ecclesie*, edited by James P. Carley, translated by David Townsend (Woodbridge: Boydell, 1985).

Keating, Geoffrey, *Foras Feasa ar Éirinn: The History of Ireland*, edited by David Comyn and Patrick S. Dinneen, 4 vols, ITS, 4, 8, 9, 15 (London: David Nutt, 1902–1914).

King's Mirror (Speculum Regale—Konungs Skuggsjá), edited by L. M. Larson, Scandinavian Monographs, 3 (New York: Twayne, 1917).

Le Lai d'Haveloc and Gaimar's Haveloc Episode, edited by Alexander Bell (Manchester: University of Manchester Press, 1925).

Land of Cockaygne, in *Anglo-Irish Poems of the Middle Ages*, edited by Angela Lucas (Dublin: Columba Press, 1995), pp. 46–72.

Laȝamon, *Brut or Hystoria Brutonum*, edited by W. R. J. Barron and S. C. Weinberg (Harlow: Longman, 1995).

Lebor Gabála Erenn: The Book of Invasions, edited by R. A. S. Macalister, 6 vols, ITS, 34, 35, 39, 41, 44 (Dublin: Educational Company of Ireland, 1938–1956).

Lebor na hUidre: Book of the Dun Cow, edited by R. I. Best and Osborn Bergin (Dublin: Royal Irish Academy, 1929).

Lestoire de Merlin, in *The Vulgate Version of the Arthurian Romances*, edited by H. Oskar Sommer, 7 vols (Washington, DC: Carnegie Institution, 1908–1913), II (1908).

Lichtoun's Dreme, in *The Bannatyne Manuscript*, edited by W. Tod Ritchie, 4 vols, STS, 2nd Ser., 22, 23, 26, 3rd Ser., 5 (Edinburgh: William Blackwood, 1928–1934), II (1928), pp. 268–71.

Lucan, *The Civil War, Books I–X*, edited and translated by J. D. Duff (London: William Heinemann, 1928).

Lucian, *The True History*, in *The Works of Lucian of Samosata*, translated by H. W. Fowler and F. G. Fowler, 4 vols (Oxford: Clarendon Press, 1905), II, 136–72.

Lybeaus Desconus, in *Codex Ashmole 61: A Compilation of Popular Middle English Verse*, edited by George Shuffleton (Kalamazoo, MI: Medieval Institute Publications, 2008), pp. 111–64.

Lydgate, John, *The Fall of Princes*, edited by Henry Bergin, 4 vols, EETS, e.s., 121–4 (1924–1927).

Mandeville, John, *The Book of John Mandeville*, edited by Tamarah Kohanski and C. David Benson (Kalamazoo, MI: Medieval Institute Publications, 2007).

Map, Walter, *De Nugis Curialium: Courtier's Trifles*, edited and translated by M. R. James, revised by C. N. L. Brooke and R. A. B. Mynors (Oxford: Oxford University Press, 1983).

Marie de France, *The Lais of Marie de France*, edited by A. Ewert (Oxford: Blackwell, 1978).

Marie de France, *Lays*, translated by Glyn Burgess and Keith Busby (Harmondsworth: Penguin, 1986).

Marie de France, *Saint Patrick's Purgatory: A Poem by Marie de France*, edited by Michael J. Curley (New York: Garland, 1993).

Navigatio Sancti Brendani Abbatis from Early Latin Manuscripts, edited by Carl Selmer (South Bend, IN: University of Notre Dame Press, 1959; repr. Dublin: Four Courts Press, 1989).

Nennius, *British History and the Welsh Annals*, edited by John Morris (London: Phillimore, 1980).

Nicolaus de Bibera, *Carmen Satiricum*, edited by Theobald Fischer, Geschichtsquellen der Provinz Sachsen, I: Erfurter Denkmäler (Halle: Buchhandlung des Waisenhauses, 1870).

Origen, *Die Homilien zu Lukas in der Ubersetzung des Hieronymus und die griechischen Reste der Homilien und des Lukas-Kommentars*, edited by Max Rauer, in *Origenes: Werke*, 12 vols, Die Griechischen Christlichen Schriftsteller, 35 (Berlin: Akademie-Verlag, 1899–1955), IX (1931).

Origen, *Homilies on Luke*, translated by Joseph T. Leinhard (Washington, DC: Catholic University of America Press, 1996).

Orpheus and Eurydice, in *The Poems of Robert Henryson*, edited by Robert L. Kindrick (Kalamazoo, MI: Medieval Institute Publications, 1997), pp. 187–222.

Partonope of Blois, edited by A. Trampe Bödtker, EETS, e.s., 109 (1912).

Patrick, *Confessio*, in *St. Patrick: His Writings and Muirchu's Life*, edited and translated by A. B. E. Hood (London: Phillimore, 1978), pp. 23–34.

Paula and Eustochium, 'Epistola ad Marcellam', in *Itinera Hierosolymitana et Descriptiones Terrae Sanctae*, edited by Titus Tobler and Augustus Molinier, 2 vols (Geneva: J.-G. Fick, 1879–1885), I, pp. 43–7.

Paula and Eustochium, 'On Visiting Jerusalem', in *Lives of Roman Christian Women*, edited by Caroline White (Penguin: London, 2010), pp. 165–75.

Pearl, in *The Poems of the Pearl Manuscript*, edited by Malcolm Andrew and Ronald Waldron (Exeter: Exeter University Press, 2002), pp. 53–110.

The Peterborough Chronicle, 1070–1174, edited by Cecily Clark, 2nd edn (Oxford: Clarendon Press, 1970).

Plutarch, *De Defectu Oraculorum*, in *Moralia*, edited by Frank Cole Babbitt (Whitefish, MT: Kessinger Publishing, 2005).

'A Poem in Praise of Raghnall, King of Man', edited by Brian Ó Cuív, *Éigse*, 8 (1956–1957), 283–301.

Pomponius Mela, *Description of the World*, edited by Frank E. Romei (Ann Arbor, MI: University of Michigan Press, 1998).

Preideu Annwfyn, in *Legendary Poems from the Book of Taliesin*, edited and translated by Marged Haycock (Aberystwyth: Cambrian Medieval Celtic Studies, 2007), pp. 433–51.

Procopius of Caesarea, *History of the Wars*, edited and translated by H. B. Dewing, 7 vols (London: W. Heinemann, 1914–1940).

Le Purgatoire de Saint Patrice: des manuscrits Harléien 273 et Fonds français 2198, edited by Johan Vising (Göteborg: W. Zachrisson, 1916).

Ralph of Coggeshall, *Radulphi de Coggeshall Chronicon Anglicanum*, edited by Joseph Stevenson, RS, 66 (London: Longmans, 1875).

Reinbrun, in *The Romance of Guy of Warwick*, edited by Julius Zupitza, EETS, e.s., 42, 49, 59 (1883; 1-vol. repr., 1966), III, pp. 631–74.

De reis van Sente Brandane, edited by H. P. A. Oskamp (Zutphen: Thieme, 1972).

Saint Patrick's Purgatory, edited by Robert Easting, EETS, o.s., 298 (1991).

Saint Patrick's Purgatory, translated by J.-M. Picard and Y. de Pontfarcy (Dublin: Four Courts Press, 1985).

The Second Branch, in *The Mabinogion*, translated by Sioned Davies (Oxford: Oxford University Press, 2007), pp. 22–34.

Serglige Con Culainn, edited by Myles Dillon (Columbus, OH: H. L. Hedrick, 1941).

Servius, *Servii Grammatici Qui Feruntur in Vergilii Carmina Commentarii*, edited by Georg Thilo and Hermann Hagen, 3 vols (Leipzig: Teubner, 1881–1902).

Sick Bed of Cuchulainn, in *Heroic Romances of Ireland*, translated by A. H. Leahy, 2 vols (London: David Nutt, 1905).

Sir Gawain and the Green Knight, edited by J. R. R. Tolkien and E. V. Gordon, 2nd edn, revised by Norman Davis (Oxford: Clarendon Press, 1967).

Sir Landevale, in *The Middle English Breton Lays*, edited by Anne Laskaya and Eve Salisbury (Kalamazoo, MI: Medieval Institute Publications, 1995), pp. 423–37.

Sir Orfeo, edited by A. J. Bliss (Oxford: Oxford University Press, 1954).

Sir Owain, in *Three Purgatory Poems*, edited by Edward E. Foster (Kalamazoo, MI: Medieval Institute Publications, 2004), pp. 109–78.

Solinus, *Collectanea Rerum Memorabilium*, edited by T. Mommsen (Berlin: Weidmann, 1895).

The Stanley Poem, in *The Palatine Anthology: A Collection of Ancient Poems and Ballads Relating to Lancashire and Cheshire*, edited by J. O. Halliwell (London: [private circulation], 1850), pp. 208–71.

The Story of Merlin, translated by Rupert T. Pickens, in *Lancelot-Grail: The Old French Arthurian Vulgate in Translation*, edited by Norris J. Lacy, 5 vols (New York: Garland, 1993), I.

Thomas of Erceldoune: The Romance and Prophecies of Thomas of Erceldoune, edited by James A. H. Murray, EETS, o.s., 68 (1875).

Thomas of Kent, *The Anglo-Norman Alexander: Le Roman de Toute Chevalerie*, edited by Brian Foster and Ian Short, 2 vols, ANTS, 29, 31 (London: Birkbeck College, 1976–1977).

'Tochmarc Becfhola', edited by Máire Bhreathnach, *Ériu*, 35 (1984), 59–91.

'Tochmarc Étaíne', edited by Osborn Bergin and R. I. Best, *Ériu*, 12 (1938), 137–96.

Tractatus de Purgatorio Sancti Patricii, in *Saint Patrick's Purgatory*, edited by Robert Easting, EETS, o.s., 298 (1991), pp. 121–54.

The Triads of Ireland, edited by Kuno Meyer (Dublin: Hodges Figgis, 1906).

Trioedd Ynys Prydein: The Triads of the Island of Britain, edited and translated by Rachel Bromwich, 3rd edn (Cardiff: University of Wales Press, 2006), pp. 259–60.

The Tripartite Life of Patrick: With Other Documents Relating to that Saint, edited by Whitley Stokes, RS, 89 (London: H.M. Stationery Office, 1887).

The Turke and Sir Gawain, in *Sir Gawain: Eleven Romances and Tales*, edited by Thomas Hahn (Kalamazoo, MI: Medieval Institute Publications, 1995), pp. 340–58.

'Uita Metrica Sanctae Brigidae', in *Early Christian Ireland*, translated by Máire and Liam de Paor (London: Thames and Hudson, 1958), p. 130.

'Uita Metrica Sanctae Brigidae: A Critical Edition', edited by D. N. Kissane, *Proceedings of the Royal Irish Academy,* 77 (1977), 57–87.

Vincent of Beauvais, *Bibliotheca Mundi seu Speculi Maioris: Vol. 4, Speculum historiale* (Douai: Baltazar Belierus, 1624; repr. Graz: Akademische Druck- u. Verlagsanstalt, 1965).

Virgil, *Aeneid*, translated by Frederick Ahl (Oxford: Oxford University Press, 2007).

Virgil, *Eclogues*, edited and translated by Len Krisak and Gregson David (Philadelphia: University of Pennsylvania Press, 2010).

Visio Tnugdali: Lateinisch und Altdeutsch, edited by Albrecht Wagner (Erlangen: Deichert, 1882).

The Vision of Tnugdal, translated by Jean-Michel Picard, with an introduction by Yolande de Ponfarcy (Dublin: Four Courts, 1989).

The Voyage of Bran Son of Febal to the Land of the Living: An Old Irish Saga, edited by Kuno Meyer and Alfred Nutt, 2 vols (London: David Nutt, 1895–1897).

Voyage of Mael Duin, edited by H. P. A. Oskamp (Groningen: Wolters-Noordhoff, 1970).

The Voyage of St Brendan: Journey to the Promised Land, translated by J. J. O'Meara (Dublin, Dolmen Press, 1976).

Voyage of St Brendan: Representative Versions of the Legend in English Translation, edited by W. R. J. Barron and Glyn S. Burgess (Exeter: University of Exeter Press, 2002).

Voyage of Tadhg Mac Cein, in *Silva Gadelica: A Collection of Tales in Irish,* edited and translated by Standish H. O'Grady, 2 vols (London: Williams and Norgate, 1892), I (text), pp. 342–59, II (trans.), pp. 385–401.

'The Voyage of the Húi Corra', edited and translated by Whitley Stokes, *Revue Celtique,* 14 (1893), 22–69.

Wace, *Roman de Brut, A History of the British: Text and Translation,* edited and translated by J. Weiss (Exeter: Exeter University Press, 1999).

The Wars of Alexander, edited by Hoyt N. Duggan and Thorlac Turville-Petre, EETS, s.s., 10 (Oxford: Oxford University Press, 1989).

William of Malmesbury, *De Gestis Pontificum Anglorum,* edited by N. E. S. A. Hamilton, RS, 52 (London: Longmans, 1870).

William of Malmesbury, *Gesta Regum Anglorum,* edited and translated by R. A. B. Mynors, R. M. Thomson, and M. Winterbottom, 2 vols (Oxford: Clarendon Press, 1998).

William of Newburgh, *A History of English Affairs, Book I,* edited by P. G. Walsh and M. J. Kennedy (Warminster: Aris & Phillips, 1988).

William of Rennes, *Gesta Regum Britanniae,* in *The Historia Regum Britanniae of Geoffrey of Monmouth V,* edited and translated by Neil Wright (Cambridge: D. S. Brewer, 1991).

Wulfstan, *Wulfstan: Sammlung der ihm zugeschriebenen Homilien nebst Untersuchungen über ihre Echtheit,* edited by Arthur Sampson Napier, Sammlung englischer Denkmäler in kritischen Ausgaben, 4 (Berlin: Weidmannsche Buchhandlung, 1883), p. 205.

Zachary, 'Die Briefe des Heiligen Bonifatius und Lullus', in *Monumenta Germaniae Historica Epistolae Selectae,* 1, edited by Michael Tangl, 2nd edn (Berlin: Weidmann, 1955), pp. 178–9.

SECONDARY SOURCES

Ackerman, Robert W., *An Index of the Arthurian Names in Middle English* (Stanford, CA: Stanford University Press, 1952).

Allen, Dorena, 'Orpheus and Orfeo: The Dead and the Taken', *Medium Aevum,* 33 (1964), 102–11.

Anderson, Benedict, *Imagined Communities: Reflections on the Origin and Spread of Nationalism* (London: Verso, 1983).

Anderson, John D., 'The *Navigatio Brendani*: A Medieval Best Seller', *The Classical Journal,* 83 (1988), 315–22.

Ashe, Laura, *Fiction and History in Medieval England, 1066–1200* (Cambridge: Cambridge University Press, 2007).

Barber, Peter, 'The Evesham World Map: A Late Medieval English View of God and the World', *Imago Mundi,* 47 (1995), 13–33.

Barthes, Roland, 'The Reality Effect', in *The Novel: An Anthology of Criticism and Theory, 1900–2000*, edited by Dorothy J. Hale (Oxford: Blackwell, 2006), pp. 229–34.

Bartlett, Robert, *England under the Norman and Angevin Kings, 1075–1225* (Oxford: Clarendon Press, 2000).

Bartlett, Robert, *The Natural and the Supernatural in the Middle Ages* (Cambridge: Cambridge University Press, 2008).

Baswell, Christopher, *Virgil in Medieval England: Figuring the* Aeneid *from the Twelfth Century to Chaucer* (Cambridge: Cambridge University Press, 1995).

Bawcutt, Priscilla, 'Eldritch Comic Verse in Older Scots', in *Older Scots Literature*, edited by Sally Mapstone (Edinburgh: John Donald, 2005), pp. 292–313.

Bennett, Josephine Waters, 'Britain Among the Fortunate Isles', *Studies in Philology*, 53 (1956), 114–40.

Bennett, Michael J., *Community, Class and Careerism: Cheshire and Lancashire Society in the Age of Sir Gawain and the Green Knight* (Cambridge: Cambridge University Press, 1983).

Bloch, R. Howard, *The Anonymous Marie De France* (Chicago: University of Chicago Press, 2003).

Bouloux, Nathalie, 'Les îles dans les descriptions géographiques et les cartes du Moyen Âge', *Médiévales*, 47 (2004), 47–62.

Bovey, Alixe, *Monsters and Grotesques in Medieval Manuscripts* (Toronto: University of Toronto Press, 2002).

Boyle, Elizabeth, 'On the Wonders of Ireland: Translation and Adaptation', in *Authorities and Adaptations: The Reworking and Transmission of Textual Sources in Medieval Ireland*, edited by Elizabeth Boyle and Deborah Hayden (Dublin: Dublin Institute for Advanced Studies, 2014), pp. 233–61.

Bray, Dorothy Ann, 'Allegory in the *Navigatio Sancti Brendani*', *Viator*, 26 (1995), 1–10.

Brouland, Marie-Thérèse, *Sir Orfeo: le substrat celtique du lai breton anglais* (Paris: Didier Érudition, 1990).

Brown, Michelle P., 'Marvels of the West: Giraldus Cambrensis and the Role of the Author in the Development of Marginal Illustration', in *Decoration and Illustration in Medieval English Manuscripts*, edited by A. S. G. Edwards, English Manuscript Studies, 10 (London: British Library, 2002), pp. 34–59.

Burgess, Glyn, '*Savoir* and *Faire* in the Anglo-Norman *Voyage of St Brendan*', *French Studies*, 49 (1995), 257–74.

Burgess, Glyn S. and Clara Strijbosch, *The Legend of St Brendan: A Critical Bibliography* (Dublin: Royal Irish Academy, 2000).

Butterfield, Ardis, *The Familiar Enemy: Chaucer, Language, and Nation in the Hundred Years War* (Oxford: Oxford University Press, 2010).

Bynum, Caroline Walker, *Metamorphosis and Identity* (New York: Zone Books, 2001).

Byrne, Aisling, 'West Is East: The Irish Saracens in *Of Arthour and of Merlin*', *Nottingham Medieval Studies*, 55 (2011), 217–32.

Byrne, Aisling, 'Fairy Lovers: Sexuality, Order and Narrative in Medieval Romance', in *Sexual Culture in Late-Medieval Britain*, edited by Robert Rouse and Cory Rushton (Cambridge: D. S. Brewer, 2014), pp. 99–110.

Byrne, Aisling, and Victoria Flood, 'The Romance of the Stanleys: Regional and National Imaginings in the Percy Folio', *Viator*, 46 (2015), 327–52.

Byrne, F. J., 'Historical Note on Cnogba (Knowth)', *Proceedings of the Royal Irish Academy, Section C*, 66 (1967–1968), 383–400.

Calkin, Siobhain Bly, *Saracens and the Making of English Identity: The Auchinleck Manuscript* (New York: Routledge, 2005).

Campbell, Mary B., *The Witness and the Other World: Exotic European Travel Writing, 400–1600* (Ithaca, NY: Cornell University Press, 1991).

Campbell, Tony, 'Portolan Charts from the Late Thirteenth Century to 1500', in *The History of Cartography*, edited by J. B. Harley and David Woodward, 6 vols (Chicago: University of Chicago Press, 1987–1994), I (1992), 371–463.

Carey, John, 'Time, Space and the Otherworld', *Proceedings of the Harvard Celtic Colloquium*, 7 (1987), 1–27.

Carey, John, 'Ireland and the Antipodes: The Heterodoxy of Virgil of Salzburg', *Speculum*, 64 (1989), 1–10.

Carey, John, 'Otherworlds and Verbal Worlds in Middle Irish Narrative', *Proceedings of the Harvard Celtic Colloquium*, 9 (1990), 32–42.

Carey, John, 'The Irish Otherworld: Hiberno-Latin Perspectives', *Éigse*, 25 (1991), 154–9.

Carey, John, 'Aerial Ships and Underwater Monasteries: The Evolution of a Monastic Marvel', *Proceedings of the Harvard Celtic Colloquium*, 12 (1992), 16–28.

Carey, John, 'The Rhetoric of *Echtrae Chonlai*', *Cambridge Medieval Celtic Studies* 30 (1995), 41–65.

Carey, John, *A Single Ray of the Sun: Religious Speculation in Early Ireland* (Aberystwyth: Celtic Studies Publications, 1999).

Carey, John, 'Tara and the Supernatural', in *The Kingship and Landscape of Tara*, edited by Edel Bhreathnach (Dublin: Four Courts Press, 2005), pp. 32–48.

Carney, James, 'Review of *Navigatio Sancti Brendani* edited by Selmer', *Medium Aevum*, 31 (1963), 37–44.

Cartlidge, Neil, 'Sir Orfeo in the Otherworld: Courting Chaos?', *Studies in the Age of Chaucer*, 26 (2004), 195–226.

Cartwright, John, 'Sir Gilbert Hay's "Alexander": A Study in Transformations', *Medium Aevum*, 60 (1991), 61–71.

Cary, George, *The Medieval Alexander*, edited by D. J. A. Ross (Cambridge: Cambridge University Press, 1956).

Caughey, Anna, '"Als for the worthynes of þe romance": Exploitation of Genre in the *Buik of King Alexander the Conqueror*', in *The Exploitations of Medieval Romance*, edited by Laura Ashe, Ivana Djordjević, and Judith Weiss (Cambridge: D. S. Brewer, 2010), pp. 139–58.

Charles-Edwards, T. M., *Early Christian Ireland* (Cambridge: Cambridge University Press, 2000).

Christiansen, Reidar Th., *The Vikings and the Viking Wars in Irish and Gaelic Tradition* (Oslo: Jacob Dybwad, 1931).

Clancy, Thomas Owen, 'Subversion at Sea: Structure, Style and Intent in the *Immrama*', in *The Otherworld Voyage in Early Irish Literature*, edited by Jonathan Wooding (Dublin: Four Courts, 2000), pp. 194–225.

Clark, John, 'Martin and the Green Children', *Folklore*, 117 (2006), 207–14.

Clarke, Catherine A. M., *Literary Landscapes and the Idea of England, 700–1400* (Cambridge: D.S. Brewer, 2006).

Cohen, Jeffrey Jerome, 'Hybrids, Monsters, Borderlands: The Bodies of Gerald of Wales', in *The Postcolonial Middle Ages*, edited by Jeffrey Jerome Cohen (New York: Palgrave Macmillan, 2001), pp. 85–104.

Cohen, Jeffrey Jerome, *Hybridity, Identity, and Monstrosity in Medieval Britain: On Difficult Middles* (New York: Palgrave Macmillan, 2006).

Cohen, Jeffrey Jerome, 'Green Children from Another World, or the Archipelago in England', in *Cultural Diversity in the British Middle Ages: Archipelago, Island, England*, edited by Jeffrey Jerome Cohen, The New Middle Ages (New York: Palgrave MacMillan, 2008), pp. 75–94.

Cole, Chera A., ' "Fairy" in Middle English Romance' (PhD dissertation, University of St Andrews, 2013).

Cooper, Helen, 'The Supernatural', in *A Companion to the Gawain-Poet*, edited by Derek Brewer and Jonathan Gibson (Woodbridge: D. S. Brewer, 1997), pp. 277–91.

Cooper, Helen, 'Introduction', in *Sir Gawain and the Green Knight*, translated by Keith Harrison (Oxford: Oxford University Press, 1998), pp. ix–xxxiii.

Cooper, Helen, *The English Romance in Time: Transforming Motifs from Geoffrey of Monmouth to the Death of Shakespeare* (Oxford: Oxford University Press, 2004).

Cunliffe, Barry, *Facing the Ocean: The Atlantic and its Peoples* (Oxford: Oxford University Press, 2000).

Daston, Lorraine, and Katharine Park, *Wonders and the Order of Nature, 1150–1750* (New York: Zone Books, 1998).

Davies, Glyn, 'New Light on the Luck of Edenhall', *The Burlington Magazine*, 52 (2010), 4–7.

de Beauvoir, Simone, *The Coming of Age*, translated by Patrick O'Brian (New York: Putnam, 1972).

Delumeau, Jean, *The History of Paradise: The Garden of Eden in Myth and Tradition*, translated by Matthew O'Connell (New York: Continuum, 1995).

Dinzelbacher, Peter, *Vision und Visionsliteratur im Mittelalter* (Stuttgart: Hiersemann, 1981).

Dinzelbacher, Peter, 'The Way to the Other World in Medieval Literature and Art', *Folklore*, 97 (1986), 70–87.

Dinzelbacher, Peter, and Harald Kleinschmidt, 'Seelenbrücke und Brückenbau im mittelalterlichen England', *Numen*, 31 (1984), 242–87.

Djordjević, Ivana, 'Saracens and Other Saxons: Using, Misusing, and Confusing Names in *Gui de Warewic* and *Guy of Warwick*', in *The Exploitations of Medieval Romance*, edited by Laura Ashe, Ivana Djordjević, and Judith Weiss (Cambridge: D. S. Brewer, 2010), pp. 28–42.

Duffy, Seán, 'Emerging from the Mist: Ireland and Man in the Eleventh Century', in *Mannin Revisited: Twelve Essays on Manx Culture and Environment*, edited by Peter Davey and David Finlayson (Edinburgh: Scottish Society for Northern Studies, 2002), pp. 53–6.

Duignan, Leonie, 'The *Echtrae* as an Early Irish Literary Genre' (PhD dissertation, National University of Ireland, Maynooth, 2010).

Dumville, David, '*Echtrae* and *Immram*: Some Problems of Definition', *Ériu*, 27 (1976), 73–94.

Dumville, David, 'Two Approaches to the Dating of *Nauigatio Sancti Brendani*', *Studi Medievali*, 29 (1988), 87–102.

Dunn, Joseph, 'The Brendan Problem', *The Catholic Historical Review*, 6 (1921), 395–477.

Dwyer, R. A., 'Arthur's Stellification in the *Fall of Princes*', *Philological Quarterly*, 57 (1978), 155–71.

Easting, Robert, 'Owein at Saint Patrick's Purgatory', *Medium Aevum*, 55 (1986), 159–75.

Easting, Robert, 'Purgatory and the Earthly Paradise in the *Tractatus de Purgatorio Sancti Patricii*', *Cîteaux: Commentarii Cistercienses*, 37 (1986), 23–48.

Easting, Robert, 'The South English Legendary "St Patrick" as Translation', *Leeds Studies in English*, n.s., 21 (1990), 119–40.

Easting, Robert, 'Middle English Translations of the *Tractatus de Purgatorio Sancti Patricii*', in *The Medieval Translator II*, edited by Roger Ellis (London: Queen Mary and Westfield College, 1991), pp. 151–75.

Easting, Robert, *Visions of the Other World in Middle English*, Annotated Bibliographies of Old and Middle English Literature, 3 (Woodbridge: D. S. Brewer, 1997).

Easting, Robert, 'Access to Heaven in Medieval Visions of the Otherworld', in *Envisaging Heaven in the Middle Ages*, edited Carolyn Muessig and Ad Putter (London: Routledge, 2007), pp. 75–90.

Echard, Siân, *Arthurian Narrative in the Latin Tradition* (Cambridge: Cambridge University Press, 1998).

Edwards, A. S. G., 'The Manuscript: British Library MS Cotton Nero A. x', in *A Companion to the Gawain-Poet*, edited by Derek Brewer and Jonathan Gibson (Woodbridge: D. S. Brewer, 1997), pp. 197–220.

Foster, Brian, 'The *Roman de Toute Chevalerie*: Its Date and Author', *French Studies*, 9 (1955), 154–8.

Foster, F. A., 'Legends of the Afterlife', in *A Manual of the Writings in Middle English, 1050–1500*, edited by J. Burke Severs (Hamden, CT: Archon Books, 1970), II, pp. 452–7, 645–9.

Freitag, Barbara, *Hy Brasil: The Metamorphosis of an Island, from Cartographic Error to Celtic Elysium*, Textxet Studies in Comparative Literature, 5.69 (Amsterdam and New York: Rodopi, 2013).

French, D. R., 'Ritual, Gender and Power Strategies: Male Pilgrimage to Saint Patrick's Purgatory', *Religion*, 24 (1994), 103–15.

Friedman, John Bloch, *Orpheus in the Middle Ages* (Cambridge, MA: Harvard University Press, 1970).

Friedman, John Bloch, *The Monstrous Races in Medieval Art and Thought* (Cambridge, MA: Harvard University Press, 1981).

Fulton, Helen, 'Magic and the Supernatural in Early Welsh Arthurian Narrative: *Culhwch ac Olwen* and *Breuddwyd Rhonabwy*', *Arthurian Literature*, 30 (2013), 1–26.

Graf, Arturo, *Miti, leggende e superstizioni del medioevo*, 2 vols (Turin: Ermanno, 1892–1893; repr. Bologna: A. Forni, 1965).

Gray, Louis H., 'The Origin of the Name of Glastonbury', *Speculum*, 10 (1935), 46–53.

Green, D. H., *The Beginnings of Medieval Romance: Fact and Fiction, 1150–1220* (Cambridge: Cambridge University Press, 2002).

Grimaldi, Patrizia, 'Sir Orfeo as Celtic Folk-Hero, Christian Pilgrim, and Medieval King', in *Allegory, Myth, and Symbol*, edited by Morton W. Bloomfield (Cambridge, MA: Harvard University Press, 1981), pp. 147–61.

Gwara, Scott James, 'Gluttony, Lust and Penance in the B-text of *Aislinge Meic Conglinne*', *Celtica*, 20 (1988), 53–72.

Hall, Alaric, *Elves in Anglo-Saxon England: Matters of Belief, Health, Gender and Identity* (Woodbridge: Boydell, 2007).

Hamp, Eric P., 'Varia X: Irish *síd* "tumulus" and Irish *síd* "peace"', *Études Celtique*, 19 (1982), 141–2.

Hastings, Adrian, *The Construction of Nationhood: Ethnicity, Religion and Nationalism* (Cambridge: Cambridge University Press, 1997).

Hayes, R. L., *The Manuscript Sources for the History of Irish Civilisation*, 14 vols (Boston: G. K. Hall, 1965–1975).

Herbert, Máire, 'Goddess and King: The Sacred Marriage in Early Ireland', in *Women and Sovereignty*, edited by Louise O. Fradenburg (Edinburgh: Edinburgh University Press, 1992), pp. 264–75.

Hiatt, Alfred, *Terra Incognita: Mapping the Antipodes Before 1600* (London: British Library, 2008).

Honey, W. B., 'A Syrian Glass Goblet', *The Burlington Magazine*, 50 (1927), 286, 289, 291, 293–4.

Hopkins, Amanda, 'Why Arthur at all? The Dubious Arthuricity of *Arthur and Gorlagon*', *Arthurian Literature*, 26 (2009), 77–97.

Hull, Eleanor, 'The Silver Bough in Irish Legend', *Folklore*, 12 (1901), 431–45.

Hutton, Ronald, 'The Making of the Early Modern British Fairy Tradition', *The Historical Journal*, 57 (2014), 1135–56.

Jaski, Bart, *Early Irish Kingship and Succession* (Dublin: Four Courts Press, 2000).

Kane, George, 'Review of Patch, *Other World*', *Modern Language Review*, 46 (1951), 475–6.

Kenney, James F., *The Sources for the Early History of Ireland: Ecclesiastical* (New York: Columbia University Press, 1929).

Kittredge, G. L., 'Launfal', *The American Journal of Philology*, 10 (1889), 1–33.

Kittredge, George, 'Sir Orfeo', *The American Journal of Philology*, 7 (1886), 176–202.

Kline, Naomi Reed, *Maps of Medieval Thought: The Hereford Paradigm* (Woodbridge: Boydell, 2001).

Koch, John T., ed., *Celtic Culture: A Historical Encyclopedia* (Santa Barbara: ABC-CLIO, 2006).

Kugler, Hartmut, 'Die Ebstorfer Weltkarte ohne Gervasius von Tilbury', in *Kloster und Bildung im Mittelalter*, edited by Nathalie Kruppa and Jürgen Wilke (Göttingen: Vandenhoeck & Ruprecht, 2006), 497–512.

Larrington, Carolyne, 'The Fairy Mistress: A Medieval Literary Fantasy', in *Writing and Fantasy*, edited by Ceri Sullivan and Barbara White, Longman Cross-Currents Series (Harlow: Longman, 1999), 32–47.

Lascelles, M., 'Alexander and the Earthly Paradise in Mediaeval English Writings', *Medium Aevum*, 5 (1936), 31–47, 79–104, 173–88.

Lavezzo, Kathy, *Angels on the Edge of the World: Geography, Literature, and English Community, 1000–1534* (Ithaca, NY: Cornell University Press, 2006).

Lawton, David A., '*Scottish Field*: Alliterative Verse and the Stanley Encomium in the Percy Folio', *Leeds Studies in English*, n.s., 10 (1978), 42–57.

Lawton, David A., 'History and Legend: The Exile and the Turk', in *Postcolonial Moves*, edited by P. C. Ingham and M. R. Warren (New York: Palgrave, 2003), pp. 173–94.

Le Goff, Jacques, *The Birth of Purgatory*, translated by Arthur Goldhammer (London: Scolar Press, 1984).

Le Goff, Jacques, 'The Marvelous in the Medieval West', in *The Medieval Imagination*, translated by Arthur Goldhammer (Chicago: University of Chicago Press, 1988), 27–44.

Lewis, Barry J., 'Celtic Ecocriticism', *Cambrian Medieval Celtic Studies*, 59 (2010), 71–81.

Lewis, C. S., *English Literature in the Sixteenth Century Excluding Drama* (Oxford: Clarendon Press, 1944).

L.[ewis,] C. S., 'Review of Patch, *Other World*', *Medium Aevum*, 20 (1951), 93–4.

Lewis, C. S., 'The Anthropological Approach', in *English and Medieval Studies Presented to J. R. R. Tolkien on the Occasion of his Seventieth Birthday*, edited by Norman Davis and C. L. Wrenn (London: Allen and Unwin, 1962), pp. 219–30.

Lewis, C. S., *The Discarded Image: An Introduction to Medieval and Renaissance Literature* (Cambridge: Canto, 1994).

Lloyd-Morgan, Ceridwen, 'From *Ynys Wydrin* to *Glasynbri*: Glastonbury in Welsh Vernacular Tradition', in *Glastonbury Abbey and the Arthurian Tradition*, edited by James P. Carley, Arthurian Studies, 45 (Cambridge: D. S. Brewer, 2001), pp. 161–77.

Loud, Graham A., 'Coinage, Wealth and Plunder in the Age of Robert Guiscard', *English Historical Review*, 114 (1999), 815–43.

Lyle, E. B., '*The Turk and Gawain* as a Source of *Thomas of Erceldoune*', *Forum for Modern Language Studies*, 6 (1970), 98–102.

MacCana, Prionsias, *Branwen Daughter of Llŷr: A Study of the Irish Affinities and of the Composition of the Second Branch of the Mabinogi* (Cardiff: University of Wales Press, 1958).

MacCana, Prionsias, 'The Influence of the Vikings on Gaelic Literature', in *Proceedings of the International Congress of Celtic Studies, Dublin, 6–10 July 1959*, edited by Brian Ó Cuív (Dublin: Dublin Institute for Advanced Studies, 1962), pp. 78–118.

MacCana, Prionsias, 'The Sinless Otherworld of *Immram Brain*', *Eriú*, 27 (1976), 95–115.

MacCana, Prionsias, *The Learned Tales of Medieval Ireland* (Dublin: Dublin Institute for Advanced Studies, 1980).

MacQuarrie, Charles W., *The Biography of the Irish God of the Sea from* The Voyage of Bran *(700 AD) to* Finnegans Wake *(1939): The Waves of Mannanán* (Lampeter: The Edwin Mellen Press, 2004).

MacQuarrie, Charles W., 'The Isle of Man in Medieval Gaelic Literature', in *A New History of the Isle of Man: The Medieval Period, 1000–1405*, edited by Seán Duffy (Liverpool: Liverpool University Press, forthcoming).

Martin, Joanna, ' "Of Wisdome and of Guide Governance": Sir Gilbert Hay and *The Buik of King Alexander the Conquerour*', in *A Companion to Medieval Scottish Poetry*, edited by Pricilla Bawcutt and J. H. Williams (Woodbridge: D. S. Brewer, 2006), pp. 75–88.

Matthews, David, *Writing to the King: Nation, Kingship and Literature in England, 1250–1350* (Cambridge: Cambridge University Press, 2010).

McDonald, R. Andrew, *Manx Kingship in its Irish Sea Setting, 1187–1229: King Rǫgnvaldr and the Crovan Dynasty* (Dublin: Four Courts Press, 2007).

McKenzie, Stephen, 'The Westward Progression of History on Medieval *Mappaemundi*: An Investigation of the Evidence', in *The Hereford World Map: Medieval World Maps and their Context*, edited by P. D. A. Harvey (London: British Library, 2006), pp. 335–44.

Merrills, A. H., *History and Geography in Late Antiquity* (Cambridge: Cambridge University Press, 2005).

Meyer, Paul, *Légendes hagiographiques en Français*, Histoire Littéraire de la France, 33 (Paris: Imprimerie Nationale, 1906).

Michelet, Fabienne, *Creation, Migration, and Conquest: Imaginary Geography and Sense of Space in Old English Literature* (Oxford: Oxford University Press, 2006).

Mills, Maldwyn, and Gillian Rogers, 'The Manuscripts of Popular Romance', in *A Companion to Medieval Popular Romance*, edited by Raluca L. Radulescu and Cory James Rushton (Woodbridge: D. S. Brewer, 2009), pp. 49–66.

Mitchell, Bruce, 'The Faery World of *Sir Orfeo*', *Neophilologus*, 48 (1964), 156–9.

Mittman, Asa Simon, 'The Other Close at Hand: Gerald of Wales and the Marvels of the West', in *The Monstrous Middle Ages*, edited by Bettina Bildhauer and Robert Mills (Toronto: University of Toronto Press, 2003), pp. 97–112.

Mittman, Asa Simon, *Maps and Monsters in Medieval England* (London: Routledge, 2006).

Morris, Rosemary, 'The *Gesta Regum Britanniae* of William of Rennes: an Arthurian Epic?', *Arthurian Literature*, 6 (1986), 60–123.

Muessig, Carolyn, and Ad Putter, eds., *Envisaging Heaven in the Middle Ages* (London: Routledge, 2007).

Muhr, Kay, 'Manx Place-Names: An Ulster View', in *Mannin Revisited: Twelve Essays on Manx Culture and Environment*, edited by Peter Davey and David Finlayson (Edinburgh: Scottish Society for Northern Studies, 2002), pp. 37–52.

Murray, Kevin, 'The Manuscript Tradition of *Baile Chuinn Chetchathaig* and its Relationship with *Baile in Scáil*', in *The Kingship and Landscape of Tara*, edited by Edel Bhreathnach (Dublin: Four Courts Press, 2005), pp. 69–72.

Murray, Kevin Patrick, '*Baile in Scáil* and *Echtrae Chormaic*', in *Ogma: Essays in Celtic Studies in Honour of Próinséas Ní Chatháin*, edited by M. Richter and J.-M. Picard (Dublin: Four Courts Press, 2001), pp. 195–9.

Musgrave, William, 'The Luck of Edenhall', *The Gentleman's Magazine*, 61 (1791), 721–2.

Newman, Barbara, 'What Did it Mean to Say "I Saw"? The Clash between Theory and Practice in Medieval Visionary Culture', *Speculum*, 80 (2005), 1–43.

Ní Mhaonaigh, Máire, 'Literary Lochlann', in *Cànan & Cultar/Language and Culture*, edited by Wilson McLeod, James E. Fraser, and Anja Gunderloch, Rannsachadh na Gàidhlig, 3 (Edinburgh: Dunedin Academic Press, 2006), pp. 25–37.

North, Richard, 'Morgan le Fay and the Fairy Mound in *Sir Gawain and the Green Knight*', in *Airy Nothings: Imagining the Otherworld of Faerie from the Middle Ages to the Age of Reason: Essays in Honour of Alasdair A. MacDonald*, edited by Karin E. Olsen and Jan R. Veenstra (Leiden and Boston, MA: Brill, 2014), pp. 75–98.

Ó Cathasaigh, Tomás, 'The semantics of *síd*', *Éigse*, 17 (1978), 137–55.

O'Loughlin, Thomas, 'Patrick on the Margins of Space and Time', in *Eklogai: Studies in Honour of Thomas Finan and Gerard Watson* (Maynooth: Cardinal Press, 2001), pp. 44–58.

O'Meara, J. J., 'In the Wake of the Saint: The Brendan Voyage, an Epic Crossing of the Atlantic by Leather Boat', *Times Literary Supplement*, 14 July 1978 (repr. in *Otherworld Voyage*, edited by Wooding, pp. 109–12).

Olsen, Karin E., 'Female Voices from the Otherworld: The Role of Women in the Early Irish *Echtrai*', in *Airy Nothings: Imagining the Otherworld of Faerie from the Middle Ages to the Age of Reason: Essays in Honour of Alasdair A. MacDonald*, edited by Karin E. Olsen and Jan R. Veenstra (Leiden and Boston, MA: Brill, 2014), pp. 57–74.

Owen, D. D. R., *The Vision of Hell: Infernal Journeys in Medieval French Literature* (New York: Barnes & Noble, 1971).

Patch, Howard Rollin, *The Other World According to Descriptions in Medieval Literature* (Cambridge, MA: Harvard University Press, 1950).

Payne, Robert O., 'Review of Patch, *Other World*', in *Comparative Literature*, 3 (1951), 366–8.

Pearsall, Derek, 'Madness in *Sir Orfeo*', in *Romance Reading on the Book: Essays on Medieval Narrative Presented to Maldwyn Mills*, edited by Jennifer Fellows et al. (Cardiff: University of Wales Press, 1996).

Pearsall, Derek, and Elizabeth Salter, *Landscapes and Seasons of the Medieval World* (London: Elek, 1973).

Pioletti, Antonio, 'Artù, Avallon, l'Etna', *Quaderni Medievali*, 28 (1989), 6–35.

Pleij, Herman, *Dreaming of Cockaigne; Medieval Fantasies of the Perfect Life*, translated by Diane Webb (New York: Columbia University Press, 2001).

Poppe, Erich, 'Imtheachta Aeniasa: Virgil's "Aeneid" in Medieval Ireland', *Classics Ireland*, 11 (2004), 74–94.

Purdie, Rhiannon, *Anglicising Romance: Tail-Rhyme and Genre in Medieval English Literature* (Woodbridge: D. S. Brewer, 2008).

Putter, Ad, 'The Influence of Visions of the Otherworld on some Medieval Romances', in *Envisaging Heaven in the Middle Ages*, edited by Carolyn Meussig and Ad Putter (London: Routledge, 2007), pp. 237–51.

Reinach, Salomon, 'Le mot *orbis* dans le latin de l'empire', *Revue Celtique*, 22 (1901), 447–57.

Reinhard, John Revell, *The Survival of Geis in Mediaeval Romance* (Halle: Max Niemeyer, 1933).

Rickard, P., *Britain in Medieval French Literature, 1100–1500* (Cambridge: Cambridge University Press, 1956).

Rider, Jeff, 'The Other Worlds of Medieval Romance', in *The Cambridge Companion to Medieval Romance*, edited by Roberta L. Krueger (Cambridge: Cambridge University Press, 2000), pp. 115–31.

Ross, Miceal, 'Anchors in a Three-decker World', *Folklore*, 109 (1998), 63–75.

Rouse, Robert Allen, *The Idea of Anglo-Saxon England in Middle English Romance* (Cambridge: D. S. Brewer, 2005).

Russell, Jeffrey Burton, *Lucifer: The Devil in the Middle Ages* (Ithaca, NY and London: Cornell University Press, 1984).

Said, Edward, *Orientalism: Western Conceptions of the Orient* (London: Penguin, 1978).

Saunders, Corinne, *Magic and the Supernatural in Medieval English Romance* (Cambridge: D. S. Brewer, 2010).

Scafi, Alessandro, *Mapping Paradise: A History of Heaven on Earth* (London: British Library, 2006).

Scanlon, Larry, *Narrative, Authority and Power: The Medieval Exemplum and the Chaucerian Tradition* (Cambridge: Cambridge University Press, 1994).

Selmer, Carl, 'The Vernacular Translations of the *Navigatio Sancti Brendani*: A Bibliographical Study', *Mediaeval Studies*, 18 (1956), 145–57.

Siewers, Alfred K., *Strange Beauty: Ecocritical Approaches to Early Medieval Land-scape* (New York: Palgrave Macmillan, 2009).

Silverstein, Theodore, *Visio Sancti Pauli: The History of the Apocalypse in Latin Together with Nine Texts*, Studies and Documents, 4 (London: Christophers, 1935).

Sims-Williams, Patrick, 'The Visionary Celt: The Construction of an Ethnic Preconception', *Cambridge Medieval Studies*, 11 (1986), 71–96.

Sims-Williams, Patrick, 'Some Celtic Otherworld Terms', in *Celtic Language, Celtic Culture: A Festschrift for Eric P. Hamp*, edited by Ann T. E. Matonis and Daniel F. Melia (Van Nuys, CA: Ford and Bailie, 1990), pp. 57–81.

Sims-Williams, Patrick, 'The Early Welsh Arthurian Poems', in *The Arthur of the Welsh: The Arthurian Legend in Medieval Welsh Literature*, edited by R. Bromwich, A. O. H. Jarman, and B. F. Roberts (Cardiff: University of Wales Press, 1991), pp. 33–71.

Sims-Williams, Patrick, *The Irish Influence on Medieval Welsh Literature* (Oxford: Oxford University Press, 2011).

Sobecki, Sebastian I., 'From the *Désert Liquide* to the Sea of Romance: Benedeit's *Le Voyage de Saint Brendan* and the Irish *Immrama*', *Neophilologus*, 87 (2003), 193–207.

Sobecki, Sebastian I., *The Sea and Medieval English Literature* (Cambridge: D. S. Brewer, 2008).

Sobecki, Sebastian I., ed., *The Sea and Englishness in the Middle Ages: Maritime Narratives, Identity and Culture* (Cambridge: D. S. Brewer, 2011).

Spearing, A. C., *The Medieval Poet as Voyeur: Looking and Listening in Medieval Love-Narratives* (Cambridge: Cambridge University Press, 1993).

Speed, Diane, 'The Saracens of *King Horn*', *Speculum*, 65 (1990), 564–95.

Tatlock, J. S. P., 'Geoffrey and King Arthur in *Normannicus Draco*', *Modern Philology*, 31 (1933), 1–18.

Thurneysen, Rudolph, *Die irische Helden- und Königsage bis zum siebzehnten Jahrhundert* (Halle: Max Niemeyer, 1921).

Tolkien, J. R. R., 'On Fairy Stories', in *The Monsters and the Critics and other Essays* (London: Allen and Unwin, 1983), pp. 109–61.

Toner, Gregory, 'Reconstructing the Earliest Irish Tale Lists', *Éigse*, 32 (2000), 88–120.

Torres, Sara V., 'Journeying to the World's End? Imagining the Anglo-Irish Frontier in Ramon de Perellós's Pilgrimage to St Patrick's Purgatory', in *Mapping Medieval Geographies: Geographical Encounters in the Latin West and Beyond, 300–1600*, edited by Keith D. Lilley (Cambridge: Cambridge University Press: 2013), pp. 300–24.

Turville-Petre, Thorlac, *England the Nation: Language, Literature, and National Identity, 1290–1340* (Oxford: Clarendon Press, 1996).

Varisco, Daniel Martin, *Reading Orientalism: Said and the Unsaid* (Seattle, WA: University of Washington Press, 2007).

Wade, James, *Fairies in Medieval Romance* (New York: MacMillan, 2011).

Wade, James, 'Ungallant Knights', in *Heroes and Anti-Heroes in Medieval Romance*, edited by Neil Cartlidge (Cambridge: D. S. Brewer, 2012), pp. 201–18.

Watkins, C. S., *History and the Supernatural in Medieval England* (Cambridge: Cambridge University Press, 2007).

Watkins, Carl, 'Doctrine, Politics and Purgation: *The Vision of Tnúthgal* and *The Vision of Owein at St Patrick's Purgatory*', *Journal of Medieval History*, 22 (1996), 225–36.

Watt, J. A., *The Church and the Two Nations in Medieval Ireland* (Cambridge: Cambridge University Press, 1970), pp. 36–40.

Wiggins, Alison, 'The Manuscripts and Texts of the Middle English Guy of Warwick', in *Guy of Warwick: Icon and Ancestor*, edited by Alison Wiggins and Rosalind Field, Studies in Medieval Romance, 4 (Cambridge: D. S. Brewer, 2007), pp. 61–80.

Wiley, Dan, 'An Introduction to the Early Irish King Tales', in *Essays on the Early Irish King Tales*, edited by Dan M. Wiley (Dublin: Four Courts Press, 2008), pp. 13–67.

Williams, David, *Deformed Discourse: The Function of the Monster in Mediaeval Thought and Literature* (Montreal: McGill-Queen's University Press, 1996).

Wilson, E., '*Sir Gawain and the Green Knight* and the Stanley Family of Storeton, and Hooton', *Review of English Studies*, n.s., 30 (1979), 308–16.

Wingfield, Emily, 'The Composition and Revision of Sir Gilbert Hay's *Buik of King Alexander the Conquerour*', *Nottingham Medieval Studies*, 57 (2013), 247–86.

Wittkower, Rudolf, 'Marvels of the East: A Study in the History of Monsters', *Journal of the Warburg and Courtauld Institutes*, 5 (1942), 159–97.

Wolf, Armin, 'The Ebstorf Mappamundi and Gervase of Tilbury: The Controversy Revisited', *Imago Mundi*, 64 (2012), 1–27.

Wooding, Jonathan, ed., *The Otherworld Voyage in Early Irish Literature: An Anthology of Criticism* (Dublin: Four Courts Press, 2000).

Wright, Thomas, *Saint Patrick's Purgatory: An Essay on the Legends* (London: John Russell Smith, 1844).

Zaleski Carol, *Otherworld Journeys: Accounts of Near-Death Experiences in Medieval and Modern Times* (Oxford: Oxford University Press, 1987).

Index

Acallam na Senórach 176
Adulterous Falmouth Squire 73 n. 23
Adventure of St Columba's Clerics 94
Aethelstan 173
Aided Chon Roí 164–5
Aislinge Meic Conglinne 49
Alexander the Great 24, 33, 62, 112
  and the Earthly Paradise 129–40
  and his flight with griffins 136–7
  human limitations of 137–8
Alfred the Great 145–6
Alliterative *Morte Arthure* 121
Amadas et Ydoine 38–40, 56, 65–6
Anglo-Saxons 28
annwfyn 16, 125, 129, 165–6
Anselm, St 146
Antipodes 11, 14–15, 18, 126, 144
apples 50, 160, 162
  and Avalon 121–2, 123, 124–5,
    159–60
  and the Earthly Paradise 136, 138
archipelagic geography 7, 24, 141–3
Arthur, King of the Britons 33, 61, 112
  and Avalon 119–29
  exhumation at Glastonbury 124–5
Ashe, Laura 83
Atlantic Ocean 35–6, 41, *see also* water
    barriers
Auchinleck manuscript 52 n. 92
Augustine of Hippo, St 44, 78, 151
Avalon 24, 36–7, 61, 112, 159, 167, 184
  descriptions of 119–23
  at Glastonbury 124–5
  in Welsh 159 n. 67

Babylonian Talmud 130
Baile in Scáil 111, 114, 163, 164
  manuscripts of 113 n. 18
  summary of 114–15
  and Uí Néill dynasty 115–16
Bannatyne manuscript 42
Barthes, Roland 30–1
Battle of Brunanburh 173
Battle of Clontarf 118
beatific vision 104
Bede 146, 151, 169
  *Historia ecclesiastica gentis
    Anglorum* 149, 154, 158, 167
  In Cantica Canticorum 146

Benedeit, *Voyage of St Brendan* 94
  treatment of the Earthly Paradise
    in 99–101
Bennett, Josephine Waters 146
Beowulf 2
Bible 69, 80, 91–2, 153
  Acts of the Apostles 150
  1 Corinthians 95
  2 Corinthians 89 n. 78
  Ezechiel 86 n. 72, 90, 92, 99–100
  Genesis 86 n. 72, 90, 101, 103, 131
    n. 73, 136, 139
  Isaiah 86 n. 72, 90
  Matthew 150
  Revelation 9, 69, 72, 86 n. 72, 87,
    91–9
Bliss, Alan J. 94
Bloch, Howard R. 33
Book of Lecan 155
Book of Lismore 101
Bosworth Feilde 180
Branwen ferch Llŷr 165–6
Britain, in literature 165, 166, 173
  classical accounts of 144–7
  climate of 146
  geographical peripherality of 143–4
  island nature of 141–3
  on medieval maps 143–4, 152–3
  and *translatio imperii* 151, 153, 157, 183
Brittany 37, 122, 128, 147
branches 160
  from otherworld 45, 54, 114, 164
Brown, Michelle P. 174
Burgess, Glynn 101

Caesarius of Heisterbach, *Dialogus
    miraculorum* 74, 127 n. 66
Calkin, Siobhain Bly 173
Cambridge University Library MS Ee. 6. 11
    79, 80 n. 40, 83
Camden, William, *Brittania* 145
Campbell, Mary B. 6
Carey, John 4, 25–6, 48, 164
Cartlidge, Neil 39–40
Cary, George 130
Catalan Atlas 148
caves (as entry points to otherworld) 1, 10,
    17–20, 28, 59, 70, 76, 108, 127, 141,
    160–1, 162

Celtic sources (for otherworld
    accounts) 6–9, 87–96, 142, 147
Ceylon 14, 144
chansons de geste 172
Charlemagne 145–6
Chaucer, Geoffrey:
    Tale of Sir Thopas 31–2, 39, 43
    Wife of Bath's Tale 6
chivalry 80–1, 181
Chrétien de Troyes:
    Chevalier de la Charette 58, 85
    Erec et Enide 50
Cistercian order 71 n. 11, 74–5, 83
Clarke, Catherine A. M. 141
Claudian 145
Cogadh Gaedhel Re Gaillaibh 118
Cohen, Jeffrey Jerome 4 n. 10, 142
Conn Cétcathach 111, 112, 162
Cooper, Helen 22, 98, 154, 179–80
Cormac Mac Airt 111, 113, 162
Crovan, Gõdred 162, 163, 178
crusades 107, 174
Culhwch ac Olwen 165–6
Cunliffe, Barry 147
cups 50, 106–7, 108–9, 111,
    114–15

Dál Cais 115
Dál Cuinn 112–13, 184
Daston, Lorraine 4
David, poem on St Brendan 71–2
    and Ireland 9
David I, King of the Scots 109
de Beauvoir, Simone 61
de Courcy, John 161
death 58–66
    in *Amadas et Ydoine* 65–6
    and the Earthly Paradise 101
    and geographical peripheries 61 n. 128,
        147, 150–1
    and immortality in otherworld 53,
        120–9
    and otherworld journeys 118–19
    otherworld warnings of 111, 131–9
    in *Sir Orfeo* 64, 96
devil (Satan) 28–9
Dicuil, *Liber de Mensura Orbis Terrae* 14
Didorus Siculus 168
dinnshenchas 34
Donatus of Fiesole, *Uita Metrica Sanctae
    Brigidae* 157–8, 169
dream poetry 30–1
drink 41, 48, 49, 50–1, 115
    taboo on drinking in otherworld 50
Duanaire Finn 161

Eachtra Thaidhg Mhic Céin 69, 97, 111
    background to 101–2
    four paradises in 103
    religious ethos of 103–5
    structure of 102
Eadmer, *Vita Anselmi* 146
Eamhain 34, 159–62
Earthly Paradise (Eden) 10, 11, 24, 33,
    40–1, 71–3, 99, 105–6, 158, 168
    and Alexander the Great 129–40
    in the Bible 90–1, 130
    in *Lebor Gabála* 155–6
    on *mappae mundi* 130, 153–6
    in *Sir Owayne* 85–7
    in *Tractatus de Purgatorio Sancti
        Patricii* 74–80
Easting, Robert 10, 74–5, 79, 84
Echard, Siân 123
echtrae (genre) 111 n. 12
Echtrae Airt meic Cuinn 113, 114
Echtrae Chonnlai 43, 48, 50, 54, 102,
    113, 118
Echtrae Chormaic 111, 113, 114
Echtrae Láegairi maic Crimthainn 118–19,
    129–30
ecocriticism 4, 9 n. 21
eldritch poems 42
Estoire de Merlin 169–72
Étienne of Rouen, *Draco
    Normannicus* 126
Etna, Mount 127–8, 141
Eustochium, St 145

Fabyan, Robert, *Chronicle* 145
fairy hunt 1, 40, 93, 128
fairy lovers 45–9, 118–19, 122–3
Flodden Feilde 180
Fomoiri 164, 176
food 19, 27–8, 48–52, 76, 79
    and gluttony 49
    and taboo on eating in otherworld 51–2
forest 25, 52, 63, 126, 128, 185
Forfess Fer Falgae 164

Gauls 14, 147
Gawain romances 182
geis 44 n. 69
Geoffrey of Monmouth 147, 148
    Historia Regum Britanniae 120–4,
        166–7
    Vita Merlini 121–2, 128, 167
Gerald of Wales 185
    De Instructione Principis 124–5
    Itinerarium Kambriae 19–20, 108–9
    Speculum Ecclesiae 125

Topographia Hibernica 54, 148, 149–50, 154–5, 163, 168–9, 173–5, 182
Gervase of Tilbury:
  Ebstorf Map and 153
  Otia Imperialia 17–19, 126–9
Giant's Ring, *see* Stonehenge
giants 166–7, 170–3, 189–90
gifts from otherworld 28, 114, 132–3, 150
Gildas, *De Excidio Britonum* 148
Glastonbury:
  as Avalon 124–5
Gormont et Isembart 172
Gorre, land of 58, 85
Green Children of Woolpit 17, 19, 105, 109
Greene Knight 181
Gregory the Great, *Dialogi* 72, 78
Gui de Warewic 173
Guinevere 124
Guy of Warwick 53, 178
  Irish translation of 52 n. 93

H[enry] of Saltry, *see Tractatus de Purgatorio Sancti Patricii*
Hahn, Thomas 182
Harrison, John, *Description of Britain* 145
Hay, Gilbert 135
  The Buik of King Alexander the Conquerour 112, 135–40
Heaven 68, 73, 76, 95, 104, 105–6
Hell 68, 73, 77, 85, 105–6, 176
Henry I, King of England 109
Henry II, King of England 28–9, 124, 126, 150, 174
Henry VI, Holy Roman Emperor 128, 141
Henryson, Robert, *Orpheus and Eurydice* 64
Herbert, Máire 115–16
Higden, Ranulf, *Polychronicon* 145, 146
horizon of expectations 21–2, 25, 34, 59–60, 112, 139, 185
hortus conclusus 54
Hugh of St Victor 151
Hutton, Ronald 17
Hy Brasil 10

Immram Brain 18, 33–6, 37, 43, 44–5, 46, 54–5, 160, 164
Immram Curaig Ua Corra 72–3, 102
Immram Máele Dúin 49, 55, 94, 102
In Cath Catharda 15
Ireland in literature:
  barbarous inhabitants of 168–9
  climate of 155

and healing 148–9, 154–6, 166–7
marvels of 149–50, 154–5
on medieval maps 73, 143–4, 152, 153
as mirror of Eden 154–6
as otherworld 142–58
purity of 148–9, 157–8
sovereignty of 115
westerliness of 150–1, 154, 156
Isidore of Seville, *Etymologiae* 122, 145, 148, 167
  on Ireland 148–9
  on islands 148
islands 143
  on medieval maps 148
  supernatural properties of 147–9
Isle of Ladies 54
Isle of Man:
  beauty of 163
  geography of 163
  history of 161–2, 178–9
  and Ireland 162, 163, 165 n. 95
  kings of 159, 164, 177–81
  as otherworld 159–64, 168, 177–8, 181–2
Iter Ad Paradisum 130–3
  authorship of 130–1
  French translation of 135
  summary of 131–2

Jauss, Hans 22
Jerome, St 168
jewels 1, 26, 41, 52, 53, 94, 141, 158
  in the Earthly Paradise 41–2, 85–6, 91, 95, 99
  as light sources 32–3, 91
Judgement Day 92 n. 84

King Horn 171
kingship 110
  in Irish narrative 114, 116–18
Kissane, D. N. 158

Ladye Bessiye 180
Lai d'Havelo 173
Lake Avernus 59
Land of Cokaygne 40–2, 49
Land of Women 34, 37–8, 45, 54–5
Lascelles, Mary 134
Lathom, Isabella 179, 180
Lavezzo, Kathy 141
Laʒamon, *Brut* 121
Le Bel Inconnu 37
Le Goff, Jacques 11, 74
Le Scrope, William 178
Lebor Gabála 102, 155–8

Lebor na hUidre 35
Lewis, C. S. 42, 185
Lia Fáil 162, 164
Lichtoun's Dreme 42–3
Lochlann 176
Lough Derg, *see Tractatus de Purgatorio Sancti Patricii*
Lucan, *Pharsalia* 14
Luck of Edenhall 107–8
Lybeaus Desconus 37
Lydgate, John, *Fall of Princes* 125 n. 56

Mabinogion 165–6
Mac Finguine, Cathal, *see Aislinge Meic Conglinne*
Mac Mathúna, Séamus 34
MacCana, Prionsias 104, 176
Manannán mac Lir 37–8, 44, 160
Mandeville, John, *Travels* 136 n. 88
Map, Walter, *De Nugis Curialium* 20, 27–9
mappae mundi 72, 130, 152–3
    British Isles on 152–4
    Catalan Atlas 148
    Ebstorf Map 153
    in Gilbert Hay, *The Buik of King Alexander the Conquerour* 136–7
    Hereford Map 61 n. 128
    in Oxford, St John's College MS 17 143–4
Marie de France 43
    Espurgatoire Seint Patriz 82–3
    Graelent 47–8
    Guigemar 55–6
    Lanval 32–3, 44, 45, 47, 48–9, 55, 62
    Yonec 54, 56–7
Matthew Paris 74
McCone, Kim 113
McKenzie, Stephen 153–4
Mediterranean Sea 18, 143, 147, 152
Melusine 44
Michelet, Fabienne 141
monsters 5, 99, 148, 157
Morgan Le Fay 58, 121, 126
Murray, Kevin 115
music 86, 190
    in *Echtrae Airt Meic Cuinn* 144
    in *Immram Brain* 44–5
    in *Sir Orfeo* 26–7

Narnia 185
Navigatio Sancti Brendani Abbatis 9, 23, 50–1, 69–72, 111, 122, 163
    compared to the *Tractatus de Purgatorio Sancti Patricii* 97
    and Ireland 9

and Promised Land of the Saints 98–101
    sceptical responses to 11 n. 28, 70–2
Nennius, *Historia Brittonum* 125
new historicism 4
New Jerusalem 41, 72, 91–2, 95
Ní Mhaonaigh, Máire 176–7
North, Richard 60

Ó Cuív, Brian 159
Ó hUiginn, Tadhg Dall 161
O'Grady, Standish 101
O'Loughlin, Thomas 150
Of Arthour and of Merlin 169
Ogier le Danois 120 n. 39
Olaf, King of Dublin 173
orientalism 175
Origen 144–5
Orpheus legend 63–4, *see also Sir Orfeo*
Otto IV, Holy Roman Emperor 127, 128

Pan 28
Park, Katherine 4
Partonope of Blois 57–8
Patch, Howard Rollin 2, 6, 21, 92, 120
Patrick, St 75
    Confessio 150–1
Paula, St 145
Payne, Robert O. 3, 23
Pearl 59
Pedeir Keinc y Mabinogi, see Mabinogion
Percy family 179
Percy Folio 177, 180–1
perilous bridge 76, 77, 85, 89
Peterborough Chronicle 39–40
Pliny 144
Plutarch 146–7
Pomponius Mela, *De Chorographia* 144, 146–7, 168
portolan charts 152
Preideu Annwfyn 16, 125, 129, 165–6
Procopius of Caesarea 146–7
Purdie, Rhiannon 173
Purgatoire de Saint Patrice, see Tractatus de Purgatorio Sancti Patricii
Purgatory 12, 70–3, 74, 105–6
    in *Tractatus de Purgatorio Sancti Patricii* 74–7
Putter, Ad 94, 106

Raghnall (Rǫgnvaldr), King of the Isle of Man
    life of 161–2
    poem in praise of 159–63
Ralph of Coggeshall, *Chronicon Anglicanum* 109, 124 n. 51

Reinbrun 52–3, 116
Renan, Ernest, *La Poésie des races celtiques* 9 n. 22
Rider, Jeff 4
Rogers, Gillian 180
romance 3–4, 17, 22, 29, 44–7, 79, 94, 154, 171, 180–1
  and the *Tractatus de Purgatorio Sancti Patricii* 69, 74–87
Rose of England 180

Said, Edward 175
Saint Patrick's Purgatory, *see Tractatus de Purgatorio Sancti Patricii*
saracens 171–3, 175
Saunders, Corinne 5, 55
Scandinavia 144
Scanlon, Larry 110
Scotish Feilde 180
Serglige Con Culainn 94
Servius 144–5
sexual desire 37, 48, 55, 57–8
  in Eden 43–4, 48
  and food 48–9
  and sin 103–4, 169
Shakespeare, William 148
Síaburcharpat Conculaind 176
Sicily 141, 184
  and Arthur 127–8
síd 15, 43, 130, 159–61, 168
Siewers, Alfred K. 4, 142
Sims-Williams, Patrick 4, 15–16, 147, 165
Sir Degaré 54
Sir Gawain and the Green Knight 38, 179
  Green Chapel in 59–61
  Green Knight in 38
  manuscript of 59
Sir Landevale 32, 36
Sir Orfeo 1, 9, 20, 26, 38, 52–3, 63–4, 65–6, 87, 116
  and Bible 93–6
  manuscripts of 96 n. 96
Sir Owayne, see Tractatus de Purgatorio Sancti Patricii
Sobecki, Sebastian I. 99
Solinus 145–6, 168
South English Legendary 83–4
Spearing, A. C. 58
Speculum Regale 154
Stanley, John 179–81
Stanley, Thomas 179
Stanley family 178–80
Stanley Poem 180–1
Stanzaic *Morte Arthur* 121
Stephen, King of England 77

Stonehenge 166–7
Strabo 54, 168

taboos 44–7
Tancred, King of Sicily 128
Tara 162
Tatlock, J. S. P. 126
Thomas Chestre, *Sir Launfal* 32, 36, 47
Thomas of Erceldoune 51–2, 105, 184
Thomas of Kent, *Roman de Toute Chevalerie* 134–5
Thornley Abbey 143
Thule 143
Tochmarc Becfhola 48
Tochmarc Étaine 43, 46
Tolkien, J. R. R. 27
Torres, Sara V. 76
Tractatus de Purgatorio Sancti Patricii 9, 10, 20, 23, 69–73, 108, 111–12
  authorship of 75
  and the Bible 89–90
  bodily journey to afterlife in 76–8
  chivalry in 80–1, 83
  and Ireland 9, 76, 88–9
  provenance of 88
  and romance genre 69, 74–87
  summary of 75–6
  translations into Anglo-Norman 82–5
  translations into Middle English 82–7
translatio imperii 151, 152–3, 157, 183
Trevisa, John, *Polychronicon* 145
Tristan and Isolde 167
Tuatha Dé Danann 164, 176
Turke and Sir Gawain 51, 177

Uí Néill 112–13, 115
Urban II, Pope 146

Vals Sanz Retour 58
van der Zanden, C. M. 84
Vikings 118, 161–2, 171–3, 176–7
Vincent of Beauvais 70
Virgil:
  Aeneid 45 n. 71, 59
  Eclogues 144–5
  Georgics 158
Virgil of Salzburg 14
Visio Sancti Pauli 89
Visio Tnugdali 9, 75, 88
  compared to the *Tractatus de Purgatorio Sancti Patricii* 81–2
Vision of Adamnán 89
Vision of Laisrén 89
visions of the afterlife 33, 68 n. 1
Voyage au Paradis Terrestre 135, 136

Wace, *Roman de Brut* 120–1
Wade, James 46
Wars of Alexander 13–14
water barriers (at entry to
    otherworld) 1–2, 76
  lakes 2, 17–18, 54, 152
  rivers 19–20, 32, 47, 59–60, 73, 76, 85,
    99, 131–2
  seas 17–18, 35–6, 55, 57–8, 97–9, 135,
    141–8.
Watkins, C. S. 105
West, the 147, 151, 152, 154–6, 157,
    167, 174–5, 183

William, King of the Scots 109
William II, King of Sicily 128
William of Malmesbury:
    De Antiquitate Glastonie Ecclesie 125 n. 59
    Gestis Pontificum Anglorum 146
    Gesta Regum Anglorum 146
William of Newburgh, *Historia Rerum
    Anglicanum* 19, 105, 109
William of Rennes, *Gesta Regum
    Britanniae* 122–3
wonders of the east 174
Woolpit, Suffolk, *see* Green Children of
    Woolpit